DATE DUE

LETTERS FROM AMERICA

LETTERS FROM AMERICA

ALEXIS DE TOCQUEVILLE

Edited, translated, and with an

introduction by Frederick Brown

Yale UNIVERSITY PRESS *New Haven and London*

INTRODUCTION

In April 1831, Alexis de Tocqueville sailed for America aboard the schooner *Le Havre.* His companion was Gustave de Beaumont, equally highborn and a fellow lawyer, who had befriended him when he first entered the legal profession four years earlier, at the lower court in Versailles. Having secured leaves of absence from the judiciary, the two young men traveled as unpaid commissioners authorized by the government to study the American penal system, with the reform of French prisons in mind.

Tocqueville declared in private that the commission was hardly more than a pretext. It would enable him to tour the New World under official auspices and observe a republic as nearly unencumbered by history as the virgin forests were undisturbed by human design. Above all, it would help him escape the troublesome consequences of a revolution that had, in August 1830, enthroned a constitutional monarch whom old-line nobles championing the deposed Bourbon dynasty—Tocquevilles and Beaumonts among them—cordially detested.[1] One such consequence was an oath of loyalty required of civil servants by the new king, Louis-Philippe d'Orléans. Unwilling on the one hand to lose his precarious footing in professional life, and on the other to salute a regime that had evicted his father, Hervé, from the Chamber of Peers, Alexis wavered between dreary alternatives. Was he condemned to be an idle aristocrat or an impious son? A hostage to the past or a traitor to his class? Eventually he took the oath, with encouragement from Count Hervé (who knew full well that the benighted Bourbon, Charles X, had brought about his own downfall). But pledging allegiance did not banish reservations. It impelled Alexis, on the contrary, to find some means of distancing himself from the regime without forswearing it. America naturally sprang to mind. "There is so much talk about America in France, it looms so large in public opinion, and so often influences our political decisions that everything connected with its social life excites the liveliest interest in us," Tocqueville wrote from New York to his cousin Félix Le Peletier d'Aunay. The United States was seen as a vast social laboratory, and books about its prisons—notably La Rouchefoucauld-Liancourt's *Des prisons de Philadelphie* [On the Prisons of Philadelphia] (a fourth edition in 1819) and Charles Lucas's *Du système pénitentiaire en Europe et aux États-Unis* [On the Penal Systems of Europe and the United States] (1828)—suggested that experiments being conducted overseas might profit France, where social upheaval and economic grief had begotten a rising population of waifs and felons. What passed for a prison system was a chaotic, often brutal, improvisation.

The "pretext" Tocqueville chose for visiting America thus went to the heart of matters in post-Napoleonic France. But, like a lie that tells the truth, it also went to the heart of a prison story that played no small part in shaping Alexis's sensibility. The prison and the guillotine were intimate specters haunting the Tocqueville family.

Alexis's family name was Clerel. In the seventeenth century the Clerels, a land-rich Norman clan whose first chronicled ancestor fought with William the Conqueror at Hastings, acquired the fief of Tocqueville on the Cotentin peninsula near Bayeux and styled themselves Clerel de Tocqueville. Enjoying all the privileges of *gentilhommes seigneurs* under Louis XIV, they enhanced their nobility and rounded out their estates with advantageous marriages, one of which, between Bernard de Tocqueville and Catherine-Antoinette de Damas Crux, produced Alexis's father, Hervé-Bonaventure, in 1772. Norman gentry typically eschewed Paris, except for schooling. Those who could afford it sent their sons to an institution founded by Normans on Paris's Left Bank, the Collège d'Harcourt, and there, with other children of privilege, Hervé spent eight years or more. This collegiate school became a prison during the Revolution. For Hervé it was already as lonely as one during the last decade of the ancien régime. He lost his father at four, his mother in 1785 at thirteen, and might have lost his way had a surrogate parent not presented himself in the person of his tutor, a benign priest named Louis Lesueur, who would, in the next century, teach and succor Alexis de Tocqueville as well.

That Tocqueville *père* lived long enough to father children and Lesueur long enough to teach them confirmed the abbé's belief in the visitations of Providence. When the Bastille fell on July 14, 1789, Hervé's maternal relatives—the Damas—fled France and exhorted him to join an army shaping up across the border, in Belgium. But Hervé, who had as little regard for the feckless nobility of Louis XVI's court as Alexis would later have for the auxiliaries of Charles X, stayed put. Like other liberal aristocrats, he vested his hopes for good government in General de Lafayette, with whose son he briefly shared rooms. By 1791 those hopes had faded, and in June of that year the royal family was apprehended at Varennes trying to escape from the clutches of a revolution increasingly swayed by radical voices. Hervé then fled to Belgium. But the spectacle of émigrés living profligately in blind ignorance of a changed world drove him back to Paris, where he enlisted in the King's Guard. The young man, still only nineteen, grew up quickly as events raced past him with unbridled savagery. The King's Guard was disbanded, the Tuileries palace was invaded on August 10, 1792, by a mob that slaughtered the defenders, a hecatomb of decapitated Swiss Guards was set on fire in one of Paris's main squares, Louis XVI was compelled to seek asylum at the Legislative Assembly and soon thereafter imprisoned, priests who had not sworn allegiance to the new Civil Constitution of the Clergy were massacred. Hervé spirited Lesueur—one such "nonjuring" priest—out of Paris to his native village in Picardy and himself found refuge there.

At that point, a prudent course of action might have been to join the community of aristocratic refugees at Coblenz or even Prince Louis-Joseph de Condé's army of émigrés. Instead, Hervé arranged, from afar, to marry Louise de Rosambo, the granddaughter of Lamoignon de Malesherbes, an illustrious member of the *noblesse de robe*—the judicial nobility—who as chief censor under Louis XV had authorized the publication of Diderot's *Encyclopédie* and had been an enlightened presence in Louis XVI's circle of confidants. This career had not endeared Malesherbes to the Jacobin leadership. Neither had his eloquent defense of Louis XVI at the king's trial in December 1792. By January 30, 1793, when Hervé appeared at the jurist's chateau in the commune of Malesherbes near Orleans to claim his granddaughter's hand, the patriarch was a marked man.

Marked though he knew himself to be, Malesherbes surrounded himself with his extended family (which included three granddaughters, one of whom had married Jean-Baptiste Chateaubriand, the writer's brother), after the fashion of Boccaccio's gentlefolk retreating to a villa during the plague year. They lived together unharmed throughout 1793. "At nine o'clock every evening everybody came together in the *salon*," Hervé later wrote.

"M. de Malesherbes would arrive and seize on one of us for a talk which went on until midnight. While talking he never failed to undo the buttons, of coat and waistcoat, of his interlocutor. At midnight he went to bed fully clothed, and slept for several hours; he was obliged to keep his clothes on because he had the habit, when an idea struck him in the middle of the night, of getting up to write it down."[2] The reprieve—how could they think that it was anything more?—lasted until December 1793, when two emissaries of the Revolutionary Tribunal arrested Louise de Tocqueville's father, Louis de Rosambo, himself a distinguished jurist, on trumped-up charges of engaging in seditious correspondence with Chateaubriand. Before long every other member of the family followed Rosambo to prison, in one of those crazed sequences that decimated the aristocracy. Rosambo was guillotined on April 20, 1794, his wife the next day, and Lamoignon de Malesherbes on the 23rd. Thanks to the fall of Robespierre on IX Thermidor (July 27), four of nine survived, among them the Tocquevilles. They walked free after ten months spent in a fetid prison awaiting their turn to mount the scaffold and were greeted by another survivor, the priest Lesueur. "Our relatives, our friends had disappeared," Hervé recalled, "and the remnants of two families had no one to rely on except a young man of twenty-two who knew little of the world and whose only experience was of misfortune." Hervé's hair had turned completely white in prison. Louise's nerves were shattered.

The white-haired young man of twenty-two bent all his energies to the task of recovering land and chattels for those two families and acquitted himself remarkably well, both at Malesherbes, where numerous creditors had to be satisfied, and at Tocqueville, where peasants had done some damage. One of the supreme ironies of the Revolutionary era worked in Hervé's favor: only the property of nobles who had fled the country was confiscated by the state for sale to bidders or parceled out to small farmers at modest rents; nobles who lost their heads often retained title to their estates. Hervé thus succeeded in saving not only Malesherbes and Tocqueville but yet another chateau, this one twenty kilometers downriver from Paris at Verneuil-sur-Seine, which had belonged to Louise de Tocqueville's guillotined great-aunt, Madame de Sénozan (née Anne-Nicole de Lamoignon). After much notarial give-and-take, Louise's relatives ceded it to her. By that time it was 1807 and the Tocquevilles had occupied it for half a decade, enlivening it with three sons: Hippolyte (born in 1797), Édouard (1800), and Alexis (1805).

Although memories of the Terror lingered at the chateau (from which Madame de Sénozan had been dragged away in her seventy-sixth year), Hervé did his utmost to make Verneuil—with its turrets, formal gardens, mirrored drawing room, private theater, and suite of sixteen master bedrooms—a model of pastoral gentility. Elected mayor of the town, he dealt willy-nilly with the world outside. His children, who grew up during Napoleon's reign, heard cannon fire only as a distant rumble, and may never have seen an Epinal print of *grande armée* grenadiers. They were the cosseted beneficiaries of what their father called "la bonne vie de chateau" [the good chateau life]. Hervé attended closely to their education, seconded by abbé Lesueur, who lived with the family. Friends, neighbors, and relatives frequently called upon them—one friend, neighbor, and near relative being François-René de Chateaubriand. It was a cultivated household, where books mattered and literature set the tone. "Literature was one of the standing subjects of conversation," Tocqueville recalled.

> Every new book of any merit was read aloud, and canvassed and criticized with an attention and a detail which we should now think a deplorable waste of time. I recollect how every-

> body used to be in ecstasy about things of [Jacques] Delille's,
> which nothing would induce me now to look at. Every con-
> siderable country house had its theater, and its society often
> furnished admirable actors. I remember my father returning
> after a short absence to a large party in his house. We amused
> ourselves by receiving him in disguise. Chateaubriand was an
> old woman. . . . Every incident was matter for a little poem.[3]

Delille, the author of elegant, lifeless verses consecrated by the
French Academy, and Chateaubriand, whose novels *Atala* and *René*
heralded the Romantic movement, made odd bedfellows. But a
post-revolutionary salon redolent of the ancien régime could easily accommodate them both. And so could Alexis de Tocqueville,
in whom a prose style more eighteenth century than nineteenth
came to serve a modern intellect and a passionate temper.

What darkened "la bonne vie de chateau" were the moods of
Madame Louise de Tocqueville. Long before Alexis knew very
much about the reasons for her melancholia and irritability—the
holocaust that had made all those empty bedrooms at Verneuil a
derision—he knew that she never stopped mourning a lost world.
"I remember as if it were today, before my eyes," he wrote years
later, "an evening [in childhood] when some family celebration
brought together a host of relatives. The servants were off and we
sat around the fire. My mother, whose voice was sweet and touch-
ing, began to sing a well-known royalist song, which had to do
with the sorrows and death of Louis XVI. When she ended we
were all in tears."[4] The restoration of the Bourbon monarchy in
1815, after Waterloo, would not put heads back on Louis XVI and
the Rosambos and Mme de Sénozan. For Louise there could be
no Restoration.

Hervé, on the other hand, thrived. Being the grandson by marriage of Malesherbes, a man whose memory was revered by royalists, he was invited to help run post-Napoleonic France and

proved highly competent at administering the affairs of various provinces—the lower Loire valley, Burgundy, Lorraine—as Louis XVIII's quasi-autocratic prefect. Louise lived apart from him after 1817, having apparently decided that her nerves could no longer stand the test of provincial receptions. At Dijon they went separate ways, he to the prefecture at Metz on the Moselle, she to the Tocquevilles' residence in Paris's aristocratic Faubourg Saint-Germain.

Inevitably, this separation affected the course of Alexis's life. Until age fifteen, he lived alone with his mother and abbé Lesueur. In 1820, Hervé plucked the shy, frail youth from the Faubourg Saint-Germain, brought him to Metz, and enrolled him at the collegiate school, where he mingled for the first time with middle-class boys, several of whom became good friends.[5]

Before long, his exceptionally keen mind earned him high honors.

It also led him to pasture outside the confines of the classical curriculum. Wandering unsupervised through his father's library, he encountered a literature—in all likelihood the work of French *philosophes*—that assailed the basic pieties of his existence. He was shaken by it. "Withdrawn into a kind of solitude during the years that followed hard upon my childhood and having only a large library to satisfy my insatiable curiosity, I gorged on a random assortment of books," he wrote toward the end of his life. "Until then . . . my days had passed in a home full of faith, where doubt had not been allowed to graze my soul. Now it entered, or rather rushed upon me, with irresistable violence. Not just doubt of this or that proposition, but doubt of everything. Suddenly I felt a sensation like that reported by those who have been through an earthquake. . . . I was overcome by the blackest melancholy, seized by an extreme disgust for the life which I had not even begun, and crushed, as it were, by distress and terror at the sight of the road through the world which lay before me."[6] What emerged from this adolescent crisis of faith, in which hormones undoubtedly fortified iconoclastic arguments (the following year, at sixteen, he impregnated a maidservant), was the Tocqueville who would always struggle with self-doubt and never let received ideas go unexamined.

Given free reign, Alexis might have become a vagabond when he was graduated from the collegiate school. England beckoned him. He dreamed of traveling abroad with Louis de Kergorlay, a beloved cousin his own age. But there would be no travel until he finished law school, which he entered half-heartedly in 1824, law being the least repugnant of several alternatives. Back to Paris he thus went, for a resumption of life with Louise de Tocqueville. Little is known about his two years at the École de Droit. Had he been disposed to complain as uninhibitedly as Gustave Flaubert, who attended courses there during the 1840s, he would have inveighed against Justinian's *Pandects* and *Institutes*, the lectures of sclerotic professors, the danger of legal gibberish destroying his aptitude for expressive language. Intellectually, it was a barren place in famished times. Two years earlier, after students protested a curb on freedom of the press, school had been suspended and the curriculum reorganized with a view to stripping it of all philosophical content. Alexis found no forum for questions he had begun to ask about the relationship of history, geography, climate, political forms, and legal codes. The successful student didn't ask questions. He soldiered on, looking neither right nor left while intoning articles of the Napoleonic code. And Alexis succeeded where Flaubert would not. In 1826 he defended two theses, one in Latin, one in French.

He was rewarded by the family with a voyage to Italy and Sicily. His brother Édouard, who had resigned a commission in the army after flare-ups of asthma, accompanied him. The young men spent four months abroad, taking notes, climbing volcanoes, and breathing free in what proved to be excellent preparation for Alexis's journey to America. When the voyage ended, professional life began. Hervé, now prefect of a region administered from Versailles, arranged to secure Alexis a niche at the lower court (the "Court of First Instance") in his new bailiwick. The council responsible for confirming such appointments included three members of the Tocqueville clan; council meetings were, to all intents and purposes, family reunions.

Alexis undertook the drudge work of a novice prosecutor with due diligence. He prepared at least sixty briefs between 1826 and 1830 and admitted to being, if not enchanted with his profession, far more interested in the practice of law than in the routine study of it. He found litigation truly antipathetic only when required to argue a case himself, as stage fright crippled him. "Generally speaking . . . I have a craving to excel which will make my life a torment. . . . I find it hard to get used to speaking in public; I grope for words and cut my arguments too short. Beside me are men who reason ill and speak well; that puts me in a continual rage. It seems to me that I am their superior, but when I want to make an effect, I know I am inferior."[7] Years later, intimates would have recognized this as an early version of Tocqueville (by then a legislator and the renowned author of *Democracy in America*) declaring plaintively that he cut an unpersuasive figure on the rostrum of the Chamber of Deputies.

Fortune favored Alexis when, at Versailles, he met Gustave de Beaumont, a more seasoned prosecutor, who valued his intellectual companionship and gladly served as his jovial go-between in the professional world. Tocqueville may have had the better mind, but Beaumont had the bump of conviviality. Their virtues were well matched, and their backgrounds similar. Gustave came from an old feudal family whose branches had spread through-out the Loire region. Like Hervé de Tocqueville, Gustave's father, Jules de Beaumont, had not joined the émigrés. Like Hervé, Jules had lived to tell the tale. He, too, had worn a mayor's sash during the Empire—in the small town of Beaumont-la-Chartre, where the family occupied a chateau somewhat less imposing than the Tocquevilles' at Verneuil. And like Hervé he presided over a household more hospitable to the arts than that of most coun-try squires. Beaumonts not only hunted but played musical instruments. Gustave, whose two older brothers received military commissions, was pledged from birth to the judiciary, these two careers being the customary options for aristocratic children of the day.

Beaumont and Tocqueville bonded so strongly than when Gustave was transferred to Paris in 1829, Alexis was grief-stricken. Until then they had shared quarters at Versailles and almost every day had conversations that reached far beyond the courtroom. Upon leaving law school Alexis had begun to study history, in particular the history of French civilization as conceived and pro-fessed by François Guizot in spellbinding lectures at the Sor-bonne. He and Gustave attended them, often together, sometimes in turn. Hugh Brogan, the distinguished biographer, notes the seminal role of this experience in Tocqueville's intellectual development: "What fascinated Tocqueville about Guizot's lec-tures was their ambition, their profundity, their scope. They were so immensely suggestive—or, as he would have put it, so full of *idées mères* [fertile ideas]. They were the inspiration which he needed; they showed him his own way forward. They were no mere chronicles."[8] The lectures were all the more alluring for hav-ing been banned between 1822 and 1827 by a reactionary govern-ment, in much the same way that philosophical thought had been purged from courses at the law school. Guizot was a leader of the liberal opposition under Charles X, and destined to occupy high office under Louis-Philippe.

The education that Tocqueville and Beaumont devised for themselves also included English and economics. Beaumont's appointment to the Paris tribunal did not interfere with it, and neither did political tumult. This curriculum gave them salutary employment when, in 1830, practicing law became for both of them a torment of divided allegiances. And it continued during the nine months of their travels in America, which may have been inspired after all as much by the prospect of learning together full time as of discovering the New World.

Still, Tocqueville was seldom of one mind about anything, and he did not view matters without ambivalence when he climbed aboard *Le Havre* on April 2, 1831, at the age of twenty-five. The turmoil of 1830 had not yet ended; it remained to be seen whether this revolution would mimic that of 1789. Questions bedeviled him. Would Tocquevilles who had escaped death almost four decades earlier survive this time around? Would he, who carried royal credentials to America, soon find himself in the vanguard of a new generation of émigrés? Was he a researcher or a fugitive? His letters from America, for all their exuberance, wit, and keen observation, reflect those anxieties.

Although my constant purpose has been to translate Tocqueville's meaning, I have taken liberties where a too-literal translation would have betrayed the admirable prose stylist Tocqueville was already proving himself to be. Deleted are unintended redundancies within a single letter, and descriptive passages that Tocqueville copied, sometimes verbatim, from one letter to another.

Gallimard published Tocqueville's letters to his family, Mary Mottley, and abbé Lesueur in 1998 as part of his *Oeuvres complètes*

[Complete Works], volume 14, titled *Correspondance familiale* [Family Correspondence], edited by Jean-Louis Benoît and André Jardin. All thirty-five of these letters are included here. The two letters to Louis de Kergorlay, Tocqueville's cousin, appear in volume 13 of the *Oeuvres complètes*. Tocqueville's letters to all others are from *Tocqueville: Lettres choisies et souvenirs, 1814–1859* [Tocqueville: Selected Letters and Recollections], edited by Françoise Mélonio and Laurence Guellec (Paris: Gallimard, quarto edition, 2003), except for the following: to Ernest de Chabrol (May 18, June 20, September 17, October 7, October 18, October 26, November 28, and December 1, 1831, and January 16, 1832), and to Eugène Stöffels (June 28, 1831), from the Beinecke Library, Yale University; to the vicomte Ernest de Blosseville (October 10, 1831), and to M. Bouchitté (October 11, 1831), from the Beaumont edition of Tocqueville's correspondence (Paris: Michel Lévy, 1866). Selections of this correspondence were published by Paula Deitz in the *Hudson Review* and Stephen Donadio in the *New England Review*.

The excerpts from Beaumont's correspondence all come from his *Lettres d'Amérique, 1831–1832*, edited by André Jardin (Presses Universitaires de France, 1978). Beaumont the amateur artist had an eye for the "picturesque," that voguish ideal he frequently invokes, and his letters as well as his sketches abound in detail missing from Tocqueville's correspondence. Taken together, their letters furnish a stereoscopic picture of the voyage. It should be noted that Tocqueville reserved almost all his impressions of their trek through the backwoods of Michigan for a long essay titled "Quinze jours dans le désert" [A Fortnight in the Wilderness]. On that subject Beaumont was not reticent in his correspondence, from which I quote exceptionally long passages.

1. During the Terror, two of Louis XVI's brothers survived abroad. With Napoleon's downfall and the restoration of the Bourbon dynasty, each ascended the throne in turn, Louis-Stanislas as Louis XVIII (1814 / 1815–1824) and Charles as Charles X (1824–1830).

2. From Hervé de Tocqueville's unpublished *Journal* in the Archives du Département de la Manche at Saint Lô.

3. From Nassau W. Senior's manuscript journal, quoted in Hugh Brogan, *Alexis de Tocqueville* (New Haven: Yale University Press, 2007), 27.

4. Alexis de Tocqueville, letter to Lady Theresa Lewis, May 6, 1857.

5. Among them, Eugène Stöffels and his brother Charles, to whom he wrote letters from America.

6. Alexis de Tocqueville, letter to Sophie Swetchine, February 26, 1857, translated by Hugh Brogan in *Alexis de Tocqueville*, 49–50.

7. Alexis de Tocqueville, letter to Louis de Kergorlay, July 27, 1827.

8. Brogan, *Alexis de Tocqueville*, 93.

LETTERS FROM AMERICA

With excerpts from Gustave de Beaumont's correspondence

Portrait of Tocqueville, courtesy of the Beinecke Library, Yale University. A political colleague of Tocqueville, Charles de Rémusat, portrayed him in his memoirs as "a small, slight man with an agreeable, regular, but sickly face shadowed by a mass of curly brown hair that preserved an air of youth about him; his sad, unanimated features assumed more expression when he talked. The livid pallor of his skin was an early sign of organic ailments and led malicious people to suspect him of being bilious, envious, and everything that follows from that. He was not at all so; only a little mistrustful, often in pain, often discouraged about himself."

THE CROSSING

Tocqueville and Beaumont sailed from Le Havre on April 2, 1831, and landed at Newport, Rhode Island, on May 9, after thirty-seven days at sea.

Alexis de Tocqueville to his mother, on board the vessel
***Le Havre,* bound for New York, April 26, 1831**

It is you, my dear Mama, to whom I wish to write first. I had intended to do so upon my arrival in New York, but I lack the courage to wait until then. Moreover, circumstances are favorable: since the wind speeding us forward is scarcely rocking the boat, my script may be no more illegible than usual. I should like to offer you a substantial letter, but I don't quite know where to begin. Not that anything of great moment has occurred since our separation, only that I feel I have millions of things to tell you. I shall therefore take the easy path and ramble.

Papa will have told you how and at what time he bid us farewell at Le Havre. What he couldn't have reported was our sadness after his departure. Never have I felt such heartache. When he and my brothers left, the bond that tied me to all of you and to France went slack; and I doubt that any American city will ever seem as foreign and deserted to me as Le Havre appeared at that moment.

After painfully killing three long hours, we boarded our vessel.

Rumor had it that we would likely remain in Le Havre for six days. You can imagine how this news thrilled us. We threw ourselves onto our bunks and fell fast asleep, lacking a better alternative. At half past midnight, awoken by some noise overhead, I climbed through the companion hatch and realized that we were under full sail. A jetty lantern was still glowing on the horizon; otherwise no land was visible in the night, and I have seen no sign of it since. I hope, however, that it exists somewhere; for I am ill disposed to live this long on water. The threat of seasickness regularly sends me below deck. While Beaumont has been his usual hale and hearty self, I spent two days in bed queasy and dejected. Only on the third did I take some interest in things of this world and on the fourth I recovered. Most other passengers fared less well than I.

We didn't really mingle until the sixth day, when everyone crept out of his hole. Let me assure you, we made a fine assemblage of pale, yellow, green faces—every color of the rainbow. I should like to acquaint you with the inhabitants of our little world, who, not counting a cow and a donkey, number exactly 181 by my reckoning, 30 housed in the cabin section, 13 in steerage, 120 in the bow, and 18 crew. I shall limit myself to a description of several cabin passengers—the vessel's aristocracy, as it were. In the cabin adjacent to our own is an important English landowner, M. Palmer,[1] who has served in the House of Commons. A very kind, knowledgeable old man, he has taken a liking to us and furnished us with useful information and excellent advice. He is the best of the lot. His roommate—a traveling salesman, to put it more bluntly than he himself might—is the buffoon. Not that he

1. Charles Palmer, a retired major general who had fought in the campaign against Napoleon. He had represented Bath in the House of Commons, and he owned considerable property there and vineyards near Bordeaux.

means to make one laugh. On the contrary, he amuses us despite himself, being a very serious personage, whose entire conversation is wine and politics. And good Lord, what politics! Everything a fool would claim to know after reading *Le Constitutionnel*.[2] His pomposity has us in stitches. He always calls France "My fatherland," as in, "I'm visiting America to sell the wines of my fatherland." People give him a wide berth. He avenges himself by opening one of his bottles every day and hoarding it.

Our other neighbor is M. Schérer,[3] a man whose countenance is such that we couldn't face the prospect of conversing with him for three days; now we cleave together like three toes. . . . Except for his looks, which would be regarded as deplorable anywhere in the world, he is an excellent fellow. To be sure, he resembles in every way a thousand wastrels loitering about the streets of Paris, but we're glad of his company. He speaks very fluently, is happy-go-lucky, and neither dim nor bright.

I must stop drawing these portraits or the letter will never end; suffice it to say that we are as diverse a conglomeration of animals as boarded Noah's ark: a Spaniard, a whole French family, two Americans, a Swiss lady and her children. Relations are, by and large, easy and considerate, if not intensely amiable. We get along with everyone, and it is well that we do, for at sea one either befriends one's companions or fights. There is no middle ground. You'd be amazed, dear Mama, at the peculiar life one leads on this large oceangoing diligence! Being crammed together, constantly exposed, breeds an informality and freedom unimaginable

2. *Le Constitutionnel* was a liberal newspaper, patriotic and anticlerical, favored by the moderately liberal bourgeoisie that gained power and influence in the Revolution of 1830.

3. Édouard Schérer, a son of General Barthélemy Schérer, who had commanded the Army of Italy in 1795, when France defeated Austria at Loano, and served as minister of war from 1797 to 1799.

on land. One lives in the midst of the crowd as if one were alone; some people read aloud, others play games or sing. While I write, my neighbor sups. If one feels impelled to do something—be it eating, drinking, or sobbing—one simply does it. Rooms are so narrow that one must step outside to dress, and, apart from putting on my breeches, I perform my daily toilette for all to see.[4] In short, we live, like the Ancients, on the public square. This is the true land of freedom. Its one drawback is that freedom can be exercised here only within the confines of a wooden box. Most of our companions therefore while away their time in the most trivial pursuits, distilling boredom drop by drop, as far as I can tell.

We haven't been contaminated and busy ourselves much as we normally would ashore, weather permitting. We rise before dawn, study until breakfast at nine o'clock; we resume work at noon and continue until dinnertime. After dinner, we speak English with whoever will tolerate our chatter, and retire at nine p.m. This is not to say that we lack all external distractions. Everything in this world is relative. Think of the nuns [in the play *Ver-vert*] all atwitter over the foul language of their pet parrot. That's precisely how matters stand with us. We watch a cloud on the horizon or the trimming of the sails with absolutely rapt attention. The other day we spotted a barrel in the sea. It caused a general stir; pistols were produced; and we used it for target practice, making an infernal racket. Mine was the shot that pierced it. This has entered our annals as "The Day of the Barrel." Another sensation was Schérer's visored cap being carried off by a wave. But unquestionably the most memorable event took place this morning when a gust of wind blew a charming little sky-blue bird, half

4. "For all to see": written as "face à Israel" in the original, or "in the presence of Israel," from "coram Israel," a common expression in the Vulgate meaning "to appear in public."

dead, into our rigging. It's a species we don't have in Europe, and the Americans aboard immediately recognized it as one of their own. You have no idea how delighted we were with the little creature, which seemed to have been sent for the express purpose of announcing imminent landfall. We caught it and put it in a cage.

One week ago, on a delicious spring evening, our ship was plowing ahead, I'm not sure how, on a windless day in calm seas. Someone proposed that we dance. So Beaumont went off to fetch his flute and a merry time was had by all, romping on the deck. If you want to know where this occurred, consult a map for the convergence of forty-two degrees latitude and thirty-four degrees longitude! There, or thereabouts, was the dance hall. Man must be an animal heedless of all that may befall him to caper as we did over a bottomless abyss, under the vault of heaven, with death on all sides. But after all, is the same not true of the best furnished salon in the Faubourg Saint-Germain?[5] And then, one accustoms oneself to everything. I assure you that I no longer scan the horizon for land as I did our first day out; I am already quite used to seeing nothing around me but a more or less closed circle, with billowy clouds floating overhead. More than once, however, we have witnessed spectacles that deserve an artist's eye. One moonless night, for example, water began to sparkle like an electrifying machine. It was pitch black outside, and the ship's prow slicing through the sea spewed fiery foam twenty feet in either direction. To get a better view, I shimmied onto the bowsprit. From that vantage point, the prow looked as if it were leaping at me with a forward wall of glittering waves; it was sublime and admirable beyond my ability to evoke it. The solitude that reigns in the middle of the ocean is something formidable. During the first ten

5. The Faubourg Saint-Germain was a neighborhood of elegant mansions in Paris, inhabited mainly by the old-line aristocracy.

days of our journey, we regularly spied other sails; large birds tracked us and often perched on our spars; the sea abounded in fish. Beginning at around 30 degrees longitude, the vessels, birds, and fish disappeared. The ocean acquired a somber cast, but its monotony impresses one as vast rather than dull.

At the approach of the Banks of Newfoundland, we were buffeted by two gales, one lasting thirty-six hours. It was a repeat performance of what we experienced on the sea of Sicily [four years ago],[6] with this notable difference that we were never in any danger of capsizing, as our sturdy vessel cleaved the tallest waves.

The real danger in those circumstances is of falling and breaking an arm or a leg. You can't imagine, dear Mama, what a toll is taken of one's energy by the continual effort to keep one's balance. I needed a sea voyage to acquaint myself with all the perils of distraction. If you daydream for a minute, you're liable to wake up on your backside, in which case you slide straight ahead until you meet a wall. At table, the diner opposite may receive a glass of wine in his face. Servants spill sauce down your collar.

Eventually, one grows used to all that. The thirty people at table end up regulating their movements and we greet one another with the most agreeable decorum. Moreover, one endures these tribulations only in very heavy weather.

But to return to the Newfoundland Banks, that is where birds and fish reappear, in particular one called the Portuguese man-of-war.[7] It's a little fish with floating transparent membranes that

6. Tocqueville had traveled in Italy and Sicily with his older brother Édouard in 1827.

7. Alvan Stewart, an American traveling from New York to Liverpool aboard the packet *Manchester* in May 1831, also observed the Portuguese man-of-war, a sea creature that resembles a jellyfish and has a powerful sting.

catch the wind like sails. Then there are fish no bigger than a pinhead; they have the same properties as glowworms and in their millions produce an electric show of the kind I mentioned earlier. After fish and birds came kelp. It is said that this sea grass played its part in the discovery of America by announcing the approach of land to the mariners who first crossed the ocean.

Today, May 4, the day on which I resume my letter, we are situated at sixty-six degrees longitude. New York is only 130 leagues away.[8] It will be a negligible distance if we strike a leading breeze, otherwise possibly a week's voyage. Meanwhile, we've already been thirty-two days at sea! Our fresh provisions are largely gone, and sugar is already rationed. Despite it all, you will believe me, I hope, when I say that my chief satisfaction upon docking at New York will not be stepping foot on American soil but receiving news from Europe. The packet from Le Havre leaving on May 15 will undoubtedly not have arrived, but other vessels that set sail eight or ten days after we did may have passed us. Only seeing you again, my dear Mama, could exceed the pleasure of reading letters from all of you.

To his mother from shipboard, May 9, 1831
(continuation of the above letter)
Yesterday evening the first shouts of "Land Ahoy!" were heard, but one needed a spyglass to sight the shoreline. Today, at dawn, Long Island came into view. We are fast approaching the coast and can already make out greensward and leafy trees. It's a delicious spectacle. I must cut this letter short to join the celebration on deck. For once, the sea is not inconveniencing anyone.

8. The league was measured differently at different times in different countries. For Tocqueville it was about three miles, or five kilometers.

Gustave de Beaumont to his father, April 25

We were to weigh anchor at noon, but, with certain details delaying us one or two hours, the tide ebbed and our vessel fetched up on a sand bank as soon as it set sail. There it remained until high tide rolled in at midnight. We were two days traversing the Channel, pushed by a stiff easterly (we logged better than nine leagues an hour). Until now, that was the high point of our voyage. It is important to distance oneself from the coastline, which we did with uncommon speed. Since then, the wind has not constantly blown our way, but we can't complain. Having sailed 800 leagues, we should, if fortune favors us, arrive in New York, 350 leagues away, in a week or ten days. At this moment we are very near the Grand Banks; every day the captain shows us our coordinates on a map. . . . What sad thoughts breed in this vast emptiness between the sky and the sea! What a frightful desert has supplanted the places in which I had a fatherland, a family, friends! And why did I flee my country? What am I going to do on foreign soil? Heaven grants us only a few years of life; one can almost count the days of youth and here I am devoting them to the hazards of an adventurous life! What am I seeking? Am I pursuing a chimera? . . .

Usually we speak only English, Americans and English being the majority on board. . . . A young American woman named Miss Edwards gives us regular English lessons, which most often take the form of her correcting our errors in long, more or less trivial conversations. Despite her eighteen years, her freshness, her niceness and physical charms, our relations are entirely *fraternal*. . . . The other Americans with us are fine people on the whole, especially the *Scarmehorn* [Schermerhorn] family, the spelling of whose name I won't vouch for. . . .

Here is how we fill our days:

Portrait of Beaumont in 1827, by Blaize

At five-thirty in the morning we are awoken by an infernal racket that drowns out both the noise of the sea and the whistling of the wind: I refer to [Beaumont's brother] Jules's alarm clock, which we have come to find invaluable. We rise as best we can . . . in the rolling and pitching of the boat, which makes it difficult to dress without banging one's head and elbows against the wall of a cramped cabin. We work until nine, when we are interrupted by the breakfast bell. Everyone takes his place at the common table and begins to eat, paying as little attention as possible to breaking glasses, falling bottles, spilling sauces, etc. We have fresh bread every day, excellent wine, Bordeaux, Madeira (one's fill of it), and often champagne. Our meals would be good if we had a decent cook; but the latter spoils everything he touches. What he touches are the ducks, chickens, and turkeys that travel with us, whose number diminishes daily. I forgot to tell you that among our traveling companions are a cow, sheep, and a donkey, all of which . . . will eventually grace our table.

After breakfast we usually climb to the deck. Loungers spend the whole day up there observing the vagaries of the weather. . . . We resume our work at eleven, which, at the moment, has us translating a book on American prisons that will be of great interest to the French government. We shall present it upon our return. Since labor of this kind is inherently rather tiresome, we leaven it with readings other than penological, which will stand us in good stead. We've already made our way through a complete history of the United States. Now we've immersed ourselves in political economy with the work of Jean-Baptiste Say.[9] It appeals

9. Jean-Baptiste Say, a Protestant from Lyon, took part in the eighteenth-century Revolution as secretary to the finance minister. Between 1794 and 1800 he edited a journal titled *La Decade philosophique,*

to us very strongly, and I can't tell you what a pleasure it is being shut up in our little cell, exchanging ideas, and making an earnest effort to seek the truth. Tocqueville is truly a man of distinction, remarkable for his loftiness of intellect and nobility of soul. The better I know him the more I like him. Our existences here are entwined; it's clear that we have and shall always have a common destiny. . . . We are meditating great projects. First we shall accomplish as best we can the mission we've been assigned; that is our strict duty and must be done conscientiously. But while studying the penal system, we shall be seeing America. While visiting its prisons, we shall be familiarizing ourselves with its inhabitants, its cities, its institutions, its ways. We shall learn the mechanism of its republican government. Europe is not at all acquainted with this government. It is spoken of incessantly in false comparisons with countries that bear no resemblance to it. What about a book that provides a precise idea of the American people, that outlines its history, that paints its character in broad strokes, that analyzes its social state and in this regard corrects many erroneous opinions? . . .

To return to our daily schedule, we dine at three in the afternoon. I speak only of the formal meals; many people, being otherwise unoccupied, eat all day long. After dinner, one strolls, trying not to lose one's balance when the sea is rough. . . . When it's

---

littéraire, et politique [The Political, Literary, and Philosophical Decade], in which he expounded the doctrines of Adam Smith. His major opus (possibly the work referred to here), *Traité d'économie politique, ou simple exposition de la manière dont se forment, se distribuent, et se composent les richesses* [Treatise on Political Economy, or the Production, Distribution, and Consumption of Wealth], was first published in 1804. Between 1828 and 1830 he published *Cours complet d'économie politique pratique* [Complete Course of Practical Political Economy].

calm and the sky is clear, we celebrate enthusiastically. I agreed to play a flute concerto, which (I note in passing) those sworn enemies of all musical harmony, the English, greatly appreciated; one thing led to another and the flute concert to dance music, with me standing on a chair conducting the orchestra like a born maestro as people performed every figure of the quadrille in swift succession: pantalon, pastourelle, poule, galop, and waltz.

In general, our diversions are full of light-hearted gaiety. Each person adds his flavor to the mix and we are soon on intimate terms. It's rather like traveling in a diligence. We cleave together less closely than coach passengers, being more numerous, but our mutual internment lasts longer.

Supper is served at nine p.m., which for me means tea. I never partake of this meal because I don't eat in the evening. I suspect my habits will change, however. Americans generally eat supper and nothing is more disagreeable than being somewhere and not doing what everyone else does.

For now, Tocqueville and I usually go to bed when our companions gather for their evening repast. With only very flimsy partitions separating us from the diners, who could easily see us if they wished, we fall asleep to the clatter of spoons and forks.

Sometimes we sleep, but at times one is so rudely tossed about that shutting one's eyes is out of the question. We count ourselves lucky when we're not thrown from our beds by a sudden, violent jolt. I've barely escaped that fate. . . .

. . . Nothing is more unpredictable than the length of crossings; the average is forty or forty-five days, but it isn't unusual for voyages to last longer. One of our fellow passengers, a young man, once spent sixty-six days at sea. He has crossed eight times and it has never taken fewer than forty-six days, almost always more. . . .

Tocqueville to his father, May 8, 1831, on board *Le Havre*

I can see the New York–Liverpool packet from here.[10] One of my fellow passengers has offered to forward a letter that will reach you by way of England. It would take much longer crossing on the Le Havre packet. I shall take advantage of this opportunity, dear Papa, to send you my news. An imminent deadline and the fear of having to pay our obliging companion a steep delivery charge will make this letter slim, but I believe that even so it will give you much pleasure. I am thriving: my stomach has coped quite well with shipboard fare, unwholesome though it decidedly is.[11]

Our voyage has been a mixture of good and bad: the beginning was all fair, the middle stormy, then contrary winds held us back. Today, we approach New York at last. Only one degree of longitude separates us and the wind is favorable, the sea superb.

We spent our time very well. Our companions demonstrated great good will and work fully occupied us during the hours we didn't spend with them. In short, our voyage was long, but very happy. God willing, the first packet from France will bring good news. You are constantly in our thoughts. I didn't need this absence to know how much I love all of you, but I didn't know how much one can suffer from long deprivation of news, when it concerns the family.

The bottom of the sheet is compelling me to finish. I've written Mama a long letter, which will come on the first Le Havre packet.

10. He was apparently mistaken. In a letter written on May 14, Beaumont noted that the two vessels had not met and that the Liverpool packet would not leave New York until the 16th.
11. Tocqueville had lifelong stomach problems.

So, adieu. I cannot tell you how much I am moved by all the ideas that these few words bring to mind. Adieu, my dear Papa. I embrace you with all my heart and Mama as well, Bébé,[12] my brothers and sisters. May God see to it that this letter finds all of you in good health.

Have Beaumont's letter posted as soon as possible.

Tocqueville to his father, New York, May 14, 1831

The attached letter couldn't leave on the Liverpool packet, which didn't come abreast of us. However, I insist that it go via England. It may thus reach you several days earlier. Anyway, it is one more chance of transmitting our first news.

The thought that you are worried about us torments me and poisons the feeling of well-being that we've experienced here. We reckoned that you would be without word of us for almost three months. I fear, knowing you as I do, that that interval will have given your imagination time enough to raise alarms about our safety. It is in fact more time than it should be. First, our voyage lasted longer than expected. Then, the maritime schedule has been changed, so that beginning this month, packets leave every ten days. As it happened, we arrived here on the 11th, the day after a boat sailed; now we must wait until the 20th. I wish this change had taken place later, but we are happy about it all the same. News from France, and above all from our families, is our over-riding need. Consider that we are not used to being so far away from home; that France's current predicament magnifies our anxiety a hundredfold; that, finally, we are living among people who

12. Bébé was a sobriquet for abbé Lesueur, the priest who had tutored Alexis's father, Hervé de Tocqueville, and remained in the family as tutor to Hervé's three sons.

are utter strangers to us and with whom we have no point of contact outside matters of a dry, serious nature.

We are therefore living more in your midst, despite the 1500 leagues separating us, than among the Americans whom we see every day. So pray, deprive us not of this resource; make sure that no packet leaves without a long, forthright, detailed letter to us. We, in turn, shall be as punctual as possible. But bear in mind two things, my dear Papa.

The first is that nothing is more unpredictable than ocean crossings; one boat will make it in twenty days, another in fifty. We returned with an American who, last year, arrived in New York sixty-six days after departing Le Havre.

Secondly, the mail service in this country is rapid but quite unpredictable. That is what our consul reiterated yesterday. So, if a letter we send from the interior goes astray or is held up, you may not hear from us for fifteen or twenty days, perhaps more.

I therefore beg of you not to worry needlessly. I give you my word of honor that everything I've just told you is the exact truth. This letter has only one purpose, to let you know that we're still alive; an enormous letter that the Le Havre packet will bring Mama contains details. Rest assured that we are in the pink of health, that we have settled in beautifully and are everywhere received with open arms.

I hope this communiqué pleases you. Adieu, my good father. A heartfelt embrace for you, Mama, Bébé, brothers and sisters.

Tocqueville to his mother, New York, May 14, 1831

When we first caught sight of Long Island, dear Mama, I hardly expected what would soon befall us. Once on deck, I realized that the wind, blowing from the east since morning, had shifted to the west. An hour later, it became violent and contrary. We were forced to tack, that is, to zigzag, but made no progress. As the morning wore on, our crew noted that the wind had settled "in a quarter," meaning that it would likely continue westerly for several days, to our dismay, for we had sick people among us, and had almost exhausted our fresh provisions; even wood and grain were in alarmingly short supply. Passengers therefore petitioned the captain to veer north and make for Newport. He agreed. So it came to pass that at nine in the evening of May 9 we dropped anchor in the outer harbor of that town, sixty leagues from New York. A fishing boat soon drew up and hailed us. Our delight at having reached land was such that all the younger folk and the captain himself crowded aboard the dory. Half an hour later, in damp breeches and on shaky legs, we were dancing jigs at Newport's dock, as happy as could be just to find ourselves back in the world. We then made our way to an inn, where the captain treated us to supper. What I personally relished most—you may not appreciate this—was the water we drank; the water on board had become undrinkable (apropos of which I must tell you that the captain, excellent man and fine sailor though he is, had horribly mismanaged everything to do with the vessel's stores and comfort). As for my companions, they ate with both feet in the trough. Then, remembering "French gallantry," they and I bought a large quantity of fresh provisions, re-embarked, and reached our vessel at midnight. No one had yet gone to bed. In triumph we hauled our booty down to the ladies' saloon, and proceeded to sup all over again. When I say "supped," please understand that I refer, in my case, only to the conversational aspect of the meal.

The following day we visited Newport. To our indulgent eyes, the town seemed quite pretty. It is a cluster of houses no larger than chicken coops but very trim. Except that such neatness would be unimaginable in France, the inhabitants are not conspicuously different from Frenchmen. They dress like us and their physiognomies are so various that one would be hard pressed to identify their national origin. I believe that this must be true throughout the United States.

After delighting for three hours in the sensation of walking on solid ground, we boarded the steamer that plies between Providence and New York. You would marvel at the interior of this immense machine. One detail will suffice: it contains three large saloons, two for men, one for women, where as many as eight hundred people eat and sleep comfortably. It completed the run of sixty leagues to New York in just eighteen hours, despite choppy seas and contrary winds.[13]

This entire coastline of America is low lying and nondescript. Hardly a tree remains standing in a region densely wooded two centuries ago. We sailed between Long Island and Connecticut, and approached New York at sunrise, entering the port from behind. I don't know whether our view was colored by the experience of thirty-five days at sea and our recent passage down a drab coast, but I assure you that cries of admiration went up when we beheld the city's surroundings. Picture a sea dotted with sails, a lovely sweep of notched shoreline, blossoming trees on greensward sloping down to the water, a multitude of small, artfully embellished candy-box houses in the background—and you have the entrance to New York by way of the Sound.

I was so struck by what I presume to be the commodiousness of these little houses and their excellent situation in the landscape that I shall try to obtain the design of several especially pretty

13. Navigation by steamboat had made great strides since Robert Fulton accomplished the round-trip river voyage between New York and Albany aboard the *Clermont* in 1807. The New York–Providence line was opened in 1822. More than 130 miles of its course took place at sea. Tocqueville's steamer, the *President,* had been put in service a year earlier. It was 413 feet long.

ones; Émilie may perhaps find them useful for Nacqueville.[14] I have already been informed that they are not expensive; we have nothing comparable in France.

I must try to describe things more succinctly lest my letters swell into quarto volumes.

Beaumont to his mother, May 14

We reached Newport at dusk. Tocqueville and I immediately had ourselves rowed to shore. When we landed, we were thrilled as never before. Unsteady on our feet, we continued to feel the rocking of the boat even on solid ground and to see all the fixed objects around us moving. . . .

Bright and early on the morning of May 10 we sought out the collector (of custom duties) for permission to unload our belongings. He granted it, provided we swear on the Bible that we had nothing subject to duty, and after paying a minimal fee of one dollar, or 5.30 francs, we obtained customs clearance. As it happens, the inspectors, unlike their French counterparts (from what I hear), examined our trunks perfunctorily. We then strolled through the town. It has sixteen thousand residents, a magnificent port, which has recently been fortified, little houses, which look as if they had been modeled after our kitchen at Beaumont-la-Chartre, but whose tidiness calls to mind an operatic stage set—they're all painted. There is also a church with a rather remarkable steeple (I've sketched it in Jules's album). We had been told that the women of Newport are famously beautiful; we found them all quite the opposite. The new population, as far as we

14. Émilie de Tocqueville was his sister-in-law, the wife of his eldest brother, Hippolyte, eight years his senior. She had inherited the chateau of Nacqueville, eight kilometers from Cherbourg and near the Tocqueville chateau.

could make out, lacks an original character: it is neither English nor French nor German, but a mixture of all nations. This culture is mercantile: the little town of Newport has four or five banks. The same holds true everywhere else in the Union. . . .

At three p.m. we boarded an immense steam-driven vessel capable of accommodating as many as 800 or 1,000 passengers, with a bed for each. We numbered only 130. It took seventeen hours to travel from Newport to New York, a distance of sixty leagues. This brief voyage was intensely interesting and fraught with near tragic circumstances. First of all, the mere navigation of such a boat and the means employed to steer it are daunting. We viewed one of the country's most picturesque coasts, to the left of us, as we traversed the Sound between New York and Connecticut. . . . The Sound is an immense body of water, but narrow enough that one can discern everything on both shores. Perched among rocks that line the water on either side are the prettiest country houses imaginable. . . . We were particularly struck by the enormous number of vessels animating this majestic scene—brigs, sloops, dinghies crisscrossing in every direction. . . .

IN NEW YORK

Tocqueville and Beaumont resided in a boardinghouse at 66 Broadway until June 30, 1831, mingling in New York society, doing research, interviewing men of consequence, and visiting prisons and reformatories, notably Sing Sing, thirty miles up the Hudson in Ossining, which had been opened six years earlier.

Continuation of Tocqueville's letter of May 14 to his mother

Here we are in New York. From a Frenchman's perspective, it looks disarmingly weird. There isn't a dome, a steeple, or a large edifice in sight, which leaves one with the impression that one has landed in a suburb, not the city itself. At its very core, where everything is built of brick, monotony rules. The houses lack cornices, balustrades, carriage entrances. Streets are ill paved, but pedestrians have sidewalks.

Lodging was a problem at first because foreigners abound at this time of year and because we sought a pension, not an inn. At last we found one that suits us perfectly, on the most fashionable street in town, called Broadway. As luck would have it, M. Palmer, the Englishman I mentioned earlier, had already found accommodations in this boardinghouse. Our shipboard friendship and especially the interest he is taking in our mission have led him to oblige us whenever and however possible. Best of all are the amenities offered by Americans. They beggar description. Men of every class seem to compete for the honor of being most cordial and useful. The newspapers, which report everything, announced our arrival and expressed the hope that people would come forward to assist us. They have outdone themselves. All doors are open and welcoming hands extended at every turn. I, for whom diligences and inns have always been the tiresome appanage of travel, find these new conditions most agreeable.

One difficulty that has hampered us ever since we left France, and which we have begun to overcome, is language. In Paris, we fancied we knew English, not unlike collegiate school graduates who think that their baccalaureate is a certificate of learning. We were soon disabused of that notion. All we had was a basic vehicle for making rapid progress. We truly drove ourselves during the ocean crossing; I remember days on a windswept deck translating English when it was difficult to hold a pen. Unfortunately, with so many French speakers aboard we could always fall back on our native language. Here the situation is different. As no one speaks French, we have had to give it up. Our conversation is entirely in English. It may sound pitiful, but at least we make ourselves understood and understand everything. Interlocutors even tell us that we show *great promise.* If we do end up mastering the language, it will be an excellent acquisition. The benefits we've already reaped illustrate for me the foolishness of a Monsieur de Belisle,[1] who travels to lands where he cannot converse. One might as well take strolls in one's room with the windows shuttered.

No doubt you would like to know, my dear Mama, how we spend our days. We rise between five and six and work until eight. At eight o'clock the breakfast bell rings. Everyone convenes punctually. Afterward we visit several establishments to interview men with knowledge of matters that concern us. We return for dinner

1. Bon Georges-Charles-Evrard de Belisle, Hippolyte de Tocqueville's father-in-law.

at three o'clock. Between five and seven we put our notes in order. At seven we go out and socialize over tea. This way of life is most agreeable, and I believe eminently sane. But it flouts all our assumptions. Thus, we were quite surprised at first to see women appearing at the breakfast table with faces carefully made up for the day. We are told that this is customary in all private houses. Paying visits to a lady at nine in the morning is not thought improper.

At first we found the absence of wine from meals a serious deprivation, and we are still baffled by the sheer quantity of food that people somehow stuff down their gullets. Besides breakfast, dinner, and tea, with which Americans eat ham, they have very copious suppers and often a snack. So far, this is the only respect in which I do not challenge their superiority; they, on the other hand, reckon themselves superior in many ways. People here seem to reek of national pride. It seeps through their politeness.

Sunday, New York, May 15
I take up my letter again, dear Mama, after returning from high mass at a Catholic Church five minutes from our residence. I carried the little book that Bébé gave me and assure you that I was thinking about all of you during mass, of him and of you, dear Mama. I can't tell you how singularly one is affected, when far from home, by all the religious ceremonies one has attended since childhood. At one point, with none but Americans around me, I fancied myself in France and was so persuaded of it that I spoke French to my uncomprehending neighbors. The church, a large one, was filled to overflowing, and the congregation more meditative than an assembly of French worshipers. We heard a good sermon on the subject of grace and were pleased to discover that we could follow it. Our intention had been to visit the bishop after

mass, but he is in Europe right now.[2] We were told that his grand vicar, a good-natured, amiable priest named Power, would receive us splendidly, but Father Power was not at home when we called; we shall return tomorrow.

Catholics are firmly established in New York. They have five churches and more than twenty thousand members. I have heard Americans say that converts are numerous. Their numbers are increasing in various parts of the Union and I should not be surprised if a religion so beleaguered in Europe made great strides in this country. Every year another fifteen or twenty thousand Catholics arrive from Europe. They spread throughout the wildernesses of the West, where the need for religion is most keenly felt. They become fervent, if they aren't already, or their children do. So indispensable is a religious doctrine seen to be on this side of the Atlantic that Protestants themselves hold lapsed Catholics in low regard.

I thought these details would interest you.

I beg you, dear Mama, not only to transmit this letter to Édouard's household, but to ask Hippolyte how the arrangement sits with them. I prefer addressing only one person at a time and pouring out all my news. The thicker a letter, the less liable it is to go astray. Clearly, Beaumont and I have had nothing to complain about thus far. Launched on the most marvelous voyage imaginable, we enjoy privileges that travelers are seldom vouchsafed. Our brains are at work, we exercise our bodies, and time

2. The bishop, Jean Dubois, had emigrated during the Revolution. At the time of Tocqueville's visit, he was in Rome raising money and recruiting priests for his diocese. John Power, the grand vicar, was an Irish priest who had been called to America in 1819 by the trustees of Saint Peter's parish in New York. He was a theologian and renowned preacher.

flies. But even the most beautiful things of this world have their dark side, and we cannot withdraw into ourselves without feeling pangs of anxiety. Almost two months and fifteen hundred leagues of sea separate us. What has become of you? What are you doing right now, as I calmly write this letter and gloat over my good fortune? What are my father's political circumstances? How is your health, dear Mama? How is good Bébé carrying his eighty years? Is Alexandrine[3] feeling better or worse? What are my brothers doing, and Émilie? What, finally, is the state of France? I ask myself these questions during the day; they return at night and prey upon my mind. We are dying to hear from you, but when we do, our happiness will be cheated by the realization that your news is five weeks old or more. How many changes, how many revolutions can take place during that interval! Last year, between July 26 and August 8, less than a fortnight, was there anyone in France whose life had not been turned upside down?[4]

I'm sure you want to know what we plan to do next, but we haven't made any definite decisions. We think we'll remain here for another three weeks or so. We would like to visit Boston, then, after coming back, to set out for a little town one hundred

3. Alexandrine was the wife of Tocqueville's brother Édouard. Her father, Auguste-Alexandre Ollivier, was an immensely rich banker and had been a peer during the Restoration. Through his marriage, Édouard became one of the two hundred largest shareholders in the Bank of France and the landlord of a manorial estate in the Oise.

4. On July 26, the Bourbon monarchy issued its last edicts. A revolutionary uprising followed on July 27–29, known as "Les Trois glorieuses." On August 8, Louis-Philippe acceded to the throne as a constitutional monarch. Tocqueville's father, who had been an important prefect during the Restoration, lost his seat in the Chamber of Peers. Unemployment was rife. Riots continued to break out in major cities, often resulting in the destruction of church property.

leagues northwest of New York called Auburn, which is the site of a very famous penitentiary.[5] In this land, there is incredible contempt for distances. The immense rivers, some of which we've seen meeting the sea, and the canals built to connect them make it possible to travel day and night at four leagues an hour, on boats as commodious as houses, with no bumps or relays. Thus, people do not say that one is one hundred leagues away from one's destination, but twenty-five hours.

My first letter went to father on the Liverpool packet, which I was sure would be the quickest, most reliable carrier. I hate to think of you anguished by our long silence and hope that M. Hottinguer has reassured you.[6] May this be a lesson to you: whatever is said about the ease with which one now crosses the ocean, it is still an enterprise fraught with imponderables. One cannot fix its duration. And besides, if a letter should miss the packet, there will be a further delay of two or three weeks, or sometimes a month.

Here I am at the end of this immense letter. I could relate many other things, for we are all eyes and ears. Eventually I shall relate them, little by little. Tell Papa, Bébé, my brothers and sisters that although the letter is not addressed to them, I had them in mind when writing it, that I think of them incessantly, that nothing in life will make me happier than clasping all of you to my bosom.

Good-bye, my good mother. I have not yet forgotten your

5. The penal system at Auburn required inmates to work during the day, together but in silence, and live isolated from one another at night.

6. Jean-Conrad Hottinguer was a prominent French banker of Swiss origin, the co-founder of France's first savings bank, the Caisse d'Épargne et de Prévoyance. Presumably more widely traveled than the Tocquevilles, he may have been in a position to explain the benign circumstances of Alexis's silence.

parting recommendation, and never shall, I hope. Beaumont almost cried when he read what Bébé wrote in the book he gave me and has asked me to tell him that he will never forget the sentence at the end, which refers to both of us.

Please keep this letter. It contains details I haven't had time to note and which I shall take pleasure revisiting at a later date.

I've folded it peculiarly in order to include one to Louis de Kergorlay; I don't know his whereabouts and am afraid my letter might go astray. Be so kind as to have it handed to him in Paris or posted out of town, if you know his address.

May 19
The April 15 packet has not yet arrived, though winds are favorable. The one that left Liverpool on the same day is here with comforting news about France. I pray that the reports shall be borne out. We can't wait for our letters.

Beaumont to his father, May 16

. . . One of our first visits was to the French consul, Baron de Saint-André, for whom we bore a letter from the foreign minister. He has a wife and children; they are amiable people and straightaway invited us to dinner. Amiability aside, there is nothing to be gained from their conversation; they know nothing whatever about the country in which they are residing and utterly lack the spirit of observation. We shall dine there again today, which annoys us because we have better things to do. M. Palmer (our fellow passenger) continues to lavish attention and care upon us. He is ferreting out everyone who might be useful to us. We have been introduced to the governor of the state of New York, the mayor of the city, the *recorder*, the *aldermen*, and almost all the judges, several of whom proffered their services before we asked for them. . . .

. . . The new society in which we find ourselves bears no resemblance to those of Europe. It has no model; its basic conditions of existence are unique, which should give pause to all would-be imitators.

That a great nation—a vigorous, enterprising country in which the government hardly makes its presence felt—lacks an army is quite remarkable. But how can Europe profit from this example? The United States has no ambitious neighbors to fear; it is more powerful than the countries surrounding it. What purpose would an army serve?

In the United States political parties are almost unknown. Government posts can be a bone of contention, but never is the fundamental system questioned. The only thing that preoccupies everyone is *commerce*. It is the *national passion* and merchants conduct their business without benefit of armed national guards and troops of the line. But what relevance does this have to states whose citizens have long been at one another's throats, where the administration must constantly call upon the army to quell internal feuds?

Americans are, as I said, a *mercantile* people. They are consumed by a desire for riches, which carries in its train a host of disreputable passions: cupidity, fraud, bad faith. Their sovereign goal is to make money. On the other hand, no or little shame attaches to bankruptcy; it is quite common in all cities.

Still, this society has two faces. Where the one I've just described is vicious, the other displays strong moral features. Hence, American mores are extremely pure. A wife who misbehaves is regarded as a rarity. I daresay, one encounters only happy couples. The winter is a season of social gatherings, but ultimately domestic life is what marriage is all about. Single men concern themselves only with single women.[7] The latter, once they're married, are absolutely pledged to their spouses. . . . In sum, the contentment exuded by families is something one would like for oneself. I should never care to plight my troth here because of the vexations likely to attend marriage in a foreign land. But seeing as how the exception in all other countries is the rule in America, Tocqueville and I could not help but conclude that if ever we should be the victims of some political catastrophe, we would come live abroad with our wives and children.

What is the source of such morality in people who, as we have seen, are not always virtuous? I believe that I shall be able in due course to answer that question more fully. But I already see several things at work, the first being the religious spirit that informs society; nowhere are religious ideas honored more than here. All forms of worship are free, but the man who belongs to no church would be considered *a brute*. . . .

Secondly, there is one class, that of merchants all sharing the same interest and all vying for the same thing—*riches.* There is no idle class; one doesn't encounter here, as one does in France, a certain number of individuals whose sole occupation is the seduction of women.

7. In *Itinéraire pittoresque sur le fleuve Hudson* [A Picturesque Voyage up the Hudson River], published two years earlier, another French traveler, the French artist Jacques-Gérard Milbert, noted the existence of brothels in all American cities, carefully identified as such and assigned to certain districts. Prostitutes who, upon leaving those districts for any reason, did not wear the "garments of moral propriety" or comported themselves "provocatively" might be severely punished. "This lawful repression," Milbert wrote, "is necessary in a country that accords great freedom to young women, even those of the upper class, who usually go about their business, visiting or shopping, unescorted; this way they need not fear embarrassing mistakes" (*Itinéraire pittoresque*, 2:228–229). New York had more than 200 brothels, as a conservative estimate.

Why are our garrison cities more immoral than others? Because a regiment increases the number of idlers. Here, commerce and industry absorb all one's time. Add to this the fact that Americans have a colder temperament than we do. . . .

. . . The Sabbath is observed with the utmost rigor. No one works and the shops are shut tighter than in Paris. The only permissible reading is the Bible.[8]

I will not undertake to describe New York because I am not yet sufficiently acquainted with the city. However, on Saturday evening, Tocqueville and I, during one of our walks, came across a church open for prayer. A few pious souls sat inside. We spied a staircase leading to the steeple. Up it we went, from attic to attic, climbing narrow, dark stairs and, after many tribulations, reached the top. There we enjoyed an admirable panorama: an island city of 240,000 inhabitants surrounded on one side by the ocean, on the others by immense rivers studded with vessels large and small. Its port is of immense proportions. Public edifices are rare and generally undistinguished.

Here the fine arts are in their infancy. The commerce and industry that beget wealth do not foster good taste. As for what Americans think about French political life, don't imagine, as you may be inclined to, that our revolutionaries excite unbounded enthusiasm. They consider the hero of two worlds[9] a man of fine

8. In France, the law of November 18, 1814, made Sabbath rest obligatory, to the consternation of liberals, who condemned it for violating freedom of conscience and freedom of work.

9. The marquis de Lafayette was sometimes referred to as the "héro des deux mondes." His lifelong allegiance to republican ideals did not sit well with aristocratic families loyal to the Bourbon monarchy. Tocqueville and Beaumont, though keenly aware of Charles X's failings, shared the political prejudice of Bourbon loyalists who remembered that Lafayette had commanded a French Revolutionary army in 1792 and, more recently, during the Revolution of 1830, appeared on a balcony of the

character but poor judgment, who wants to dress a nation in political theories that don't fit properly.

I note, besides, that here as elsewhere the aristocracy of money aspires to distinction. Much is made of family trees. I was quite surprised to hear these proud champions of equality call themselves *honorable esquires.* They display coats of arms on their carriages and their seals.

Wherever one goes there is talk of superiority. The self-esteem of Americans verges on conceit. I attribute this to the accolades their government receives in Europe. The result is that one must praise them lavishly to remain on good terms with them. I do it whole-heartedly, without compromising my perception. National pride leads them to do their utmost to fascinate us and show us only the attractive side of things. But I hope that we shall learn the truth. . . .

Tocqueville to Louis de Kergorlay,[10] New York, May 18, 1831

. . . Up to now, not everything I see fills me with enthusiasm, because I ascribe more to the nature of things than to the will of men. That sums up my present view. Still, the spectacle before my eyes is enormous. Never have a people been blessed with such happy, dynamic conditions of existence. Human freedom dis-

---

Paris town hall alongside Louis-Philippe wrapped in a tricolor flag. Tocqueville scorned him not as a traitor to his class so much as a naïf who would have crudely wed France to American institutions.

10. Comte Louis de Kergorlay was a cousin of Tocqueville. Having graduated from the École Polytechnique during the Restoration, he served in the artillery, fought in the battle for Algiers, and remained a staunch supporter of the Bourbon monarchy after its fall in 1830. He was arrested in 1832 for participating in a plot to overthrow Louis-Philippe. He and Tocqueville remained close throughout their lives even though they were politically at odds.

ports itself in all its fullness and power, drawing energy from whatever benefits each individual, but at no individual's expense. One cannot fail to see that there is something *feverish* about the movement of industry and thought here. So far this fever seems only to have invigorated people without compromising reason. However strenuously one exploits the resources presented by physical nature, nature always matches one's efforts. As accomplishments grow, the not-yet-accomplished grows proportionately. New York, which had 60,000 souls at the time of the Revolutionary War, now has 200,000 and each year adds immensely to its size. We hear that the Mississippi wilderness is being populated even more swiftly. Everyone tells us that it has the most bountiful soil in America and stretches out forever. It seems to me that this incredible material movement eclipses political issues. The latter are on the surface and do not deeply perturb the masses. Our informants assure us that the government has considerable difficulty luring people into public service from private enterprise. The fact is that this society walks on its own, and promises not to encounter any obstacles; the art of government seems to be in its infancy. . . .

Tocqueville to Ernest de Chabrol,[11] New York, May 18, 1831

. . . We have not yet received any news from France. You cannot imagine, dear friend, how painfully deprived we feel. We left our country, and everyone dear to us, in such a critical situation that we don't enjoy a moment's peace of mind.

11. Ernest de Chabrol was a childhood friend of Tocqueville. He, too, had graduated from law school, and he replaced Beaumont as deputy prosecutor at Versailles, an appointment he owed to the influence of a great uncle, the comte de Chabrol, who was the minister of finance under Charles X.

What has become of you? When we parted you were on the verge of taking a big step. Did you indeed take it? Will you introduce us to Madame de Chabrol when we return? All that interests me greatly. I am sending you a thick letter for Marie.[12] I can't tell you how often her memory has come to mind since my departure. You may regard it as a quirk of the human heart, but I assure you that I love her more than ever since I've ceased to see her. Perversely, distance has drawn me closer. The fact is that I didn't believe I was so attached to her. Please go on about her at length in your reply, my dear friend; tell me what she's about, what she's doing. Does my name occasionally come to her lips? I thank you in advance for details.

That isn't the only favor I have to ask of you. Laughable though you may find it, Beaumont and I would like you to tell us at great length what the French think of this country. Since we've left France, we have consorted only with Americans—either on the boat that brought us here, or on shore—with the result that little by little we have insensibly grown accustomed to the new order of things. We have already shed most of our national prejudices about this nation. And yet you can appreciate that it behooves us to acquaint ourselves with opinions prevailing at home if we mean to modify them and study most particularly matters apt to help us enlighten our compatriots.

So, in so far as possible collect your thoughts on the subject, and those of others, and send them along. Thus, for example,

12. Mary Mottley, whom Tocqueville had met as a young attorney in Versailles, where she and the unmarried aunt who had brought her up lived as members of an expatriate English colony. Born in 1801, she came from a naval family, her father having been bursar of the seaman's hospital at Gosport. Tocqueville, who always called her Marie, married her in October 1835. Chabrol served as the letter box in Tocqueville's correspondence with her.

what idea do the French have of political institutions in the United States, of the national character, of the different classes of society, of the commercial state, of the future of this country, of its religious position? . . . What are your thoughts about the power of the Congress over the Union in general and over each state in particular? To what do you attribute the prosperity of this nation—to its political institutions or to material and industrial causes? To what degree of civilization do you suppose this nation has attained, and precisely what forms does its civilization assume? Where do matters stand here as to the spirit of society, the literary culture, the pleasures of the imagination, the fine arts?

Do you believe that there are political parties in the United States? To what extremes is the spirit of equality carried? Do people adhere to that spirit because they are bound to do so by law or does it profoundly inform their minds and mores? What form does it take?

How do you conceive freedom of the press in the United States, freedom of enterprise, electoral rights or eligibility?

Chat about all that in your reply, chatter on about it, expatiate. . . .

I have one more favor to ask of you. We cannot find here a book essential to our project of disassembling American society: the lessons Guizot has given in the last three years on Roman Society and the Middle Ages.[13] They have all been printed as brochures, which I've stored in a box on a shelf of my hanging library. Could you kindly wrap them up and send them here, as always in care of M. Prime?[14] I don't really know how one goes

13. This refers to François Guizot's lectures on the history of French civilization at the Sorbonne that Tocqueville had regularly attended while serving his legal apprenticeship.

14. Nathaniel Prime was a director of New York's biggest bank, Prime, Ward, and King. He was exceptionally kind to the young

about doing this, but people in charge of the coach service will instruct you.

That is the last of my commissions; I hope you won't resent all the trouble they will have caused you. Not knowing where my family is just now, I dare not put them to the task. You, on the other hand, are almost certain to receive this letter at Versailles.

Poor, dear Versailles! I swear I think about it more than once a day; ever present in my mind are memories of the tranquil existence I enjoyed there, the pleasures of a true, open-hearted friendship, the proximity of Saint-Cloud.[15]

Sometimes I also think about a few good colleagues with whom I spent very agreeable moments. Mention me especially to Dalmassez and to the attorney general, and remember me to Chauteamps and Février.[16] As for Élie, he knows how matters stand between us, without being told.

Don't assume that I am on anything less than my best behavior when I tell you that we are leading a very pleasant life here. Our letters of introduction and the publicity surrounding our mission have opened all doors. We are showered with attention. This facilitates research and makes the voyage doubly agreeable. We are still hobbled by language but are beginning to understand everything, and I hope we will reach the point of being able to express everything. It is important that we do so, for French is not in common use here.

. . . We have just received the April 16 issues of English news-

---

Frenchmen, inviting them to soirées in New York City and to his country house on Long Island Sound.

15. The royal residence outside Paris, at Saint-Cloud, where Charles occasionally resided during his reign, and from which he fled on July 31, 1830.

16. Dalmassy, Chautemps, Février, and Élie were all young lawyers, along with Tocqueville, at the court in Versailles.

papers. French government securities had risen by eight francs in just a few days and it was said that the ministry seemed to be on firmer ground. But perhaps everything will have been thrown into confusion again by the time you receive this letter.

That is the misfortune of being so far apart. Distance magnifies all of one's anxieties a hundredfold and poisons the pleasures of daily life.

Whatever happens, don't forget that I have commended our neighbor to you.[17] I will be more touched by the services you render her than if they were rendered to me personally.

Tocqueville to Mary ("Marie") Mottley, from America, date undetermined

. . . And what would I reproach you for? For having introduced me to the only real happiness I've known in this world, for having enabled me to develop a great interest in existence, for having endured uncomplainingly the rough edge of my violent and autocratic character, for having subdued me with sweetness and tenderness. To my knowledge, those are the only reproaches I can summon. You have done still more for me, my beloved friend, another service I've kept for last. You have steered me away from a path that might have been my undoing. You have opened my eyes to what there is of nobility, generosity, and I daresay, of virtue in true love. It is my belief, I swear it, that my love for you has made me a better man. I love what is good more for love of you than for any other reason. The thought of you elevates my soul; I would like to make you proud of me and give you fresh proof every day that you were not mistaken in choosing me. Finally, I have never been more disposed to think of God, more convinced

17. The neighbor referred to was Mary Mottley.

of the reality of another existence, than when I think of you. You have been able to observe with what singular pleasure I converse with you about the gravest questions of life. You alone in the world, *without exception,* know how matters stand in the deepest recesses of my soul; you alone are acquainted with my instincts, my hopes, my doubts. If ever I become Christian, I believe that it will be through you. What I write here, Marie, is not an improvisation; these are thoughts long harbored. . . .

Haven't you noticed, my tender friend, that we experienced our happiest moments when we spoke least. I have often thought that during those instants something happens that is said to happen after death: our two souls chime without having recourse to the senses. Each of us enjoyed his own happiness and the other's; our souls communicated sensations, sentiments, ideas, a thousand times more swiftly than in words and yet the most profound silence reigned between us. How can one understand such pleasures when one has never loved? How can one ever forget them once one has felt them? For myself, if I were unfortunate enough to die before seeing you again, dearest one, what I would miss most would not be the pleasures that attach most men to life, no, assuredly not, I would experience only one desperate regret: that of not being able to feel again this delicious tristesse of love, of no longer hearing that inner voice of the soul. I would miss not the joys of the world but the very sorrows of a loving heart and the soft sighs it cannot stifle.

I love you as I have never loved in my life. My reason and my heart are at one in adoring you. I wasn't suddenly taken captive: you won me gradually by revealing a little more of yourself each day. You conquered my soul, you made it yours; you now reign over it as absolute mistress. I love you as one cannot love at sixteen, and yet I feel, when I think of you, all the generous passions, all the noble instincts, the absolute detachment from self that are normally the attributes of love only at that age.

I don't know why, Marie, men are fashioned after such different models. Some foresee only pleasures in life, others only pain. There are those who see the world as a ballroom. I, on the other hand, am always disposed to view it as a battlefield on which each of us in turn presents himself for combat—to receive wounds and die. This somber imagination of mine is home to violent passions that often ravage me. It has sowed unhappiness, in myself no less than in others. But I truly believe that it gives me more energy for love than other men possess.

Beaumont to his brother Jules, May 26

We always get up early. . . . We breakfast at the customary hour of eight. We then go to the Atheneum, which is a kind of public library at which one finds French, English, and American newspapers. This establishment was opened to us gratis, as well as another library of the same sort, where one finds even more interesting works. We spend as much time as we can spare doing statistical research there on the state of the population, on public establishments, and on all the political topics that concern us. . . .

Our interests are many, but we never lose sight of the special object of our official mission. We expressed the desire to meet the wardens of various prisons in the city and its environs. Authorities wished to show us particular respect; consequently, we were invited in the name of the municipal council and high-level functionaries to pay a solemn visit to the prisons and charitable establishments. This visit would be followed by another big, formal dinner. The ceremony took place only yesterday, May 25. Occupying the seats of honor in carriages prepared specially for us, we departed from City Hall at ten a.m. First we visited an asylum that houses young delinquents, an establishment already known in Europe, and the model for one being constructed right now at Melun. . . . The same carriages then took us to Bloomingdale, an insane asylum.[18] There I saw a madman who calls himself, and believes himself to be, the emperor of America. A young man, who has completely taken leave of his senses and is only twenty years old, had been brought there three days earlier by his father; he went mad over a twenty-four-hour period without anyone knowing the reason why. In the hospital as well was a charming young woman, perhaps fifteen, whose head had been turned by religious ideas. This problem isn't uncommon in the United States, where religious enthusiasm runs high. Otherwise, most forms of madness are the result of drinking strong alcoholic brews to excess. . . .

Upon leaving Bloomingdale, we went first to an institution for the deaf and dumb, then to a hospice for the poor. We couldn't linger, so our visit was superficial. In the hospice, which resembles a palace, we and twenty-three others were served a very good meal. If you had seen Tocqueville and me treated with the greatest respect by the foremost magistrates of the country's biggest city, if you had seen us occupying places of honor, receiving every kind of courtesy, being the cynosure of all eyes, in a word truly playing *star roles,* you would certainly have felt your fraternal amour-propre agreeably stroked. You might also have thought that Americans are not well versed in matters of political import, since small fry such as we bulk so large in their estimation! . . .

Our outing ended with a visit to Blackwell Island, a penitentiary where three or four hundred convicts are employed in the

18. The Bloomingdale insane asylum was located at the present site of Columbia University, in the village of Manhattanville.

construction of another prison next to the one in which they are held. Witnessing the care and zeal they bring to the task, one can hardly believe that they are at work on the edifice in which they will be interned. At last, after taking two or three charming excursions on the East River (the Sound) in canoes, we were escorted back to New York by all these *honorable gentlemen* in five crowded carriages.

Tocqueville to his sister-in-law Alexandrine, New York, May 28, 1831

The note you attached to Édouard's message, dear sister, was not what stirred me least in the thick sheaf of letters delivered by the Le Havre packet. I don't know how you manage it, but you have a certain way of expressing sentiments that goes straight to the heart of your correspondent. I am sure that you will not understand a word of the above; you will have forgotten what you told me three months ago. All I ask is that you retain the warm friendship you expressed so well at the time.

You have learned, from the voluminous letter I wrote Mama on arriving here and which I expressly wished to have you read, that our voyage was, if not altogether happy, at least free of danger. Here in New York we found trees in leaf (I shall not mention flowers, and for good reason), admirably clement weather, houses as neat as if Madame Ollivier[19] herself had had a hand in tidying them up, and good, genial hosts. With all that, we continue to sniff the air for a scent of what's going on in France: that's where we still live, despite the distance separating us. We have fled from you in vain, you are still pulling our strings, and it's all up to

19. Alexandrine's mother, Louise-Denise-Eustache de Lécluse, wife of Auguste-Alexandre Ollivier.

you whether we be the happiest men in the world or succumb to despair. I address this remark to you in particular, dear sister, you who have already availed yourself more than once of the privilege of worrying me. Remember that we are farther away now than where we were last summer.[20] And please don't make me impatient, as you did then, of receiving a letter that takes six weeks to arrive.

On April 12, that is almost two months ago, you were neither better nor worse off than when we sailed. I heard that you planned to stay at Madame de Brévannes',[21] the thought being that country air would do you good. Here the page is torn out of the book and I must wait another fortnight to find out what came of that voyage, how you are now, what you are doing. And my little niece, what is she up to these days? I often think about her and rejoice at the prospect of seeing her walk on her two little legs when I return.

I have been informed that Monsieur Ollivier[22] has expressed no intention of returning to Paris; I am pained—for him and you alike—by his long absence. Kindly mention me in your letters to him. Remember me to your entire family and in particular to Ch. de Brévannes. I shall not go on at length today because I am also writing to your husband, and time is short; we leave New York tomorrow morning for a week. So farewell, my good sister, I embrace you with all my heart, as well as the little one. Please believe that it isn't about you that I wish to speak just now. I beg you to forgive me for the insolence that ends this letter.

20. Tocqueville and Beaumont had traveled through Italy the previous summer.
21. Alexandrine's younger sister, Françoise-Adélaide Ollivier, who had married Amédée Lepileur de Brévannes.
22. Alexandrine's father, Auguste-Alexandre Ollivier, who was staying in Geneva and thought of settling there.

Tocqueville to his brother Édouard, New York, May 28, 1831

I thank you, my dear friend, for the letter that crossed on the April 15 packet. You know how precious your communications are to me, and especially one that comes from so far away. You are, as I said to Alexandrine, more present in our mind than what we see every day. Do not fail, therefore, to write us long, very detailed letters whenever the opportunity presents itself. It's the surest way of making us happy. Moreover, you can well believe that in our present state, we want to know more about French politics than we extract from newspapers. The latest reports bode well for the preservation of peace. I hope to God that they are right. Our last French paper dates to April 15, when government securities were rising, the Austrians were evacuating the Papal territories, and the ministry seemed to be growing stronger, although the language of the press was quite violent and there is still mayhem in the streets. Yesterday we received the April 24 issue of English papers; we learned, to our utter astonishment, that the Chamber of Deputies was *suspended* and not *dissolved.* This measure took us completely by surprise and, insofar as one can judge such matters from abroad, I do not consider it wise. It seems clear to me that the present Chamber does not sway public opinion in the least, and that newspapers, by exploiting the legitimate case to be made against it, will lose no time casting discredit on the very *moderation* that this Chamber represents. The radical press will step backward the better to spring forward. I believe that there has never been a more propitious time for elections than now: everything points to the disadvantages of anarchy and the lower classes are more fearful of disorder than of the privileges enjoyed by the upper crust.

But I recur to what I said above, that it is impossible to judge from afar. I am anxious to know the language of French papers;

they must be gushing over the top. Apparently, England hasn't fared brilliantly either. The whole nation is embroiled in a terrific struggle and there's no telling where the movement will stop.

Here we are truly in another world. Political passions are only superficial. The one passion that runs deep, the only one that stirs the human heart day in and day out, is the acquisition of wealth, and there are a thousand ways of acquiring it without importuning the state. To draw comparisons between this country and Europe and to entertain the idea of adapting to one what works for the other is blindness, in my opinion. I thought so before leaving France; I am confirmed in that belief the more I examine the society in the midst of which I now find myself. This is a world of merchants who give some thought to public affairs only when their work affords them the leisure to do so. By the time we return to Europe, we will, I hope, have acquired all we need to address this subject knowledgeably: no one is better set up for the study of the American people than we are. Our mission and our letters open all doors; we rub shoulders with all classes; all possible documents are furnished on demand; we have come for only one reason, to accomplish a serious goal. Our minds are constantly straining for the acquisition of useful knowledge; it is an immense labor, but not at all painful because ideas are entering us through every pore and as many of them in a salon or on a walk as in the privacy of our study.

But will we have enough time to bring this enterprise to fruition? One need not be clairvoyant to foresee events that may call us home. We ponder that every day and the thought often leaves us momentarily disgruntled with our labors.

My dear friend, I must ask a favor of you and beg you to do it as soon as possible, though it will put you to some inconvenience. Among other things that are exorbitantly expensive in this country are gloves and articles of silk. Ballroom gloves that cost forty-five sous in Paris cost six francs here and are shoddy. Since we are forever attending social functions and will be even more sociable this winter, you can imagine that we would be ruining ourselves if we had to purchase new gloves every two or three days. We shall be saving money by having them sent from Paris, despite the postage and custom duties. What I need are two dozen yellow kid gloves, the best possible, and half a dozen brown wool gloves. Please include a pair of silk openwork stockings for evening wear and one or two black silk neck cloths. Here, black neck cloths are worn at soirées.

Beaumont will enlarge upon what he would like, and Monsieur Hagdé will give you money for his purchases. You would pack everything in a tight little case and send it to me in New York—I'm not entirely sure how, but it should be easy. As for my hand measurement, you will certainly find some old gloves in my room, and in any event, our hands are almost identical. As for Beaumont, he claims that if you go to his haberdasher in the Palais Royal, Chez Irlande, the shopgirl on duty knows his hand perfectly well. Of course, you would send this package only if the state of affairs in Europe should lead you to believe that our sojourn in America will not be cut short.

Adieu, my good friend; I embrace you lovingly and swear that not a day passes without my thinking about you, your wife, or your daughter. . . .

Tocqueville to abbé Lesueur, New York, May 28, 1831

You cannot imagine, my dear friend, how happy we were a week ago, upon receiving the sheaf of letters that brought us news about all of you. Letters were in our dreams; they were our idée fixe. As soon as we heard that a packet from Havre had been sighted we ran to the port. It was the *Charles Carroll*, which we had visited in

France. It could deliver letters only to postal officials, so we contented ourselves with asking the captain for political news. Well, this devil, unable to separate the reports he had received about flare-ups in Paris before his departure and the inferences he had drawn from them, told us that a revolution had taken place. Although we did not place great faith in these tidings, we were all the more eager to lay hands on the blessed packet. An hour later, our banker, Monsieur Prime, had it delivered to us. We immediately locked ourselves in our room and shared our riches.

I cannot describe, dear Bébé, how affected I was by the sight of familiar handwriting. I read the first lines of each letter before finishing any of them, then set about reading them all calmly from beginning to end. I cannot thank you enough for having sent me collective proof that my dearest ones remember me; I am extremely touched. No one knows better than you how much we need word from home here. The pleasure we got from letters when in Italy and Sicily, however great, was not comparable.

Everyone noted that you are in good health, which was especially gratifying to me. May it please God that this remain so. Your letter amused us no end: I say "us" because I read it to Beaumont, who hastens to thank you himself for remembering him. We had a good laugh over your calculations about our progress, and laughed the louder because we calculated likewise before our departure from France: i.e., "Having covered a certain distance today, we shall progress so far in a week," and so forth.

Unfortunately, there is no such reckoning at sea. One must say to oneself: I've traversed one hundred leagues in two days, I shall perhaps need eight more to cover the next ten. The wind is favorable now, the night is calm, but before I've had time to climb the companion-ladder the wind will probably have shifted, the boat will be rocking, and we will be preparing to give up the ghost. I don't know another life more apt to take one's mind off thoughts of the morrow; it's a course in practical philosophy that must, I assure you, have some merit.

But at this moment I am revolving a thought that makes me even more exasperated by the distance between us. Shall I refer to things in your letter which you have probably already forgotten? We still have our say, but, being so far removed from each other, we can no longer converse; when a reply arrives, the question has already been forgotten and when I want to second one of your ideas, you, being preoccupied by a thousand other matters, will not know what I'm talking about.

I shall therefore speak about something bound to interest you and make it clear straightaway that it's all coming from me. When I wrote my last letter, I told you, I believe, that we had a good trip and were comfortably settled in New York. Our satisfaction has not diminished and, except that questions about what may be occurring in Europe prey on our minds, we would deem ourselves quite happy.

Let me say, to begin with, that you can't imagine how well received we are in this country. As I told Mama, the papers have announced more than once the purpose of our mission (which is uncommonly flattering to the national pride of our hosts). The result is an eagerness that never ceases to astonish us. All public places are open to us, but in addition all documents are placed at our disposal and the directors of institutions produce them for us in person.

Yesterday the mayor of New York and his *aldermen* or deputies, numbering twenty-five or thirty, led us on an elaborately ceremonial tour of the city's prisons and almshouses. Afterward we were invited to an enormous dinner, the first of its kind we have attended, which I may have some difficulty describing. The guests disposed themselves around a long table fit for a refectory, at the head of which the mayor, flanked by two servants, had seated himself. They were all excruciatingly solemn. Laughter is seldom heard on this side of the Atlantic.

As for the dinner, it was the art of cooking in its infancy: vegetables and fish before meat, and oysters for dessert—as much as to say complete barbarism. My first glance at the table set my mind at rest—I saw no wine, only the usual water and brandy. I therefore sat down with suitable gravity on the mayor's right and waited for events to unfold. Alas, wine was brought out the moment soup was whisked away. The mayor then drank to our health in the English manner, which meant filling a little glass, raising it as he looked at me, and drinking it—all these gestures performed unsmilingly. The honoree must respond by doing exactly the same thing. So each of us drank his glass, always with perfect aplomb. Up to that point, everything was proceeding well.

But our nerves began to quiver when we saw that each of the guests felt duty-bound to honor us the same way. We looked like hares with a pack of hounds on their scent, and the fact is that they would soon have done us in if we had allowed it. But at the third glass, I resolved to take only one sip and thus happily reached what in France we call the end of dinner. As it turns out, the end is just the overture here: after most of the dishes were removed, lighted candles were brought forth and a quantity of cigars served on a plate. Each diner possessed himself of one and, with a cloud of smoke enveloping us, toasts commenced. The gentlemen unbent ever so little, and indulged in the world's most ponderous joviality.

You now have a good picture of formal dinners in America. I confess I couldn't help laughing up my sleeve during this august ceremony at the difference that fifteen hundred leagues of sea make in the status of a man. I thought about the subaltern role I played in France two months ago and the comparatively lofty situation we enjoy in America, about the scant notice our mission received at home and the fanfares over it here, all on account of that little expanse of water.

I assure you, however, that we don't put on lordly airs. Far be it for us to regard the attention we receive as our due. We make the best princes in the world. But these people, who have no great political interests to debate and see nothing worthier of a government's attention than penal legislation and the state of prisons, persist in viewing us as exceptionally distinguished young men, charged with a mission of signal importance. Even the French agents treat us with great respect, the more so because of our family names, and give us useful pointers. You ought to know that in this republican land, people are far more impressed by nobility, titles, crosses, and all the gewgaws of Europe than in France. Where laws are concerned, the greatest equality prevails. One might get the impression that such equality informs manners and mores as well. But make no mistake, the Devil lurks underneath, and in the deepest recesses of the soul pride has a secure home. We sometimes laugh, Beaumont and I, over the posturing of acquaintances anxious to establish their relationship with European families and their enormous investment in such social distinctions as lie within their reach, however trivial.

Tomorrow morning we go to Sing Sing, a village ten leagues from New York and situated on the North River. We shall remain about a week to study the regimen of a huge prison recently constructed there. What we have seen until now is enough to persuade us that prisons draw widespread attention in America and that in several respects they are superior to those in France.

For us, there is more on our minds than prisons. Going to Sing Sing will be a positive pleasure. You can't imagine anything more beautiful than the North River or the Hudson. Its immense breadth, the productive activity on one bank and the steep cliffs bordering it on the other make an awesome spectacle.[23] But not even that is the America I want to see. Every day we envy those Europeans who discovered the mouth of the Hudson two hundred years ago and sailed upriver when its banks were still covered with immense forests, when all one saw at the present site of New York's 200,000 bustling inhabitants was the smoke of Indian fires. Man will never be content with anything; there's nothing for it.

To return to more practical considerations, I say that this is a most singular country. Room and board don't cost more than in Paris, but everything of human manufacture is prohibitively expensive. One pays two hundred francs for a coat, fifty for trousers, forty for boots, and so forth. It doesn't much matter to me as I have clothes enough for the entire voyage and shall have shoes specially made.

But here is what may put us to considerable expense: a pair of kid gloves costs six francs here. You are well aware of the fact that such gloves can be worn only once at most,[24] that one cannot move in society without wearing them, and that we socialize every evening. It therefore occurred to us that we would be saving quite a lot by having them sent from Europe, that with duties and postage they would still cost only two-thirds of their price here. I am asking Édouard to purchase gloves and send them to New York, following instructions he will receive from the postal service in Paris. I am asking him to include a pair of silk openwork stockings for evening wear and one or two black silk neck cloths —silk here being unaffordable. Papa will reimburse him.

So far, we are satisfied with the state of our finances, or at least confident that we cannot have lived any more frugally. Tell Papa

23. Describing the productive activity as taking place on the "north" bank and the palisades as rising on the "east" bank, Tocqueville may not yet have sailed upriver, or hadn't yet oriented himself correctly.

24. The gloves could be worn only once because, in all likelihood, they soiled easily and could not be restored to pristine condition.

for me that we restrict ourselves to what is absolutely *necessary*, in every sense of that word. After a month here, I'll send him a rough account of our expenditures. I assure you that I shrink from the idea of burdening him financially and shall do everything to avoid it.

I'll stop here because Beaumont wishes to add a word. You know that I embrace you whole-heartedly and include mama and papa. I hope that my letter from Liverpool arrived in time to dispel your anxiety. Adieu, my good friend.

Tocqueville to his father, Sing Sing, June 3, 1831

You will never guess, my dear father, where on earth I have ensconced myself to write this letter. I sit at the top of a rather steep hill. In the foreground, one hundred paces below me, is a country house, where we lodge. Beyond it, the hill slopes down to the Hudson. More than a league wide[25] and covered with sails, the great river runs north into a range of high blue mountains and disappears. Its banks are a scene of bustle and prosperity delightful to observe. And overhead is an admirable sun whose rays, filtering through the humid atmosphere of the region, bathe everything they touch in soft, transparent light. You may infer from this lengthy description that its author has a panoramic perspective. Indeed he does, for an enormous sycamore shades the summit of my hill, which rises higher than others round about, and I am perched in its branches to avoid the heat. That is where I am writing to you. Beaumont is down below drawing what I've just described. You see what a nice fit we all make.

Now I must tell you where we are, and why we have come. Sing Sing, thus named after an Indian chief who lived here sixty years

25. What he literally wrote here is "five quarter leagues," or more than three and a quarter miles.

ago but whose tribe has since retreated farther inland, lies on the Hudson eleven leagues north of New York. The town has a thousand or twelve hundred inhabitants. Its famous prison, the largest in the land, houses nine hundred inmates, and abides by the American penal system, which it is our mission to study in depth. We have been here a week already and feel an extraordinary sense of well-being. The hectic life we were obliged to live in New York, the number of visits we made and received every day, began to tire us. Here our days are at once blissfully serene and well employed. We live with a respectable American family, who show us every possible courtesy. We have made the acquaintance of several villagers whom we shall see again when we are free to do so. The rest of our time is spent in visiting the prison, in taking notes, and collecting all the practical ideas that the penal system can provide. The alacrity with which government agents supply every kind of document we may require makes our task much easier. Unfortunately not everything has been documented. Broadly speaking, I would say that, where administration is concerned, this country and France have gone off the edge, but in opposite directions. While among us, government meddles in everything, here there is not, or appears not to be, any government at all. Alike the virtues and defects of centralization are seemingly unknown; there is no mainspring regulating the machine's moving parts, with the result that in many specific ways overall performance cannot be judged. One issue of paramount importance is recidivism. There are no records that would help us determine satisfactorily the number of convicts reformed by prison life. You will appreciate that for us such information is vital.

Our impression of the prisons we have visited makes a very long story. I'd rather not launch into it with you, lest you conclude that our eyes are fastened to the penal system and to nothing else in America. That is not the case, I assure you; on the contrary, our time here is employed in many different occupations, which may be why it seems to be slipping away so terribly fast. I believe that even if we don't produce something acceptable about the United States, we shall not have wasted our time by devoting ourselves to the study we have undertaken. Our one aim since we've come here has been to comprehend the land we are exploring. We cannot accomplish that goal unless we disassemble society a priori and identify the elements that constitute it in France so as to pose questions useful for an understanding of America. The enterprise is difficult but alluring: it has enabled us to discern a great many details that go unseen when one doesn't analyze the mass and suggests any number of practical ideas that would not otherwise have crossed our minds. Knowing as we do exactly what we want to ask, the most humble conversation is instructive, and I daresay no man, whatever his social rank, is incapable of teaching us something.

This life, which is a boil of physical and intellectual activity, would make us quite happy were it not for the chasm that separates us from France. The thought of your remoteness spoils everything. I have said it already, dear father, but I feel compelled to repeat myself—living so far from those one loves is being only half alive. Given our cerebral existence, in which the heart counts for little, I despair of conceiving anything but arid impressions.

Since we are now little more than "probing instruments," you will perhaps ask me, dear father, what we find most noteworthy in this land. I would need a volume to tell you everything. Or to tell you what I think today. Tomorrow I may no longer agree with myself, for we are definitely not systematizers. Among ideas that preoccupy me, two bulk large, the first being that this population is one of the happiest in the world, the second that it owes its immense prosperity less to its characteristic virtues, and even less to a form of government intrinsically superior to all others, than to its peculiar conditions, which result in perfect accord between its political constitution and its needs and social state. This may sound a bit metaphysical, but you will understand better what I mean when I observe, for example, that nature provides so well for human industry that there is no class of theoretical speculators. Everyone works, and the vein is still so rich that all who work it succeed rapidly in gaining the wherewithal to achieve contentment. Here, the most active minds, like the most tranquil characters, have no void in their lives to fill by troubling the state. Restlessness, which harrows our European societies, seems to abet the prosperity of this one. Wealth is the common lure, and a thousand roads lead to it. Politics therefore occupies only a small corner of the canvas. I have no doubt that it does more stirring up in the most ostensibly peaceful European state than in the entire American confederation. No newspaper, among those we read every day, devotes as much space to matters of general import affecting government as to the price of cotton. What space remains is monopolized by discussions of local interest, which feed public curiosity without in any way causing social turmoil.

To resume, the more I see of this land, the more convinced I am of this truth, that there are virtually no political institutions radically good or bad in themselves and that everything depends on the physical conditions and social state of the people to whom they are applied. I see certain institutions work here that would predictably work havoc in France; while others that suit us would have evil effects in America. And yet, unless I'm sadly mistaken, man is not different or better on one side of the Atlantic than on the other. He is just differently placed. At some later date I shall tell you what strikes me in the American character.

Right now, I bear a strong resemblance to "Master crow,

perched in a tree,"[26] don't you think? On that note I shall finish my oration. I am so *snug* on my branch that I run the risk of falling asleep—in which case I might, like my friend Robinson Crusoe, shout "My dear parents!" and wake up on the ground. I have therefore decided to climb down. I shall finish the letter tomorrow.

Tocqueville to Le Peletier d'Aunay,[27] New York, June 7, 1831

My dear cousin,

The last time we had the pleasure of seeing you, my dear Cousin, you told us to write to you. We do so with great pleasure, all the more for being reminded each day of the people without whom we could not have undertaken a voyage that has proved useful and agreeable.

In America we have found a spirit of hospitality and enlightened benevolence that enables us to accomplish easily the mission with which we were charged and clears the path for all necessary research. Availing ourselves of these excellent conditions, we have visited New York prisons; during the past week we have resided in the little village of Sing Sing, where a huge penitentiary, America's biggest, is located. And, except that we don't sleep in cells and aren't lashed for our sins, we lead much the same life as the inmates. Which is what I call throwing oneself into one's work.

26. The first line of a fable by Jean de La Fontaine, based on Aesop's "The Fox and the Crow."

27. Félix Le Peletier d'Aunay (1789–1855) was a deputy with liberal tendencies in the Chamber of Deputies under Louis-Philippe and a protégé of the philosopher-politician Pierre Royer-Collard, who had been instrumental in preparing the ground for a constitutional monarchy. Le Peletier d'Aunay had prevailed upon the minister of justice to offer Tocqueville and Beaumont their American commission.

As you can well believe, our research is too incomplete to allow of a settled opinion about all that we have been able to examine. However, we have a number of notions and impressions that I would like to communicate without delay. The best way to do it succinctly is to resume the pros and cons, and rely upon your judgment, my dear Cousin, to draw the definitive conclusion that still eludes us. As you see, I haven't forgotten my lawyerly vocation.

The penal establishments we've visited so far are of two kinds: one is intended to reform boys younger than sixteen, the other to correct older criminals. About those belonging to the first category, which are called houses of refuge, we have nothing but good to say. The young men we see interned there appear to be healthy, obedient, and studious. One might have thought oneself in a school rather than a prison, and the official reports we've been given agree that, since the establishment of these houses, the number of young delinquents has diminished by almost half in New York. Of all the establishments we have observed, this is the one, I believe, that France would find most compatible. The idea behind it is simple, its execution is easy and doesn't require costly construction. I doubt, however, that results as good as those in America are to be expected in Europe. A reformed delinquent is more likely in France than here to be dogged by prejudice associated with the memory of his offense. And here the need for manpower is so imperious that children who emerge from houses of refuge every year find employment right away. Idleness and indigence never supervene to undo the achievements of reform.

As for the regular prisons we've visited so far, it is difficult to give a satisfactory account of them. In certain respects they surpass our expectations; in others, they fall far short. Generally speaking, Europeans who criticize or praise them know little about them. At first glance, they make the most favorable impression. We are living here in the midst of nine hundred inmates, who—supervised by twenty-two guards, with no chains shackling them, no wall penning them in during the day, and no hope of saving money for a nest egg—work from morning to night like laborers on the job, in total silence. We've observed them closely for ten days, during which neither of us has caught them even once exchanging words or knowing glances; they seem to have completely and irrevocably sacrificed their will. I remember seeing something of the sort among Trappist monks, but I would never have believed, if I hadn't witnessed it, that force alone could have achieved a like result.

There are other effects no less extraordinary than these. *It is a fact* that the mortality rate is lower among inmates than in the population at large. *It is also a fact* that prisons thus administered *earn* money for the state instead of costing it. The doubts we had on this score have been dispelled by official documents.

That is the positive side of the picture. Now for the negative.

First of all, I doubt that the discipline yielding such unforeseen results could easily be implemented at home, even if it were materially possible in our prison system to isolate inmates at night, which is a key provision. In order to enforce complete obedience with so few real means of repression, and at the same time to make prison work useful, the Americans have undertaken to convince each inmate, by isolating him, that he stands alone against a body of warders. *Silence* and *continual work* are their agents: the silence that separates the individual from the crowd, the work that absorbs all his moral and physical strength and diverts him from mischief. That is the secret of the system, but there's more to it. For if relentless work abets silence, how does one get an inmate to work relentlessly? We puzzled over this question in France when we were studying books about the penal system. Those that described American prisons always reminded me of Hindus who place the world on a tortoise, the tortoise on a horse, the horse on an elephant, but never tell you what it's all resting on.

The principle that underlies work and silence—the admirable discipline we have witnessed—consists simply in the arbitrary, unrestricted power to inflict corporal punishment, power conferred upon people who serve their own best interests every day by not abusing it and using it to maintain strict order within the prison. This power is vested in the establishment's director, who delegates it and delegates it effectively (at Sing Sing anyway) to every last one of his employees; they in turn have the right to administer whippings, unappealably and unobserved. It is a far cry from what Europeans imagine takes place.

However, some reflection is in order. I doubt that without such power the discipline to which the establishment owes its security and prosperity could be maintained. On the other hand, I ask myself whether it is humane, or for that matter secure, to place unrestricted power in so many hands. And finally I find it difficult to believe that a French government could do the same even if it wanted to, given the present state of mores and climate of opinion.

Moreover, you may accept the extraordinary power vested in guards but still wonder how their attention can possibly be sustained enough to impose relentless work and enforce unbroken silence. I confess that we ourselves wonder about it and remained perplexed, though we see it in operation every day. Here are our guesses. First, all responsibility resides with one man (the director, *the agent*): the law requires him in vague, general terms to keep order and to make the prison productive, all *by whatever means he deems appropriate;* there isn't even a written code. It is he who attends to all administrative details; it is he who appoints all employees. If you consider also that in a society as restrained and calm as this one public attention is trained on prisons, that these establishments are still few in number, that the implementation of the penal system is of quite recent origin, that the rivalry it excites among the different states is great, then you will understand that a prison administrator here must take measures likely to be regarded as imprudent elsewhere.

That isn't all. There is, I believe, a more general cause, one that I may have some difficulty conveying. My impression is that Americans have resorted to a very dangerous, but very effective means of getting guards to maintain the vigilance that rigorous discipline requires. On an open field they assemble several hundred stout inmates, at whose disposal they place the deadliest tools. Obviously, if discipline did not prevent these men from acting in concert, if work did not occupy all their waking moments, the life of the guards as well as the order of the establishment would be constantly imperiled. It can therefore be stated that guards must be punctilious, watchful, and fair under pain of death. And I assure you that when one sees them at work, it is quite clear that they aren't toiling for the love of God alone.

In general, what has struck me most up to now about this society is the artfulness with which the public and private interest are made to advance the same goal. Thus, almost all the good of which men are capable is elicited from them, often without their knowing it.

But I won't digress from the penal system. Don't you think, my dear cousin, that this disciplinary method asks for trouble? What I mean is that Americans are placing themselves smack in the middle of grave danger in order to avoid it. So long as the whole apparatus functions as it should, their prisons run admirably well; but I'm afraid that if one little cog breaks down a terrible catastrophe will ensue. So, should a government adopt a system whose success requires such difficult conditions, and whose failure would be perilous? Will the American government itself be able to continue along the path it marked out for itself only a few years ago?

One question continually on our minds, which we find exceedingly difficult to resolve and which is of capital importance, has to do with recidivists. Does the penal system reduce the number of crimes? That is indeed, as you told us when we departed France, the criterion by which the virtue of this operation must be measured. Would you believe that we have yet to discover an official document addressing this subject generally, and that the government of New York has undertaken to change all its prisons and every year pursues its work without having precise data on the efficaciousness of the new system being introduced? We had read M. Ch. Lucas's treatise[28] and made note of the fact that Auburn produces six times fewer recidivists than French prisons. We now realize that this figure is based upon the number of men who, having been imprisoned in Auburn, *returned* there. Well, since Auburn is not the only American prison and only one of New York's, it is obvious that this method of analysis doesn't hold water. To obtain a closer approximation, we have undertaken to examine the records of all the principal prisons in New York and contiguous states. We're well along in our work on New York; the worst of it is therefore behind us.

I also hope that we shall be able, upon our return, to give a very exact account of how much it costs the state to build new prisons or improve those that already exist, as well as to furnish the means of comparison and generally all documents that can render this knowledge profitable to France.

In the delving we've had to do for information on this point

28. *Du système pénitentinaire en Europe et aux États-Unis* [On the Penal Systems of Europe and the United States] by Charles Lucas, published in 1828.

and many others, it has become increasingly clear that America and France run to opposite extremes. At home, critics fulminate about excessive centralization; here, on the other hand, government is invisible, and this is not all to the good, whatever people say. One almost never encounters an idea guiding an enterprise of public interest, or a focal point for administrative action. And furthermore, administrative power, which impresses us as terribly restricted and incomplete, is vested in men who succeed one another so quickly that we don't see how there can be any permanence of view or continuity of effort.

That, my dear cousin, is where matters stand with us. I would like to have enabled you to judge them in the same light as we do; I've tried anyway.

To resume:

1. We know beyond a doubt:
   a) that the American penitentiaries we have visited so far cost the state nothing and often turn a profit, notwithstanding that the salaries of employees are very high,
   b) that mortality has been reduced to a negligible figure,
   c) that discipline is rigorously enforced and succeeds in isolating the inmate from the crowd, which prevents him from leaving prison worse than he was when he entered.
2. We believe (we are not in a position to affirm it categorically) that the American system reduces the number of recidivists.
3. In our view, the supposition that it will continue to function as it does today isn't altogether convincing, and we doubt that France could, or would wish to, adopt the discipline which is its backbone, even if agreement were reached on the expenditures required to launch it. Soon our ideas on these various aspects of the matter will come into sharper focus: in a week we travel to Boston, which is the site of a famous prison, and

thence to Philadelphia. But New York will continue to be our headquarters, and it is there that our correspondents continue to send their letters.

You can well imagine, my dear Cousin, that while scrutinizing the penal system we sometimes cast inquisitive glances at the multitude of other objects all around us. There is so much talk about America in France, it stands so tall in public opinion, and so often influences our political decisions that everything connected with its social life excites the liveliest interest in us. We have therefore, since our arrival, become the world's most ruthless questioners. But our research doesn't always bear fruit. Sometimes an examination leads to clear results, as for example when we are familiar with the general principles of a particular subject or when we know the state of things in France and can clarify our ideas by drawing comparisons. When we don't enjoy this advantage, we often find ourselves groping in the dark. Thus, to cite only public administration, we can see that everything in general is different here: the number of administrative authorities, their powers, their duties, and their means of action. Unfortunately, we don't know which details would serve to help us comprehend the differences: what works better here, what less well, or what is simply different than in France. If you should happen to have some time on your hands—a rare event, to be sure—and not find the prospect of guiding us in our research excessively tedious, we would have one more reason, besides those of which you are well aware, to be grateful. You are familiar with the difficulties that plague every administration, the practical and theoretical questions to which the art of governing societies can give rise. Among discerning minds, yours is the one most qualified to point a Frenchman in directions he would find it profitable to follow in America. That you so readily give us advice and encourage us to solicit it makes it doubly valuable in our eyes.

I conclude, my dear Cousin, where I should have begun, by congratulating you on the choice of the new member of your family. I have never had occasion to meet M. Séguier,[29] but his reputation as a man of distinction is too well established for me not to rejoice in advance at having him as a relative. I beg of you to convey these sentiments to him.

Beaumont to his mother, June 7

Tocqueville and I left for Sing Sing ten days ago, according to plan. We returned yesterday and devoted that entire interval to the penal system. We had hardly arrived at Sing Sing, shepherded by a very distinguished lawyer from New York, than people came by, offering every imaginable service. The prison warden, the guards, all the employees, waited on us hand and foot. All doors were opened for us, all records as well. We were lodged in a room normally reserved for inspectors and made ourselves at home there, working every day. We observed a lot and did much research. The disciplinary system established in the Sing Sing penitentiary is without a doubt most remarkable. It holds nine hundred inmates, serving sentences of various lengths. They are forced to work either in the prison courtyard, which is not enclosed, or in quarries not far from the establishment. Wearing neither manacles nor leg irons, they are perfectly free, yet work diligently at the most laborious tasks. The fact that attempts at escape are extremely rare seems so incredible that one can only puzzle over the fact. It seems inexplicable, but there is a key to the secret of this wondrous discipline. It involves several essential principles:

29. Armand Pierre, baron Séguier, a young appeals court judge, had married Le Peletier d'Aunay's daughter. The Séguiers belonged to France's legal aristocracy.

The first is the *absolute silence* to which all inmates are condemned: they are not free to talk and the truth is that during my entire stay among them I heard no one utter a single word.

The second basic principle prescribes harsh punishment for violations of the first rule. One is confident that such punishment will be applied rigorously, because prison discipline lies within the exclusive jurisdiction of the warden.

On the other hand, guards are well aware of their numerical inferiority and, as they are thirty against nine hundred, must live in fear of a revolt. Because of this, they treat the prisoners fairly, knowing that any injustice on their part, anything like draconian behavior, could provoke an uprising. . . .

There is one general consideration that transcends all others and may provide the ultimate key. Undeniably, nine hundred bandits are more powerful than thirty individuals responsible for guarding them. . . . But while they are materially stronger, do they have the same moral strength as the smaller group? No, because they are isolated from one another. Strength lies not in numbers but in association, and thirty individuals *united* by constant communication, ideas, common projects, schemes, have more effective power than nine hundred people whose isolation is their fatal flaw.

Enough of nattering on about the penal system. I'm afraid I've bored you. But how can I not talk about something that has preoccupied me for a fortnight? Just to finish up with it, I shall tell you that, despite our admiring tribute, we have many doubts about the system's solidity and effectiveness. It strikes us as slippery ground on which even staunch, able men who manage to keep their footing could easily fall. . . .

I must absolutely tell you one more thing about prison—the peculiar way in which reform is promoted by religious and moral instruction. Every Sunday, prisoners hear a sermon at religious service. This is proper and to be expected. Less conventional is the fact that services are conducted one week by a Presbyterian, the next week by an Anabaptist, then by ministers belonging to different Christian confessions. Attendance is compulsory and all inmates sit together, without necessarily knowing anything about the different sects to which the preachers belong. If they don't, so much the better for them; if they do, they must have a hard time deciding which is best and truest. Nothing is more characteristic of Americans than their indifference to *the nature of religions;* but this doesn't prevent an individual from embracing his chosen sect with great fervor. It is something I do not yet understand, how such extreme tolerance of religions in general can be reconciled with each person's zeal for his own in particular. I should very much like to know how one can have equal respect for religions predicated upon different dogmas, and how the religious spirit of Americans colors their moral conduct. . . .

. . . [Tocqueville] and I always take a little walk at five o'clock in the morning; at eight-thirty, after breakfast, we take another walk; and in the evening, at seven, we bathe in the Hudson. I've learned to swim reasonably well; Tocqueville gives me lessons with all the gusto of a friend who understands full well how awkward my position would be if I accidentally fell into some great American watercourse. . . . As for English, we are making progress. Still, not a day passes that we don't have some misunderstanding; we're never quite sure what we're being told. Misunderstandings are one thing in an inconsequential conversation, but quite another when, say, we're being invited somewhere. . . . Recently, a *socially prominent gentleman* of the neighborhood, a member of the Livingston family,[30] went to great trouble and expense arranging a splendid dinner in our honor, with many guests. The dinner was scheduled for three o'clock. He waited for us until five

30. The Livingstons were one of the foremost families of New York. The gentleman who had invited them was Edward Livingston, who had been mayor of the city and in 1831–1832 served as Andrew Jackson's secretary of state.

and we didn't come. Alas! At that moment we were happily ensconced in our rooms, completely unaware of the gathering. . . .

Tocqueville to Ernest de Chabrol, New York, June 9, 1831

I thank you, my dear friend, for the letters that you have already written to me and the care with which you transmit those of the neighbor.[31] I assure you that it is not the packet I open last. I would like to reward the great service you are rendering me with an interesting description, but up to now my ideas have been in such a state of confusion, I perceive so many things at once, that I don't know how to go about putting them in narrative order.

I don't mean to say that I'm experiencing an embarrassment of riches. I'm simply dazed by all I see and hear and can't decide what might prove to be of interest. However, I must say something, or there would have been no point in crossing the ocean.

For openers, my dear friend, imagine a society compounded of all the nations of the world: English, French, Germans. . . . People each having a language, a belief, different opinions; in a word, a society lacking roots, memories, prejudices, habits, common ideas, a national character . . . and a hundred times happier than ours. More virtuous? I doubt it. What binds such diverse elements together and makes a nation of it all? Self-interest. That is the key. The individual's self-interest, which isn't bashful; it displays itself openly and propagates itself as a social theory.

It must be admitted that this is a far cry from the ancient republics. And yet the nation is a republic and I'm quite certain will remain one for quite some time, being the best of governments for America. How so? My only explanation is that the country enjoys a physical and political advantage so remarkable

31. "The neighbor": Mary Mottley.

that private interest never runs contrary to the general interest, which is emphatically not the case in Europe.

What is it, in general, that leads men to trouble the state? On the one hand there is the desire to gain power, and, on the other, the difficulty of creating a happy existence for oneself by ordinary means.

Here there is no public power, and, the truth is, no need for one. Territorial divisions are very limited; the states have no enemies and consequently no armies, no taxes, no central government; the executive power is only the transient executor of the will of elected bodies: it dispenses neither money nor power. So long as things remain as they are, who would want to torment his life by making politics his goal?

Now it follows that if the political career is more or less closed, a thousand others, or ten times that many, invite human activity. I have the impression that the entire world here is made of a malleable material that men can turn and shape to their will. It is an immense expanse almost entirely open to enterprise. Aspiring to enjoy the sweet pleasures of life is not unreasonable; if one loves work, one's future is assured.

Thus, in this happy land, the restlessness of the human spirit does not mobilize political passions. On the contrary, everything draws it toward an activity that leaves the state alone. I should like people who dream of an America for France to come here and see what the republic is.

This last reason, which is supremely important in my view, also explains the two salient features of this nation: its mercantile spirit and its instability of character.

Nothing is easier than enriching oneself in America. The human spirit, which needs a dominant passion, naturally turns toward thoughts of gain; as a result, these people put one in mind of merchants who have convened as a nation just to do business. And the more one delves into the national character of Americans, the clearer it seems that they seek the value of all things of this world in the answer to only one question: "How much money will it fetch?"

As for instability of character, it shows through in a thousand places: an American takes something up, lets it drop, takes it up again ten times over during his lifetime; he is constantly changing houses and embarking on new enterprises. He fears compromising an acquired fortune less than any other man on earth, because he knows how easy it is to acquire a new one. Moreover, change seems to him man's natural state. And how could it be otherwise? Everything around him is moving: laws, opinions, public functionaries, fortunes. Here the earth itself wears a new face every day. In the midst of this universal commotion, the American could not stand still.

So here is not a place to look for that family pride or those ancient traditions of honor and virtue bred into various of our old European societies. A nation that seems to live only to enrich itself could not be a virtuous people in the strict sense of the word. But it is "disciplined." It has none of the vices that attend idle wealth: its habits are regular; people have little or no time to sacrifice to women, who are apparently valued only as mothers and household managers. Morals are pure, no doubt about it; the European roué is quite unknown in America, as the passion for making a fortune engulfs all others.[32]

You can appreciate, my dear friend, that everything I've told you is "approximate." I've been in this country only a short while. But I've already had ample opportunity to educate myself. I'm sure my father told you that we've been received with great good

32. Although Tocqueville reported a conversation about prostitution in his notebooks, he does not seem to have recognized its prominent place in urban life.

will. We have found strong support among officials, and private citizens have thrown open their doors to us; if we have anything to complain about, it's the multitude of social obligations imposed upon us by zealous hosts.

Thus, mingling from morning till night with men who belong to every social class, speaking broken English but knowing the language well enough to understand almost everything we hear, and possessing boundless curiosity, we are in a position to absorb a great deal. Still, I hope that you don't interpret what I've just told you as anything but a first draft, which I myself may revise some day.

I would like to dismount from the general ideas I've just set forth and walk you through a more detailed landscape, but I wouldn't know where to begin. Ask me questions and I'll answer them as best I can.

I read in the papers that Carné finally made it to Paris. Do you think that he's paid a steep price for this promotion? In what categories do his new and former political friends place him now? I've also learned that Hardoin was wildly applauded for his résumé of the December conspiracy.[33] The truth is, I'm completely at sea. Is he too getting ready to knuckle under? I think you acted commendably in refusing to be named King's Prosecutor. One must continue to stay in the background. Adieu, my good friend. I love you and embrace you with all my heart.

33. Louis de Carné had been attached to the ministry of foreign affairs since 1825. Formerly a hard-core Bourbon royalist, he had begun to accommodate himself to the new regime. The "December conspiracy" refers to a violent protest in December 1830, during the trial of the prince de Polignac, the last prime minister to serve Charles X before the Revolution of 1830. Organizers of the riot were brought to trial on charges of attempting to change the form of government, but they were acquitted by a jury of magistrates under the presidency of Hardoin.

Tocqueville to his sister-in-law Émilie, New York, June 9, 1831

Heartfelt thanks, my good little sister, for the two warm letters I've already received from you. All your kind endearments are balm to my soul, and be assured that I repay your affection in equal measure. I don't know what species of animal could say that absence cools the heart. Nothing could be further from the truth; I, at least, experience the opposite every day, loving all of you as I do even more now than when we were together under the same roof. This land of strangers who regard me indifferently puts me in mind of the happiness I enjoyed in the midst of my family. The intimacy of the hearth, the freedom it nurtures, the sincere interest excited there by one's ordinary words and trivial actions, the memory of all that, dear sister, follows me everywhere, often despite myself, taxing the pleasure of travel. It's a pity; if not for these irrepressible memories, we would be entirely satisfied with our work, of which we have only as much as sustains our interest; with society, which we enjoy or shun as we please; and with our material arrangements, which keep us on the move. Our tasks and diversions are many and sundry. A whole new world is unfolding before our eyes like images projected by a magic lantern. You are familiar enough with your correspondent to know how nicely this suits his character. Then too, there is the weather—magnificent, if a little warm—and an admirable landscape.

Now, about the landscape, I don't know whether you've been told that country houses in the outskirts of New York made me think about your Nacqueville barony. There are no chateaux here; fortunes aren't large enough, what with patrimonies being divided too many ways for any one heir to contemplate a vast and very durable establishment. Instead, Americans build inexpensive houses, whose form and disposition are extremely elegant and picturesque. They situate them on a favorable lie of land, looking out to the sea when possible. There is nothing fresher and more graceful than these dwellings. I should think that a house of this kind would lend great charm to your property. The problem is, how to help you picture them in detail. Beaumont is a passable draftsman, and I shall try to have him sketch some of the prettier examples. Rich families in this region all have one such residence, for summering. Since we've already received several invitations, it won't be difficult.

We are living, my dear sister, in the most singular country in the world. You have heard it said that in England wives lead a sedentary life, while young unmarried women enjoy great freedom. Well, fancy this: America, from our French perspective, gives English extremes an air of moderation. Here, when a woman marries, it's as if she were taking the veil, except that bearing children, and even many children, is not frowned upon in the conjugal convent. Her existence is nun-like: no more balls, almost no society, and a cold, estimable husband for exclusive company, until she goes to her eternal reward. The other day I dared ask one of these recluses to tell me, briefly, what an American woman can devote herself to in her leisure time. She replied with perfect composure: "To admiring her husband." *À admirer son mari*—a literal translation of the English verb "to admire." I report this so that, should you ever get bored at home, you will know what to do.

So much for spouses. You will find the deportment of young women even more outlandish. Picture the daughters of prominent families, dolled up at one in the afternoon, blithely scampering through all the streets of New York, from shop to shop, or riding horseback unescorted by a parent, by an uncle or aunt, or even by a servant. But there's more. Say a young man (and this has happened to us several times) crosses paths with one such equestrienne. If they already know each other, they stop, and chat amicably for a quarter hour at a boundary-post. The young woman thereupon invites him to visit her and tells him when she will be home to receive. He proceeds to call upon Mademoiselle So-and-So at the stated hour and often finds her alone in her father's drawing room, where she does the honors. We are told that this way of carrying on has none of the objectionable consequences one might expect, since—if (ahem!) we can believe what our informants assure us—the tête-à-tête is normally spent talking about the price of wool and cotton. . . . We've grown quite familiar with young men and women who have a so-called understanding. What they understand is that they will get married in several months. Meanwhile, they are always together, enacting the primmest of courtships. It is clear that one dare not flit about amorously here. Drat it! The moth would soon get singed by the candle. Straightforwardness is the rule. People assign the most literal meaning to words, and unless one bites one's tongue seven times before speaking, as the wise man counsels us to do, one may find oneself in a very delicate position.

You see how I natter on. The fact is that I would say much more if not for the impending departure of the mail coach. But there will be sequels. Farewell for now; I embrace you with everything my heart holds dearest and beg you to prove, from time to time, that you haven't forgotten me completely.

Beaumont to his brother Achille, June 18

. . . Despite the oppressive heat, we do not relax our efforts. We are in good health; I myself have never felt better. I've acquired all the habits of the native-born American and now drink tea. This adaptation was indispensable, since wine, if one can find any, costs a fortune. Although we lead perfectly comfortable existences, we don't spend much, and I doubt that our expenses will increase when we've left New York. . . .

. . . Every day we make new acquaintances. We have met with all sorts of people of distinction, most recently M. Galatin [Albert Gallatin], America's former ambassador to France, England, and Russia. A remarkable man is M. Galatin. . . . He speaks French fluently. Our conversations with him clarified many points we had been puzzling over. Then there is chancellor Kent.[34] As the author of a famous commentary on the laws of the United States (which he presented to us along with a very nice letter of homage), he is the American Blackstone.

One day we attended a kind of ball in the home of Colonel Fish, and the next day a dancing party in the home of M. King. . . . We also dined at the country house of M. Schermerhorn,[35] barely a league outside the city. It is a charming place, situated near the Sound, on the banks of the East River. M. Schermerhorn had reunited all our companions from *Le Havre.* There we encountered Miss Edwards again; we leapt and danced and capered, without benefit of music. . . . Even more enjoyable was the soirée given yesterday by M. Prime to celebrate the marriage of one of his daughters. He is a country neighbor of M. Schermerhorn, but his residence is incomparably more beautiful and commodious. There was an incredible swarm—all of New York's fashion plates attended. It

34. James Kent (1763–1847) was Columbia College's first professor of law. He became chief justice of the New York State Supreme Court and in 1814 was appointed chancellor of New York. He was noted for his *Commentaries on American Law* in four volumes.

35. Colonel Nicholas Fish—a jurist, a friend of Alexander Hamilton, and a companion-in-arms of George Washington—had distinguished himself at the battle of Yorktown. He was married to Peter Stuyvesant's descendant Elisabeth Stuyvesant and figured prominently in New York social circles. The banker Rufus King had also played an important part in the Revolution. One of his sons became the governor of New York, another the president of Columbia College, and a third the chairman of the New York–Erie Railroad. The Schermerhorns were another prominent New York family, descended from Dutch colonists who had gained wealth as traders up and down the Hudson in the seventeenth century.

was the first time we had seen a great many ladies mingling. Some impressed me as very pretty, but I'm not quite sure, for only one commanded my attention throughout the evening, Miss Fulton, who, with good reason, is thought to be New York's reigning beauty. We took some charming walks in the moonlight. Odds are a hundred to one, alas, that I'll ever seen her again. She is the daughter of the famous [Robert] Fulton, inventor of the steamboat. . . .

This evening we shall attend a banquet at the home of M. Emmet,[36] son of the famous lawyer in whose honor Americans have raised a monument. It's a nuisance and I wish we could dodge it. What particularly sets our teeth on edge are the political toasts: if one is offered to *the health of republicans,* we have made up our minds to remain silent. I'm only a little bit worried, however; Frenchmen who know us here have probably spread the word about our *political line.* Never or almost never do people mention La Fayette in our presence. Anyway, the hero of two worlds seems to have lost much of his glitter in the public imagination: when people do speak about him, they vaunt his good faith and unselfishness, but picture him as a deluded man whose views endanger his country.[37] . . .

Tocqueville to his mother, New York, June 19, 1831

I shall not send you a long letter today, my dear Mama, since time is short and, besides, a thick sheaf of my pages, which left a week

36. Thomas Addis Emmet was the brother of the famous Irish rebel Robert Emmet, who led the United Irish Society and organized an uprising in 1803, for which he was hanged by the British. Thomas, trained as a physician, became a lawyer to defend his insurgent compatriots. He was expelled from Ireland in 1802 and, after a sojourn in Paris, settled in America, where he made a great name for himself as an eloquent lawyer.

37. Five years later, in 1836, Beaumont married Clémentine de Lafayette, granddaughter of the famous marquis.

ago by the last mail, should soon land at your doorstep. However, I don't want the vessel that sets sail tomorrow to depart without something on it for you. I want above all to thank you, dear Mama, for the two letters you've already written, as I know that you have great difficulty writing in your present condition.[38] Believe me when I say that I fully appreciate this mark of tenderness. Any word from you, however brief, is precious to me. With each mail delivery I look for the script of those dear to me; it speaks more persuasively than their categorical assurances of well-being.

Knowing that in all probability our first letters have reached you lets us breathe much easier. I fear that this past fortnight has been a terrible ordeal for you. Being without news for six weeks was difficult enough for me; for you, three months must have seemed interminable. Then, too, one can hardly take comfort in the thought that navigation is safer than ever. There are still more than fifteen hundred leagues of sea to cross between four planks of wood, and no doctor aboard.

It's been a month since my first letter left for England; if M. Prime's correspondent in Liverpool has fulfilled his charge, it must have reached you. I assume it did. And were you entertained at all by my long letter written on shipboard, dear Mama? I would love to be told so. I think incessantly about my first news arriving after this long silence; I can picture the family gathering, with anticipation written on every face. And this tableau thrills me. Generally speaking, I can say that all of you have never been more in my thoughts than during our separation. My love is not greater than before, but I believe I find more pleasure in protesting it, and take lively interest in everything you recount, down to the most trifling incident.

38. Tocqueville's mother, Louise, was a woman whose nerves were delicately strung and may have been even before her traumatic incarceration during the Terror.

We continue to be admirably well received here and lead an agreeable life. However, all good things must come to an end and we plan to depart New York later this month. Our intention at first was to visit Boston, but we have completely revised our plans. Instead of heading north, we shall go west as far as a small town named Auburn, which, if you consult your map, you will find a little below Lake Ontario. Situated there is the most remarkable prison in the United States. We shall stay ten days or so, as we did at Sing Sing, then visit Niagara Falls, not far away, and board the Lake Ontario steamship for a two-day trip to Quebec. From Quebec it's a skip and a hop to Boston and thence to New York. This distance, which seems immense on the map, is traversed with remarkable speed. *It's the fashionable circuit* hereabouts; we shall be making it at a leisurely pace, as we intend to stop at Albany, Auburn, Montreal, and Quebec. Canada piques our curiosity. The French nation of Louis XIV's day survives there unspoiled in its mores and language. It was Monsieur Power, the aforementioned grand vicar of New York, who urged this voyage upon us. He lived for a long time in Canada and has offered us letters of introduction.

M. Power is an amiable man, raised in France and almost as fluent in French as in his native language. About the progress of Catholicism in this part of the world he has told us much of great interest, which I shall communicate when I have more time. It was partly on his advice that we decided against going west this fall, when one runs the risk of contracting tertian fever because of all the water there, some of it pumped up by the summer sun. Coastal regions and Pennsylvania are the healthiest places all year round. My only complaint is that they are too warm; the heat is beastly, though nothing out of the ordinary for America where, in general, seasons are more sharply defined than in Europe. New York, for example, has Italian summers and Dutch winters. It seems that the human body flourishes in these transitions, or so say doctors claiming that the climate is the main reason for the longevity of the inhabitants.

I would love to squeeze a letter to Alexandrine into this mail. I don't know whether I'll have time to write one. That poor little sister and her big, bouncing daughter are always in my thoughts. Alexandrine, Édouard, and Denise[39] are three beings so close-knit that whatever afflicts one will almost inevitably be felt by the others. May God arrange to have the sun now broiling us in America warm Alexandrine's delicate nerves and help her recuperate from the stress of her life. You know that I wish the same for you, dear Mama.

I received an announcement in the mail that Monsieur Ollivier planned to remain in Geneva; a subsequent announcement informed me that he was returning. Which should I believe? I've plumped for the latter, since it's what I want to hear. As it will be a long time before France enjoys real tranquillity, it seems to me that voluntarily remaining outside the country now is condemning oneself to remain an expatriate forever. Then, too, one whole year is no insignificant fraction of a lifetime! One must have strong motives for deciding to spend it in a ticklish situation and without pleasure of any kind. That is what I understand Monsieur Ollivier's predicament to be in Geneva.

I was delighted to learn that you are going to spend the summer at Saint-Germain, dear Mama. I shall anxiously await word that you are settled there, you and good Bébé, whom I have very much in mind! The country air, the quiet, all of that will do both of you good, I'm sure.

I'm attaching to this letter another, long one that we felt we

39. Denise, born on December 6, 1830, was the first child of Tocqueville's brother Édouard and his wife, Alexandrine.

ought to write to Félix d'Aunay, by way of keeping faith with a man who in recent months has been such a benevolent advocate. We are glad for this opportunity to congratulate him on the marriage of his daughter. The fact is that Séguier fils is held in high esteem. Will he make a good husband? That I can't say, but I know no one better qualified than he to offer his wife *mathematical proof* that she must be a submissive partner.

I wanted to send you one of the newspaper articles about us; I thought it would amuse you. But I don't have time to translate it. I shall therefore limit myself to sending you the paper on which I transcribed the original.[40] Chabrol, or someone else, will translate it for you; the English is fairly simple. You will see that the journalist is not sparing of compliments. Chabrol will do it. Besides, I should like him to see it.

Adieu, my dear, good Mama. I embrace you with all my heart, Papa as well, and Bébé, brothers, sisters, niece, the lot of you.

40. The article, datelined "Sing-Sing, June 7, 1831," was inserted in all of New York's newspapers. It read: "It will be recollected that, a few weeks ago, we noticed the fact of a commission's having been appointed by the French government to visit this country with the view of acquiring an intimate knowledge of the system of prison discipline practised in the United States. Messrs. de Beaumont and de Tocqueville, the distinguished gentlemen composing the commission, have spent the last two weeks at this place, and after a most laborious and careful inspection of the prison here, its construction, its order, cleanliness, discipline and regularity, together with a strict investigation into all the minutiae of its government and operation, we are gratified with the opportunity of stating that they are highly pleased with the institution and do not hesitate to pronounce it superior in many of its branches to any which they have ever visited.

"They are gentlemen of engaging manners, and of first rate talents and acquirements. We trust that the attention and kindness of the American people, who cannot but feel flattered with the object of their mission, will render their visit throughout the union both pleasant and profitable."

Tocqueville to Ernest de Chabrol, New York, June 20, 1831

I shall not write you a long letter, my dear friend, but I don't want to entrust you with a letter for the neighbor and not include a token of remembrance for the bearer, who is, by the way, often in my thoughts and almost as often the subject of conversation with my traveling companion. Apropos, we agree that you are a peculiar fellow. When I left you, you were preoccupied with what I took to be arrangements for a marriage. Since then, you haven't breathed a word about it; it's clear that you aren't married, but why? How come? Fill in this blank the next time you write.

We are here for about ten more days. We shall thereupon plunge headlong into the wilderness, and God knows when we'll reemerge. The fact is that our projects are not yet settled; all we know for sure is that we leave New York at the end of June. My next letter will you tell you more. Say nothing of our departure plans to my parents: I sent them in England a newspaper article about us, and told them that you would explain it. So go see them; try to pinch the article and show it to Marie: it will make her laugh. The life we lead here would be entirely to our liking, were it not for the penal system, which we've begun to find wearisome. We've slaved over it. Will our enormous labors prove useful? I don't know; but I flatter myself that our account of it will be complete. We've gone to great pains to furnish ourselves with general documents. The reason is that there is really no government in this happy land; no one has bethought himself to obtain from each region within each state the information needed for a minimally satisfactory record. Nor does anyone have the right to do it. This task therefore falls upon our shoulders, and I assure you that it has cost us blood and sweat.

However, we do allow ourselves occasional distractions. Yesterday, at the invitation of the "district attorney" (le Procureur du

Roi), we went to high court to attend the trial of a famous thief. Sitting in reserved seats was the best part of it. Unfortunately, the defendant had not had time to subpoena an important witness, much to the dismay of the attorney and the court, who wanted to show off for us. It was hoped that by harassing the poor devil he would allow himself to be judged then and there. I was afraid that they would condemn him for our sake, without letting him testify. But they were compelled after an hour and a quarter to postpone the trial until the next session. You see that men on this side of the Atlantic don't differ all that much from those on ours.

After that big case collapsed, three or four little ones were dispatched in our presence. At bottom, we are alike, France and America, but here justice is served with fewer formalities. One jury is chosen for all the cases on the day's docket, unless a defendant objects to any of its members. There is neither a bill of indictment nor an examination; what it resembles most closely is our court of summary jurisdiction. The lawyer and the prosecutor have absolutely the same instincts as in France; they are indeed defending two "causes." Impartiality doesn't count. The judge resumes the proceedings in a few words, expresses his view, instructs the jurors; the latter opine out in the open—they have no private chamber. And in a twinkling the man is condemned. Sentence is passed only at the end of the session.

There's good and bad in these arrangements. I believe that ours are better for big cases, but I am convinced that if the jury system is ever applied in small ones, which is bound to happen sooner or later, we shall be forced to imitate the Americans.

In any event, I hope that we shall never behave with the casualness that prevails here: the prosecutor keeps his hands in his pockets when he speaks, the magistrate chews tobacco, and the defense attorney cleans his teeth while questioning witnesses. I doubt that these manners are absolutely inherent in the proper administration of justice. It is evident, moreover, that the bench and the bar are indivisible. Strictly speaking, there is no judiciary, there are only lawyer judges. As far as I can tell, this state of affairs does not have the nefarious consequences we would naturally expect it to have in France; in general, lawyers here occupy a very different position from what you imagine. I don't have the time to tell you why; suffice it to say right now that they form the "resistance," in other words, the "stay-put class."[41] I'll explain this another time.

Adieu, my good friend. I love you and embrace you with all my heart.

Speak about me to all our friends.

Tocqueville to his sister-in-law Alexandrine, New York, June 20, 1831

Dear sister,

I didn't think I would write to you today, or rather, I didn't think I could, for the will to do so never falters, but I have half an hour left after my letter to mother and shall take advantage of it to chat. I constantly have you in mind, good sister. These aren't empty words. I am quite certain that not a day passes without Édouard, you, or your little daughter entering my thoughts, and whoever appears first summons the others. I wonder how all three of you are getting on, where you are, what you are doing. I like to hope that the sun shining over America is also brightening your world; that it has routed the gremlins of winter. I see you under a shade tree at Vaumorin. I can make out the family scene from here: your little girl is near you, lying quietly in her cradle; you are

41. Tocqueville used the word *stationnaire*, by which he meant pledged to the status quo.

reading; Édouard is drawing. But is it all imaginary? That possibility wrenches my heart. I am convinced (to digress for a moment, dear sister) that there is an element of egoism in fraternal friendship, that the confusion between one's own interest and one's brothers' is such that one can hardly separate them. This is often my predicament when I think of you and Édouard. I have some very close friends, and I welcome news of their good fortune. But I surprise myself actively desiring what may be useful and agreeable to you, quite as if I myself were the beneficiary. A singular phenomenon, which we philosophers can explain only in light of the above.

I hear that Monsieur Ollivier will soon be coming home. Praise the Lord! The thought of him spending so much time in voluntary exile deprived of the joys of family life so necessary to him was insufferable. If he is already near you, be sure to remember me to him.

We still lead the same life: *study and soirées.* We have busy days and long nights. So you see, you need not fret over us. The other day we attended something resembling a ball. The custom here, and it's a sensible one, is for a young woman to inform all her acquaintances, several days after her marriage, that she wishes to see them and will receive on a given day. Once this announcement is made, everyone somehow connected to the family flocks to her house or to her parents' and all post-nuptial calls are thus gotten over with in one fell swoop. We were at just such an assembly as this. It took place two leagues from New York, at a charming country house on the shore, surrounded by tall trees. The lawn on which the house stands slopes down to the water and a fresh breeze came off the sea. The evening was magnificent. Here in America there are flies that emit as much light as glowworms, and so many of these little creatures filled the woods round about that it looked as though a thousand sparks were flying through the air.

It was extraordinary. We could have dispensed with only one thing—the music. Don't take me for a philistine. I say we could have done without it because it resembled the music in fairground huts. Where intonation is concerned, these people are surely the most disorganized imaginable. Some awareness of how off pitch they are would be partly redeeming. But there isn't any. We are often subject to caterwauling that the Old World cannot conceive. What the young ladies who perform for us like best in this music are its difficulties. Do they aim to produce clashing and discordant sounds? If so, their success is complete. In addition, one can never be sure that the song is over when the music stops; it always ends like a book whose last page has been ripped out. At first I thought that the singer had stopped short and I continued to listen instead of applauding.

You probably think that I sound *indignant.* I am, for consider that apart from the grating of dreadful music on ears at least minimally acquainted with good, we have the feeling of moral violence inflicted on us by our having to listen whether we like it or not, and, what is more, to look well pleased.

On this subject, I had an amusing fit of absent-mindedness the other day. We were at the home of a lady who began to sing a popular song the air and words of which are very droll. After the first stanza, everyone laughed, myself included—it was a way of applauding. When she launched into the second stanza, my mind began to wander. It went so far astray that I lost touch with everything around me. In the midst of my aerial voyage I heard the song ending, remembered that one must laugh, and laughed, rather loudly in fact. At this outburst of jollity everyone stared at me. I soon learned why, to my chagrin. The farcical song had ended five minutes earlier, and the one that had just made me so gleeful was the most *chromatic,* the most tearful, the most plaintive romance in the entire American repertoire.

With this I must quickly take my leave. Adieu, good sister. I love you and embrace you with all my heart. Remember me to Denise.

Tocqueville to Eugène Stöffels,[42] New York, June 28, 1831

Here we are, very far removed from each other, my good friend, but our hearts span the interval. I myself feel as strongly as ever, perhaps more than I did in France, that we are bound for life, and that in whatever situation fortune places us, we can always count on each other for all the friendship and aid that one man can ask of another.

When we were at the collegiate school, and later when we were studying law and practicing it in secure positions, who could have guessed that a political tempest would separate us by a hemisphere? And who knows what else the future holds in store? Here we are— I at least—cast upon a boundless sea: God only knows where and when I shall make landfall. I would not even murmur complaints if I were alone, but crowding my imagination and darkening my view of the future are parents, friends, a family that includes old people and invalids.

[In the body of this letter, Tocqueville repeats the account he has given other correspondents of the ocean crossing and his first impressions of New York.]

You can appreciate that I haven't yet formed an opinion about Americans. At first glance, they resemble every other nation in presenting a mixture of vices and virtues that defy classification and baffle the portraitist. What I see so far is that they abide strictly by their moral conventions. Above all, the marriage bond

42. Eugène Stöffels and his brother Charles had been schoolmates of Tocqueville at Metz.

is more sacrosanct here than anywhere else in the world. Respect for religion is carried to a fault. For example, no one would allow himself to hunt, to dance, or even to play an instrument on Sunday; allowances are not made even for foreigners.

I have seen the streets in front of churches cordoned off during the services.

These republicans hardly resemble our French liberals. Other differences abound—in manners, ideas, material circumstances, but I don't have time to elaborate.

That's the good side. The bad is an immoderate appetite for wealth, and a desire to get rich quickly. Bound up with this are a perpetual fickleness, a continual need for change, the total absence of old traditions, ancient mores, a commercial and mercantile spirit applied to the most incongruous things. There you have a complete picture of New York.

[Tocqueville then describes his future itinerary.]

The news of France we've received by various packets appears to bode well. If the Périer ministry[43] shows resolve I believe it will prevail, for the time being anyway. Once people have forgotten their terror of the Republic, the spirit of opposition may, I fear, throw the nation, unwittingly, into the arms of republicans. When this letter reaches you, the results of general elections will be known. If they favor moderation, as I hope they do, we may have tranquillity for a while (assuming royalists in the west sit tight).[44]

43. Casimir Périer had been leader of the moderate opposition under Charles X and assumed the office of premier in March 1831, with a view to restoring order in the turbulent aftermath of the July Revolution.

44. Tocqueville is referring to the Vendée region of Brittany, a traditional stronghold of royalist sentiment.

I hope, for the sake of the general public and for yours in particular, my dear friend, that the revolutionary fever harrowing
Metz has begun to abate. You are often in my thoughts.

Tocqueville to Louis de Kergorlay, Yonkers, twenty miles from New York, June 29, 1831

I begin my letter here, my dear friend, but I don't know when and
where I shall finish it. I didn't write earlier because I had nothing
in particular to say; talking about France from this great distance
is exasperating. By the time my letter reaches you, you would have
forgotten the events to which it refers; during the interval the
political situation might have shifted heaven knows how many
times. And as for this country, I didn't want to say anything about
it until I had come to know it better. I realize now that I didn't
gain much by waiting. A foreign people has a certain external
physiognomy that one discerns at first glance and easily fixes in
one's mind. When one then tries to go deeper, one encounters
unforeseen obstacles; progress is frightfully slow, through gathering doubts. Right now my head is a jumble of contradictory
notions. What I can't find—and the search has exhausted me—
are several perfectly clear, conclusive points. This correspondence
does me good. The obligation to formulate my ideas may help me
sort them out a bit; which isn't to say that I would hesitate to send
you doubts and vaporous reveries if that's all I could offer. One of
the advantages of our friendship, of knowing each other as well as
we do and trusting each other implicitly, is that our "budding"
opinions will be taken for what they are; neither too much nor too
little will be made of them.

You asked me in your last letter if there are any "beliefs" here.
I don't know exactly what meaning you ascribe to that word, but
I am struck by one phenomenon, and that is the broad commu-

nality of certain opinions. It's the thing I find most enviable in America. Thus, for example, I have yet to hear anyone, whatever his social rank, publicly express misgivings about the republic being the best of all possible governments or challenge the proposition that a nation has the right to live under a government of its own choosing. The vast majority understands republican principles in the most democratic sense. To be sure, some individuals betray a certain aristocratic penchant, which I shall attempt to explain in due course, but no one—neither priests, nor magistrates, nor merchants, nor artisans—doubts that the republic is a good government, that it comports with the very nature of human society. So general is this opinion, so seldom is it discussed, even in a country where freedom of speech knows no bounds, that one could almost call it a belief. There is a second idea that shares this character: "faith" in man's good sense and wisdom, faith in the doctrine of human perfectibility. Here again one would be hard pressed to find skeptics. While everyone acknowledges that the majority may err on rare occasions, no one questions the necessary rightness of its decisions in the long run, or disputes the fact that it is not only the sole legal judge of its interests but also the surest and most infallible. What flows from this idea is the conviction that one cannot spread enlightenment broadly enough, that it should be lavished upon the populace. You know how often we in France (and we are far from being alone) have wracked our brains over the desirability or danger of educating every rank of society. A matter so difficult of resolution for us seems not even to have crossed people's minds here. I've broached it time and again with the most thoughtful men; I gathered from their curt replies that it was not something they had ever pondered, and merely voicing it as an issue struck them as rather shocking and absurd. Enlightenment, they say, is the only safeguard we have against the waywardness of the multitude.

There, my dear friend, you have what I would call the "beliefs" of this country. They sincerely believe in the excellence of their government; they believe in the wisdom of the masses, assuming the latter are well informed, and appear to be unclouded by suspicions that the populace may never share in a special kind of knowledge indispensable for governing a state. As to what we generally mean by "beliefs"—ancient mores, venerable traditions, deep-rooted memories—so far I have seen no trace of them. I even doubt that religious opinions hold as much sway as I originally thought they did. There may be nothing more intriguing about this nation than its religious circumstances, and I shall try to examine them when I resume my letter. I must interrupt it now, for several days perhaps.

Calwell [Colwells], Forty-five miles from New York
My mind has been so exercised by the letter I began this morning that I feel the need to continue it, without quite knowing what I want to say. About religion, I was struck upon arriving here by the precise practical measures associated with religious worship. The Sabbath is strictly observed. I have seen streets opposite churches roped off during service. The law absolutely requires these things, and even stronger than the law is opinion, which compels everyone to show up at church and abstain from all entertainment. Unless I'm sadly mistaken, these external forms conceal a reservoir of doubt and indifference. Irreligion isn't imbued with political passion, as in France; but religion does not wield more power for all that. Faith is obviously inert; what was once a strong impulse is growing feebler by the day. Enter any church (I refer to the Protestant kind) and you will hear sermons about morals; not one word about dogma—nothing at all likely to fluster one's neighbor or awaken the idea of dissent. But the mind gripped by a belief thrives on dogmatic abstractions, on

discussions that fall in with some religious doctrine. From what I can see, this alleged tolerance amounts to good old indifference; so extreme is it, that in public establishments such as prisons and reformatories for young delinquents seven or eight ministers representing different sects spell one another in chapel. How do the men and children who belong to one sect feel about being preached to by the representative of another? My confident reply is this: since these several ministers deal only with moral commonplaces, they don't cramp one another. It is clear, moreover, that on the whole, religion doesn't move people to the depths of their soul. In France, believers manifest their belief by sacrificing time, effort, money. One feels that they live under the sway of a passion whose instruments they have become. To be sure, alongside them are brutish types for whom the very word "religion" is anathema and who have trouble distinguishing good from evil. Neither of these classes seems to exist over here, in the mass of Protestants. Religion is observed much the way medicine was taken by our fathers in the month of May: it may not do any good, but neither can it do any harm, and anyway, people seem to say, it's best to abide by the general rule. In the final analysis, one may ask whether matters could have turned out differently. The sixteenth-century reformers made a compromise that has its political analogue today. They said: such and such a principle is bad insofar as it has this specific outcome; otherwise we stand by it and require you to do the same. But there were ardent, logical minds that chafed at being halted in mid-course, with the result that an immense new pasture was opened to the human mind, and I assure you that the latter took full advantage of it. In America, Protestantism is astoundingly fissiparous: sects have divided into an infinite number of subsects. Picture if you will concentric circles around a fixed point, which is the Catholic faith; with each successive circle, religion draws that much closer to pure deism.

Under these circumstances, how does one cope? As far as I can tell, almost all thinking Protestants find themselves mired in doubt. The reformed religion is clearly a species of compromise, the religious equivalent of "representative monarchy"; it may span one era or bridge two, but it is only transitional and is nearing its end. What will replace it? I have no answer, but for examining the question—a very *human* question—this country, where the religious and anti-religious instincts that polarize men develop freely, provides invaluable resources. If you were to witness this curious spectacle, you would recognize the struggle of two principles elsewhere dividing the world of politics. Protestants of every persuasion—Anglicans, Lutherans, Calvinists, Presbyterians, Anabaptists, Quakers, and a hundred others—form the core of the population. They are practicing and indifferent; they live from day to day, grow accustomed to a peaceful "middle ground," in which the proprieties are satisfied, if not much else. These sectarians live and die in the wishy-washy, without worrying about the heart of things; they no longer proselytize. Above them are a handful of Catholics, exploiting the tolerance of their former adversaries but themselves remaining as intolerant as ever, intolerant in the way that "believers" are. For them there is only one fixed point of truth; eternal damnation lies to either side. They live in the midst of a civil society but won't associate with the religious groups around them. I already see that their tenets on freedom of conscience comport with those of the European Church and suspect that they would start persecuting if they had the upper hand. These people are mostly poor, but zealous. Their priests are pledged to the cult of sacrifice they've embraced, quite unlike Protestant ministers managing religious affairs in a cut-and-dry way. And the Catholic population has multiplied. Many immigrants from Europe add to the number; but conversions abound. New England and the Mississippi basin swarm with them. It is clear that Protestants who are naturally inclined to religion—the blunt, earnest sorts who have grown weary of sectarian complication but who need religion—despair of finding the truth, and deliver themselves, neatly tied up, into the arms of "authority." Their critical faculty is a burden that weighs upon them, and they happily cast it off. They become Catholics. Moreover, Catholicism excites the senses and the soul: it appeals more strongly to common people than the reformed religion. Most converts therefore belong to the working class.

That's one extreme. At the other is a Protestant sect that is Christian in name only, called "Unitarianism." Among Unitarians —that is, among those who deny the Trinity and recognize only one God—J.C. is seen as an angel, a prophet, or a Socrates. They are pure deists. They invoke the Bible because they would rather not scandalize a largely Christian public, and they hold religious service on Sunday. To judge by the service I attended, one hears verses of Dryden or other English poets about God and the immortality of the soul, then a speech making some moral point. And that's the end of it. This sect is gaining converts as successfully as Catholicism, but it recruits them from the upper classes. Both thrive at the expense of Protestantism. It is clear that citizens given to argumentation—Protestants with dispassionate, logical minds, and men of intellect and learning—welcome the opportunity to embrace a philosophical sect that thinly veils their deism. In no way do its members resemble our Saint-Simonians.[45] Aside from the fact that their point of departure is utterly different, there is nothing puffed up or cock-eyed in their doctrine and cult; quite the opposite, they do their best to appear

45. Saint-Simonianism was a French political and social movement of the early nineteenth century, utopian in nature and predicated on the belief that science would supplant traditional authority. It reflected the ideas of Claude-Henri de Rouvroy, comte de Saint-Simon.

a Christian sect, which helps fend off ridicule. They are neither driven nor hobbled by a spirit of factionalism. Gravity and simplicity mark their every feature. One therefore sees the two absolute principles of "reason" and "authority" breaching the walls of Protestantism, itself an amalgam of reason and authority. Close observers may find the spectacle pretty much everywhere; but here it is flagrant. Because no institution or body of opinion in America hinders the progress of intellect and passion in this regard, they follow their natural bent.

As I see it, the two extremes are bound to confront each other before long. What will be the ultimate outcome? Here my mind enters a dense fog, and I lose sight of the horizon. Will deism ever suit all classes of a nation, especially those most in need of religion's interdictions? I'm not convinced of it. I must say that what I observe makes me more inclined than in the past to believe that natural religion, as it is called, can suffice for the upper classes—provided it stands staunchly behind the two or three great verities it teaches, and, with the trappings it borrows from established religion, enables its adherents to profess those truths openly. But the populace, unless it undergoes some radical transformation, will conceive this natural religion to be merely the absence of belief in the afterlife and fall plumb into a doctrine based on self-interest.

But coming back to the present state of the United States, you should not interpret what I've just told you too literally. I spoke about the obvious "tendency" of minds, and not of faits accomplis. It is clear that Christian religion has stronger underpinnings here than in any country I know of, and I'm sure that it influences every political administration. Ideas aren't aired on this side of the ocean unless they're well-buttoned and morally groomed; the spirit of innovation is held in check; reckless moves are discouraged, and rare is the disposition, so common among Frenchmen, to leap across obstacles *per fas et nefas* [by fair means or foul] toward a particular goal. However ardently it wishes to achieve its ends, a party would feel obliged to do so by means that have a nominal appearance of "morality" and would not openly flout religious beliefs of a more or less moral nature, even when they are dead wrong.

Admirable, isn't it, the feebleness of our nature. One religion sways people's wills, dominates the imagination, and begets real, profound beliefs. But it divides the human race into the blessed and the damned, creating divisions on earth that ought to exist only in the next life; it fosters intolerance and fanaticism. The other religion preaches tolerance, cleaving to reason, which it makes its symbol, and what is it?—an inert fellowship, feckless and almost lifeless. Well, enough of this subject. I am compulsively drawn to it, and it will drive me mad if I dwell on it any further. Besides, I have other things to tell you.

Do you know what, in this country's political realm, makes the most vivid impression on me? The effect of laws governing inheritance. At the time of the American Revolution, colonists enjoyed political equality, but not patrimonial. The English had exported their laws of primogeniture, according to which the eldest acquired three-quarters of the father's fortune. This resulted in a host of vast territorial domains passing from father to son and wealth remaining in families. My American informants tell me that there was no aristocracy but, instead, a class of great landowners leading a simple, rather intellectual life characterized by its air of good breeding, its manners, and a strong sense of family pride. . . . A certain number sided with England and were consequently responsible for the revolution. This was less than sixty years ago. Since then, inheritance laws have been revised.

Primogeniture gave way to equal division, with almost magical results. Domains split up, passing into other hands. Family spirit disappeared. The aristocratic bias that marked the republic's early years was replaced by a democratic thrust of irresistible force. Today, fortunes are disintegrating; how rapidly they change hands is beyond all imagining. I've seen several members of these old families and readily noted in them signs of great discontent with the new order of things. They regret the loss of everything aristocratic: patronage, family pride, high tone. But they have resigned themselves to the inevitable and admit that they are now nothing more than one unit among others in the state. All this is done with rather good grace, for if they are no longer favored above others, at least their former advantage does not sentence them to pariahdom. Since their families took part in the revolution and they themselves fought only indirectly against the extension of democracy, public opinion has never stigmatized them in any systematic way.

Before leaving Europe I heard that America had aristocratic leanings. I will affirm unreservedly that those who say as much are wrong. In some states democracy is on the march, in others it has progressed beyond that, affecting every aspect of life. It informs the mores, the laws, the opinion of the majority. Its opponents hide their true colors if they wish to make their way in the world. In New York, only vagrants are deprived of electoral rights. Moreover, the effects of a democratic government are visible: a perpetual instability in men and laws, an external equality pushed to the limit, a uniform style of comportment and way of conceiving ideas. There can be no doubt that the inheritance law is responsible in some considerable measure for this complete triumph of democratic principles. The Americans themselves recognize it; they complain about it or rejoice in it, but agree that "it has made us what we are, it is the foundation of our republic."

That is the language we hear every day and I have been led to reflect seriously upon the matter. If the equal division of goods should, as an inevitable consequence, bring about the destruction of families and family spirit and the complete annulment of aristocratic principles (which now appears quite clearly to be the case), wouldn't all nations in which such a civil law was established rapidly move to either an absolute or a republican form of government, with no chance of their being *decisively* thrown off one course or the other? When I apply these ideas to France, I cannot resist the thought that Louis XVIII's charter[46] was, perforce, an ephemeral document; it created aristocratic institutions in political law, but within the domain of civil law gave shelter to a democratic principle so vigorous that it was bound before long to destroy the foundations of the edifice it raised. Charles X's flaws undoubtedly accelerated the process, but we were well on our way without him. We are moving toward an unrestricted democracy. I don't say that it is a good thing; what I see in this country has persuaded me, on the contrary, that it would not suit France at all. But we are being propelled in that direction by an irresistible force. All our efforts to arrest this movement will only bring about pauses, because there is no human power capable of changing the law of inheritance, and with this change our families will disappear, possessions will pass into other hands, wealth will be increasingly equalized, the upper class will melt into the middle, the latter will become immense and shape everything to its level.

I regard the refusal to embrace these consequences as a weakness; the Bourbons, instead of trying strenuously to uphold an aristocratic principle that is moribund in France, should have done the utmost to endow democracy with incentives for order and stability. As I see it, the communal and departmental system

46. After his first restoration to the throne, in 1814, Louis XVIII granted France a "Charte," or charter.

should have commanded all their attention from the outset.[47] Instead of passively allowing Bonaparte's communal institutions to remain in force, they should have lost no time modifying them, associating inhabitants with their own affairs, giving them a vested interest in local concerns, and above all, fostering, if possible, such *habits and legal ideas* as are, in my opinion, the only possible counterweight to democracy. Had they done so, the movement now under way might have been rendered more innocuous to them and to the state. It seems to me, in brief, that democracy will henceforth be a fact that a government may pretend to *regulate*, but not to *halt*. I assure you that I have not arrived at this conclusion painlessly. What I see in America leaves me doubting that government by the multitude, even under the most favorable circumstances—and they exist here—is a good thing. There is general agreement that in the early days of the republic, statesmen and members of the two legislative houses were much more distinguished than they are today. They almost all belonged to that class of landowners I mentioned above. The populace no longer chooses with such a *sure hand*. It generally favors those who flatter its passions and descend to its level. This effect of democracy, combined with what else I note about it—the extreme instability of all its elements, its absolute lack of perseverance in treating matters of state—reinforces my conviction that the most rational government is not the one in which *all concerned* participate, but the one directed by the most enlightened and moral classes of society.

One cannot deny, however, that all in all this land presents an admirable spectacle. I will say straight out that it has impressed me with the superiority of free governments over every other

47. The "communal and departmental system" refers to administrative divisions instituted during the reign of Napoleon. The "commune" is the smallest division, corresponding in territory to a town or village.

kind. I am more convinced than ever that not all people are made to enjoy it to the same extent; but I tend more than ever to think that this fact is regrettable. You can hardly conceive of the universal satisfaction with which the existing government is regarded. The common man undoubtedly stands higher on the moral ladder than his counterpart in France; he abounds in a sense of his independent position and individual dignity. This doesn't always make relations with him agreeable, but it definitely prompts him to respect himself and others. There are two things I especially admire here. The first is extreme respect for the law; without benefit of pomp and police, it exercises irresistible command. Why? —because people make it themselves and are able to change it as they see fit. Think of thieves—they violate all the laws of their country but scrupulously obey those of their own devising. I believe that something similar occurs in the populace. The second thing I envy here is the facility with which people dispense with government. Every man regards himself as having a vested interest in public safety and the exercise of laws. Instead of counting on the police, he relies only on himself, with the result that the public constabulary is nowhere seen and everywhere present. I assure you that it is something truly incredible to behold, how common people maintain order among themselves in consequence of the belief that their only safeguard against themselves lies within themselves.

You see that I'm giving you as full an account as I can of my impressions. On balance, they are more favorable than they were at the beginning of my sojourn. Much is flawed in the American scene, but as a whole it grips the imagination. Above all, I can easily see it acting forcefully upon logical and superficial minds— a combination not all that rare. The principles of government are so simple, their consequences are deduced with such perfect regularity, that one runs the risk of being subjugated and carried away. One must struggle with oneself, one must go against the grain to perceive that institutions so simple and logical could not accommodate the needs of a great nation—strong internal government and a well-anchored foreign policy; that they are not durable by nature; that the people who have adopted them must be accustomed to living in freedom and possess an abundance of the *true* lights men rarely acquire, and then only in course of time. Having said all that, one wants to say again that such government is a fine thing; it is regrettable that the moral and physical constitution of man prevents him from enjoying it everywhere, and forever.

I would very much like to hear from you about all this, if you have the time and are disposed to ponder theoretical matters. Until now we have been communicating but not conversing. I have yet to receive an answer to the first letter I sent you. Amidst all the theories with which I keep my imagination entertained, the memory of France is like a cankerworm. It suddenly starts gnawing me by day, when I'm working, and when I wake at night. I devour newspapers and letters from abroad. The last news I received was worrisome, as it seemed to indicate great unrest in the west. You know that I've never believed that an insurrection would succeed, so I'd die of anxiety if proven wrong. We've been in New York for almost two months; now we've gained some distance from it, but not enough to prevent us from returning in a week if need be. Vessels depart for Europe every five or six days. I'm in a position to do what suits me best. I am more than ever of the opinion I expressed to you when I left. As long as Louis-Philippe is there, my hands are tied.[48] But no matter who takes his place, I shall resign my public appointment and be master again of my conduct and my actions.

48. Tocqueville was bound by an oath of loyalty to the king and the Charter.

Farewell, dear friend. Not knowing what your fate is weighs upon me oppressively. I was pained by the sadness and disgust with humanity that colored your last letter; not a day passes that I don't wish I were with you, sharing your fortune, for good or ill. Once again, farewell. I embrace you with all my heart. Keep this letter. It will be of interest to me later.

Tocqueville to abbé Lesueur, New York, June 30, 1831

I hope, my good friend, that this letter finds you in fine fettle. The last news I received from France, dated May 12 and informing me that everyone's health was sound, made me happy. But that was so long ago I dare not rejoice too exuberantly.

About your letters, we have them to thank for a most charming excursion we took the other day. When we received them it was six o'clock and the evening air was turning cool. After reading the first lines, we seized upon the idea of enlarging our pleasure by reading the rest at some quiet spot in the country.

Thus, we clutched the precious parcel and made straight for the city's outlying neighborhood. We crossed the East River, entered Long Island, and discovered a lovely valley opening out onto the port of New York. There we took off our hats and ties, sat down under a shade tree, propped ourselves against it, and began slowly to peruse our correspondence.

It was a truly *epicurean* scene. We remained there for an hour, living more with you than in New York. Night had fallen when we returned to our quarters and we agreed that since our arrival this had been our best evening yet.

We plan to leave the city tomorrow, my dear Bébé. We have now seen everything it had to show us of interest regarding people and things; the six weeks we've spent here will leave us with a very agreeable memory.

Our intention is to sail upriver as far as *Albany* and then travel overland to *Auburn,* a city situated in the territory above Lake Ontario. We shall probably remain there ten or twelve days to inspect a famous prison. Afterward we visit Niagara Falls and return to Boston by way of Montreal and Quebec. This is what's called *the fashionable tour* here, the "promenade à la mode." During the summer, throngs of people do it. It generally lasts a month or five weeks but will take us a bit longer as we will make several stops along the way.

To give you some idea of the speed with which one travels, we board a steamboat at Fort Niagara and disembark at Montreal thirty-six hours later. Your map will tell you that that is quite some distance. The region of Lake Ontario, which was deserted twenty years ago, is now thick with towns and villages. One must transport oneself a hundred leagues inland to find real wilderness. We would contemplate the modest expedition on which we are now embarking without qualms were it not for the prospect of receiving no news from abroad and, above all, being unable to time the dispatch of our own letters. You can understand that so far removed from New York we will have no way of making sure that our letters arrive here before packets bound for France weigh anchor, which they do now every ten days. Thus, there will necessarily be letters held until the next sailing, and vessels that bring you nothing. I tell you this because I know how fretful your affection makes you and how easily your imagination conjures up all manner of perils for us.

Moreover, winter is not far off and during that season we will both, perforce, grow accustomed to receiving news at wide intervals. The French consul in New York told us again very recently that there was one period of seventy days last winter when no boats came from France. On the seventieth, a favorable wind blew in three all at once.

I was very happy to learn from recent letters that our poor Alexandrine is feeling better. I now impatiently await the next bulletin. When will it arrive? I have absolutely no idea and am despairing.

The Hippolyte household had yet to leave Paris in May. Émilie wrote me a very warm letter. I see that this poor sister of mine is no more satisfied with the state of her health than Alexandrine. I assume she is now on her way to Nacqueville.

French politics, inasmuch as I can judge of the situation from afar, seem to have taken a reassuring turn. No doubt, the great electoral contest has already been waged. I hope that the moderate liberals emerged victorious and that, if so, subsequent unrest will not be of long duration.

You have no idea, my dear friend, how hungry we are for news from France. I am more convinced than ever that we would not stay here if trouble starts to brew overseas. But if France muddles on as it is now, in a more or less settled state, we are glad not to be at Paris and Versailles, cutting awkward figures.

Americans, by which I mean the enlightened public, have a more reasonable understanding of France's position than I would have thought. I assure you that although they are republicans at home, they believe no more than we do that the republic can establish itself in a great nation.

However, opinions on the subject of La Fayette are more divided than I guessed. In general the upper classes judge him as we do. That is hardly known or suspected in France.

I have been at pains to learn more about the great voyage undertaken by Ludovic.[49] I fear that he will one day repent of it. His father must be stricken.

49. "Ludovic" is Louis de Kergorlay, and the "great voyage" refers to a plot hatched by die-hard royalists (otherwise known as "legitimists") envisioning a new Restoration, with Charles X's daughter-in-law, the

After all this time, I have yet to receive a letter that constitutes a proper *reply*, dear Bébé. Until now we have been playing a game of interrupted monologues. We don't converse. I hope that you will exactly describe all the circumstances that attended the receipt of my first letter: when and how it arrived; what you said and thought upon receiving it. I want to know as much as possible.

The next letter will not reach you by regular mail. It will be brought by one of our friends, who is leaving for France on July 10. I am notifying you so that you expect a delay. You know how long it takes for *occasions* to present themselves. Despite this, I believe I did well to make this arrangement; he will deliver the letter himself and you no doubt will welcome the chance to talk with someone who has just left me and been where I have been. The messenger is Monsieur Schérer, whom my father met in Le Havre. I beg you to receive him as hospitably as possible. . . . Be warned, however, that he will portray America in an unfavorable light. The truth is, his voyage was utterly fatuous. He had no purpose in coming here, and now, after two months of aimless rambling, still ignorant of the language and customs of the country, he is obliged to depart, with nothing to show for two arduous crossings. He is very much out of sorts, as you will discover. Yesterday evening we visited the vessel on which he's booked for the eastward voyage, to help him choose a cabin. Later, Beaumont and I felt sad and resolved not to do anything of the sort again. The visit, the sight of someone about to sail for France—all of that painfully aggravated our consciousness of being on foreign soil. I daresay that we greatly envy Schérer's fate. And the idea that he may be with you in six weeks caused me more grief than

---

duchesse de Berry, as regent for her young son. They hoped to bring her back from Naples, where she lived in exile, to land at Marseille and incite an uprising.

anything I've felt since coming here. I must leave you, for lack of paper. Adieu, dear old friend. . . . I embrace you warmly and thank you for your prayers, which, until now, have been answered.

Embrace everyone for me. Tell Louis if you see him that when I've finished my letter to him it will be voluminous.

Beaumont to his brother Jules, July 4, answering a question about the manners and mores of the rich in America

Bear in mind, first of all, that the state of New York doesn't have any *rich people* as we understand the term. Generally speaking, we mean by "rich people" those whose sole occupation is spending their fortune, who live on unearned income—property owners who have retired to their country estates or consume their revenue in the city. Here everyone is actively involved in commerce and industry. Such are the resources furnished by an immense and bountiful hinterland and the outlets provided by this country's great rivers and its maritime position, that anyone can set up as a trader and make a fortune.

Normally, a country has consumers and manufacturers. Here I see only the latter; consumers are found in the lands to which New York sends its agricultural and industrial products. As the port serving all of Europe and the source of supplies for every region of North America, it enjoys a great advantage. You can imagine how this state of affairs influences the habits of a people: all is hustle and bustle. And money is the universal divinity. . . .

You will perhaps object that since it is so easy to enrich oneself there must be *rich people* and consequently people living on income from their property. Well no! At least not in the state of New York. In the first place, fortunes made with amazing rapidity are dissipated just as rapidly by inheritance laws that enshrine the principle of equal division. Secondly, a man who has devoted his entire life to business seldom retires from it, even at an advanced age. Lastly, the man who has made a great fortune by working is disposed to have his children work as if their livelihoods depended on it. We therefore see the most distinguished *American gentlemen* commute between the marketplace and the ballroom. In the morning they are behind a counter measuring the length of cloth you've bought and in the evening they are dancing opposite you in a quadrille.

This mercantile mentality, which is deeply inbred, affects manners and habits. Men are obliged to get up early in the morning. Breakfast is therefore served at seven-thirty or eight, meaning that women cannot slumber. Nothing is more commonplace than the sight of them walking about at seven a.m. By ten or noon at the latest they are in full regalia. Since a woman's sole occupation is her spouse, she walks a lot, when not caring for the family. Young, unmarried women are relentless walkers. On a street named Broadway, between the hours of noon and three p.m., one is sure to meet all of fashionable New York. The demoiselles walk unescorted. If a young man of her acquaintance passes by, he approaches unabashedly, chats with her, and strolls at her side as long as he pleases. But they cannot stroll arm in arm unless they are what Americans call "fiancés," that is, unless the man has plighted his troth with her. On the other hand, there is no formal engagement; there is a rather long courtship, followed by an "agreement" and the nuptials. When a young man and young woman are seen arm in arm, it's as if they were publishing the banns. . . .

Members of the fair sex pass the time of day lounging, reading, playing music, etc. My initial impression was that they had no bent for needlework, but I have seen them do beautiful embroidery. The work they incline toward is more of the head than the imagination. Almost all of them know or have learned French; some speak it well. They generally hew to the opinion that their education would not be complete without a knowledge of our language. As far as their music making is concerned, it is simply barbaric. . . .

People dine at two or three p.m., take tea at seven, and eat supper at ten. In the evening, visits are paid or visitors received. As a rule, when you go to someone's house, you spend the entire evening with your host; if you leave after an hour, there is open astonishment at your hasty retreat.

On the whole, American women dress rather sumptuously, but without taste. They imitate French fashions in everything. All the articles of their toilette come from Paris, and it is even an immensely profitable branch of commerce for France. But they often borrow what is least good in our fashions, and make it worse by exaggeration. The ornaments they encumber themselves with are badly distributed around their persons: they overindulge in jewels and objects of various colors, all loud. The whiteness of their complexions is remarkable, but I have yet to see a perfect beauty. . . .

What, you ask, are their amusements?

They have few. I understand that during the winter there are many balls. . . . As for now, summertime, the most fashionable and common diversion seems to be horseback riding. No one owns his own horse. They are hired. Some are very fine and cost only seven or eight francs for half a day. Every evening you encounter in town and in the outskirts a multitude of female equestriennes and their squires.

In our New York boardinghouse we encountered two very pretty women, daughters of the landlord who, as such, were obliged to serve us all day long—providing fresh linen, setting the table, etc. At day's end, a complete metamorphosis took place: they donned elegant riding habit, put on plumed hats, and pranced through town with a triumphant air. Upon their return in the evening, they would prepare us a glass of sugared water.

Theater is a meager resource for society. Going to the theater isn't fashionable, theaters are bad, and when there's music, it doesn't pass muster.

You have some idea now of how Americans live. It doesn't take much to amuse them, because they lead such busy, active lives. The women don't lack refinement, but the men do. They are either rude and coarse or, on the contrary, polite to a fault. Their good offices can sometimes be cloying, and when they have a mind to help you, there's no escape.

The fine arts here are in their infancy. Americans have no natural endowment for music; nor, I believe, for art. You ask if there is a museum in New York. There are doubtless several. But do you know what one finds on display? The magic lantern and some stuffed birds. Tocqueville and I had a good laugh when, seeing the sign "American Museum" on the facade of a building, we entered and found the above items instead of paintings.

There are a few public libraries, but they contain twenty thousand volumes at most and go unfrequented. Moreover, literature is not held in high regard. People learn to read, to write, and to calculate; in a word, to acquire as much knowledge as enables them to conduct business. But belles lettres hardly matter. We are told that things are different in Boston and Philadelphia. We shall see.

There is one kind of literature that circulates widely— newspapers. You find them as well in the cobbler's shop as in the home of the rich banker. Even humble domestics read them. Few people have private libraries; newspapers are the household's common provender. They are almost entirely devoted to commercial interests. . . . Generally speaking, the commercial and mercantile spirit holds sway. Political discussions are all about trade. The big quarrel at this moment pits the North against the South in the matter of tariffs. Newly established factories in the North would have great difficulty surviving without the help of tariffs imposed on foreign goods. Southerners who have no industry would suffer as a result, having to pay more for the manufactured goods they need.

UPSTATE NEW YORK AND WEST

Tocqueville and Beaumont departed New York at the end of June, sailing up the Hudson to Albany. After research in state archives, they made their way westward to Buffalo, visiting the Finger Lakes en route, and stopping at Auburn for a compulsory inspection of the famous prison. From Buffalo, their improvisations took them across Lake Erie to Detroit, through the Michigan backwoods with an Ojibwa guide, and up Lake Huron to Lake Superior aboard The Superior, *a tour boat carrying several hundred passengers. No sooner back in Buffalo, they set out for Niagara Falls and looped across Canada to Quebec before returning to Albany early in September.*

Tocqueville to his father, Albany, July 4, 1831

I won't write to you at length, my dear Papa; the bearer of this letter will give you news of me in greater detail than I myself could in ten pages. I'm sorry that Schérer is leaving us but am delighted that he will call upon you and fill you in. I know how much value I would attach to conversation with a man who had just seen you and I imagine that you are of like mind. I therefore rejoice in advance over the pleasure you will experience. I beg you to receive Schérer hospitably. He was a very good companion for us during the sea voyage and has remained one ever since; being familiar with your reputation as a public servant, he seems excessively eager to make your acquaintance.

Schérer belongs to the class of moderate liberals pushed further left than they wished to go by the Revolution of 1830. You see then that one can talk politics with him.

About politics, the latest news strikes me as generally favorable, except for something worrisome apparently brewing in the west. I tremble at the thought that royalists may attempt desperate maneuvers there. I am as convinced as ever that an insurrection would only result in the useless spilling of precious blood and divert the government from the course of moderation it seems to have charted.

But not everyone shares these ideas and, unless I'm mistaken, there will be an armed rising before the year is out. I hope to God I'm wrong, both for France's sake and for ours! At this immense distance from events, we would be a thousand times unhappier than people actually embroiled in them.

The city from which I date this letter borders the Hudson, about fifty leagues from New York, or twelve hours away by steamboat. With a population of at least twenty-five thousand it is the seat of state government. That is the only reason why it has drawn our attention. Stored here are a great many documents not to be found anywhere else; we have spent four or five days with them and leave tomorrow for Saratoga Springs, about fifteen leagues off to the west. Here, as elsewhere, officials have been immensely considerate. All printed documents are actually *given* to us (we shall be bringing back a *trunkful*).

Otherwise, the central government amounts to almost nothing. Its authority encompasses only matters that concern the nation as a whole, for localities manage their own affairs unfettered. This is what makes the republic work. With personal ambition finding an outlet locally, it doesn't endanger the state. I imagine that if the Bourbons, instead of fearing communal organization, had sought little by little, from the beginning of the Restoration, to confer more importance on townships, they would have been able to overcome the mass of passions stirred up against them.

We will stay only two days at Saratoga, which probably resembles all the watering places in the world and will thus be more a diversion for us than a useful source. From there we go to Auburn. We have already done immense research on the prison system. I believe the most difficult work lies behind us and we are greatly relieved, if not altogether satisfied with our yield. We will have facts and new ideas in abundance but very few that lend themselves to practical application. In any case, you can be sure of one thing—we will know our subject inside out.

I must stop here, dear Papa, and rely upon the bearer of this letter to give a fuller account of our life. He will do so cheerfully once you've put him at his ease.

Adieu, I embrace you with all my heart, and Mama as well, and Bébé and tutti quanti.

Absence has begun to weigh heavily on me. I am daunted by the expanse of time remaining before we reunite. It was three months ago yesterday that I bid farewell to you and my brothers. I shall never forget that departure; never has my heart been so wrenched.

Adieu once again.

I'm sending you an immensely long letter for Louis. Although I've written it haphazardly, it contains details precious to me as my only record of them. Take all precautions in having it delivered to him. I don't know what he is doing or where he is now.

Beaumont to his father, July 4

. . . We left New York on June 30, the first order of business being to visit a M. Livingston, who lives seven or eight leagues from

New York on the banks of the Hudson. We intended to take a steamboat, but service was interrupted that day. As luck would have it we found a sloop going in our direction; we boarded it and after two or three hours of pleasant sailing arrived at the village of Yonkers, quite near M. Livingston's residence. Well, what do you know, the Livingstons were not at home! So we returned to Yonkers in befuddlement . . . and whiled away the time there as best we could. After a modest meal, we took to the hills, Tocqueville with his rifle, I with my sketchbook. And while I sat on a rise drawing the Hudson, from a perspective wide enough to include the village and our sloop, . . . Tocqueville waged all-out war on American birds.

These birds are generally quite charming. Many are blue, others are black with a pretty yellow ruff. Both are quite common hereabouts. We haven't often had occasion to shoot any since we forgot to bring our rifles to Sing Sing. Of course we had more important business to attend to on that occasion.

About Yonkers. When the shadows grew long, I closed my sketchbook. We walked downhill and at the riverbank plunged into the Hudson for a very refreshing dip. I swim rather well now, thanks to lessons from my persistent friend Tocqueville. . . .

We spent the night on two bad beds in an attic so hot and airless that I thought we'd suffocate during the night. We were rescued early the next morning by the steamboat making a run from New York to Preskill [Peekskill]. Our plan was to disembark at Callwell [Colwell's], a pretty little village on the left bank of the Hudson, and, later that day, board another steamboat to West Point. We did in fact arrive at Callwell [sic] and had a grand time there walking in the woods and among the rocks and panting our way up a steep mountain for what turned out to be a magnificent, sweeping view of the Hudson Valley. From that summit we beheld mountain chains on every side, and right in front of us a bay called *le Nez d'Antoine*,[1] which owes its name to its wonderfully picturesque shape. We waited until nightfall for a steamboat. It arrived at nine p.m., sailing at a fast clip, as usual. The captain didn't bother to dock it where we stood because that would have taken too much time, but instead sent a canoe, into which we were heaved like two parcels, along with our trunks, and towed us until we caught up. This abduction happened so quickly, in such darkness, and on such a vast expanse of water that there was something magical about it. Yet another surprise awaited us shortly afterward, when we arrived at Newburgh, a few leagues upriver from Callwell. There we suddenly saw fireworks shooting out of the steamboat, and soon, by means of some combustible material consisting of sulfur and resin (if I'm not mistaken), the vessel was so brilliantly illuminated and cast so much light on everything round about that midnight looked like high noon.

Picture us passengers witnessing this unexpected spectacle on a river one league wide, flowing between cliffs a thousand to fifteen hundred feet high. Add to this scene the little town of New-burgh, all lit up, with its houses quite visible and its inhabitants crowding the shoreline to see us pass. They answered our fireworks with their own.

We didn't know the reason for these festivities. It was July 1. At first we thought that they were celebrating the anniversary of the Declaration of Independence, which took place on a July 4th. But why not wait another three days?

At last we learned that we were racing another steamboat, which had left New York at the same time. Ours, the *North America*, had forged ahead and was celebrating its lead. And since the

1. Beaumont mistakenly describes the mountain called Anthony's Nose, on the eastern bank across the river from Bear Mountain, as a bay.

race had been announced, the river bank was alive with people who wanted to witness it.

One disappointment tempered these interesting events. We had no sooner boarded the steamboat than we told the captain that we were going up to West Point. He told us in reply that he couldn't stop there en route to Albany. . . .

[*In Albany, the two Frenchmen were plied with documents by Azariah Flagg, New York's secretary of state, whom Beaumont portrays as a little man with the scruffy look of a underpaid clerk. "He wears blue stockings and the rest of his outfit is no less negligent." His wages were so modest that he made do by renting quarters at an inn, Beaumont noted.*]

Beaumont to his sister Eugénie, July 14

. . . On July 4 . . . the anniversary of the Declaration of Independence (1776) was to be celebrated in Albany, as in all of America's cities. Artillery salvos announced the event at an early hour and flags were draped from every window. At ten, the militia, the civil authorities, and delegations representing all of the city's trades assembled and paraded into a church where the Declaration of Independence was read and a speech delivered.

The authorities are ranked differently here than in France: officers of the militia led the parade. Behind them marched high functionaries of the civil order such as the governor, the chancellor, the secretary of state, the comptroller, etc., and finally, trailing behind, came members of various administrations and deputations. Furthermore, no law determines precedence. Who should precede whom is decided by a congregation of citizens or their representatives on the eve of the festivity. The following year they may revise the order. It would have piqued your curiosity, had you witnessed the Albany parade this past July 4, to see two very distinguished men brought there by chance and positioned conspicuously between the governor and the chancellor: these two great men were none other than Tocqueville and yours truly. The governor and the secretary of state fetched us at our hotel and left us no choice but to figure in the ceremony from beginning to end.

There is nothing resplendent about this festivity. If brilliance were the sole measure, it would not suffer comparison with the least of our political or religious ceremonies. But there is a certain grandeur to its simplicity. Don't expect beautiful uniforms and braided tunics; the celebration is meant to evoke memories of the great event with palpable emblems. So, for example, great pomp surrounds the presentation of an old, bullet-ridden American flag that survived the War of Independence; and much is made of three or four old veterans of Washington's army, whom the city preserves like precious relics; and further on is a richly decorated chariot bearing the press used to print the first copy of the Declaration of Independence. Industrial and commercial trades fly banners identifying themselves as the "association of butchers," the "association of apprentices," or something else. It would be easy to ridicule these signs, but consider how appropriate it is that people who owe their prosperity to commerce and industry should march behind them. The Declaration of Independence was read in the Methodist church (a Protestant sect) by a magistrate who, in America, corresponds to the king's attorney. He read with warmth and dignity: it was truly an admirable performance and the feelings it stirred in those present were not insincere.

Before this reading, a Protestant pastor recited a prayer. I recall the detail because it is so characteristic of America, where nothing is done without the sanction of religion. I don't believe matters are any the worse for it.

A young lawyer then delivered a political speech that sounded like boilerplate rhetoric invoking all the countries of the world. The gist of his harangue was that people everywhere are rallying, or will one day rally, to the cry of liberty. As proof that he left nothing out, I offer in evidence the fact that he even mentioned our mission in America.

At last the ceremony ended with a hymn to liberty, sung to the strains of the "Marseillaise." It was rendered more or less badly by amateurs belting out the couplets each in turn and chanting the refrain in unison. . . . When I heard the orchestra play a ritornelle after each couplet I could hardly contain myself, for this orchestra consisted of a single flute and you can't imagine how frail the poor instrument sounded in a large hall. . . . But again, good taste and distinction are not to be sought at such popular events. This observance with its cortege in bourgeois dress, with its commercial insigniae and its solitary flute made a deeper impression on me than our great celebrations in France—our military reviews, our masses of the Holy Spirit, our pageants, our rejoicings over the birth of the prince, etc. Our festivals are more dazzling; those of the United States ring truer. . . .

On the evening of July 4 we boarded a stagecoach for Auburn.

Beaumont to his sister-in-law Eugénie, July 14

. . . Should you ever have a yen to travel, I advise you against choosing the part of America from which I am now writing to you. The roads are frightful, appalling, and carriages offer no protection: so crudely made are they that the strongest bones rattle inside. . . . I had the impression during this voyage that I was traversing a forest on the only road through it. I can't express my thought more plainly. The natural state of the earth here is to be covered with woods; such was the state of untamed nature and nature still reigns untamed in these regions where civilization has been making inroads for only forty or fifty years. The woods are the emblems of this savageness (we don't have a term to convey the idea expressed so well by the English word "wilderness"). It is therefore against woods that all the energy of civilized man is unleashed. We in France cut wood in order to use it; here it is destroyed. Prodigious efforts are made to obliterate woodland, and often for naught, as vegetation, mocking the pretensions of mankind, grows back so rapidly. Inhabitants of rural America spend half their lives felling trees and children are taught at a very young age to confront the enemy with an ax and a billhook. Trees generally excite hatred, which is why one doesn't always find them shading lovely country houses. It is thought that the absence of trees signifies civilization. . . .

. . . Houses, most of which are wooden, do not lack elegance: they often incorporate classical Greek motifs. Inns are especially remarkable in this respect. The small isolated dwellings one encounters here and there in the midst of the woods are called "log houses," consisting as they do of logs placed on top of one another. . . .

. . . From Utica we headed for Syracuse, to meet M. Elam Lynds, founder of the penal system.[2] It was between Utica and Syracuse that I saw my first Indians: there is a small village called Oneida Castle wholly populated by an Indian tribe that remains more or less unspoiled by the civilization surrounding it. It is left to its own devices and abides by the laws of the country. Should one of its members commit a crime, he is brought to book in an American court.

2. Lynds, a former army captain, was the warden of Auburn. In 1825 the New York legislature assigned him the task of building a newer, more modern prison. After considering such sites as Staten Island and the Bronx, he decided to locate it at Sing Sing.

I didn't stop at Oneida Castle. However, on the way there I passed two Indian women walking barefoot. Their hair is black and dirty, their skin is coppery, their features are extremely ugly. They carry wool blankets on their backs, even in the heat of July. I was reminded of paupers in France, the dirt poor. At least these savages used to have dignity; there was something noble and grand about them in their state of nature. Here they are now, demeaned and debased. They can't do without clothes or without the liquors that stupefy them. What they get from civilization are its vices and its rags. Farther west, in the territories most of tribes have withdrawn to after being flushed out of their native habitat, I shall pay the closest attention to their mores, to their relations with American settlers, to how the uprooted cope in the middle ground between barbarism and civilization, between that which they no longer have and that which they have yet to acquire. I can think of nothing more worthwhile.

. . . From Syracuse we set out for Auburn and passed two lakes en route—Lake Onondaga outside Syracuse, near Salina, and Lake Skaneatheles halfway to our destination. We've been here for five or six days, devoting almost every waking hour to the penal system. Auburn is unquestionably the foremost establishment of its kind in America, so we've decided to leave no stone unturned in searching for documents that may be useful to us.

A few days ago we paid a visit to M. [Enos] Throop, the governor of New York state, who is residing at this moment in a small country house one league from Auburn. He is a man of great simplicity and of modest means, whom the state pays only twenty thousand francs per annum, meager compensation for someone in his office. He therefore spends only five or six months a year in Albany (the state capital), when the legislature is in session, and the rest of the time on his property, which is in fact a working farm. The house he inhabits barely has room enough for him and his wife. Its charm is its site. Lake Owasco laps its garden and open forest surrounds it on the other side. He took us for a walk in the woods. While admiring the beauty of the trees, we spotted a squirrel; the governor scampered home to fetch his rifle and returned out of breath. The little beast had patiently stood still, but the great man missed his target four straight times.

This governor is a very decent man, but without superior qualities. M. Elam Lynds, who came to see us in Auburn, shares my opinion. "Why then," I asked him, "did the people of New York choose him as their governor?" M. Lynds replied that "men of great talent would not accept such employment; they prefer commerce and occupations in which one earns more money." There, in a nutshell, is the American character.

Tocqueville to Ernest de Chabrol, Auburn, July 16, 1831

Here I am in Auburn at last, my dear friend—the famous Auburn about which people concerned with the French penal system have had so many fine and false things to say. Not that the institution isn't indeed fine, only that it isn't as our excellent friends in France, the philanthropists, imagine it to be.

They claim that at Auburn discipline is admirable, that the health of the inmates is exceptionally good, that the work they do more than defrays the cost of the establishment. They are right, but they don't point out that these results are obtained not by suasion but with the aid of an instrument that Americans call "the cat" and we the knout (if I'm not mistaken). The knout— that is what M. Lucas has been advocating for a decade, what he tender-heartedly demands in the name of philanthropy. As Monsieur Jourdain exclaimed: "Zounds, you have some tricks up your sleev!"[3] Jokes aside and disregarding our theory mongers, I can tell you that the penitentiary here is admirable. I won't yet expatiate upon the reasons for my judgment. Suffice it to say that more of what we've seen surpasses our hopes than falls short of them. After two months of research, we are more or less settled in the opinion that the American system could work at home. Keep this to yourself. We don't want it known that we have made up our minds.

Marie must have explained that I couldn't write you a letter before the last mail went out; time was short. Today I have more leisure and want to make amends by recounting a public ceremony I recently attended in Albany, the details of which will interest you. It is the ceremony held on July 4 to commemorate the signing of the famous Declaration of Independence in 1776. This was its fifty-fifth reprise. We were invited to join the parade and we accepted with pleasure.

If I draw a faithful picture of this spectacle, you will see vulgar, even ludicrous details enmeshed with a loftiness of purpose that spoke to the heart.

Leading the parade was the "militia"—the national guard of a country to which the martial spirit is absolutely foreign. As soldiers go, these upstanding citizens cut droll figures: they looked like raw recruits. Next came veterans of the War of Independence riding in several carriages. It was a brilliant stroke to have them participate in the ceremony—old men who had seen the American cause triumph and who embodied memories of the heroic age.

After the carriages artisans of every kind marched in serried ranks. Each craft formed up beneath its banner, as in feudal

3. "Corbleu vous nous en faisiez voir là de bonnes!" Tocqueville mistakenly attributes the line to the hero of Molière's *Le Bourgeois gentilhomme.* Its source is not known.

times, the important difference being that here the association or guild was free and had only as much power over its members as the latter agreed to vouchsafe it. All these people were so remarkably calm, so taciturn, that one might have mistaken the civic festival for a funeral procession. I didn't sense any joy in the event. But reserve is the prevailing attitude here. Individuals seemed to be marching each in his own head, businesslike: no dressing up for show; no armed escort; authorities lost in the crowd; a few constables with white truncheons at the ready. Altogether, a scene of perfect order.

We thus proceeded to a church, in which a podium had been erected. With my French ideas, I assumed that this space was meant for the state governor and municipal officials. No, it was set aside for the guild banners, the county colors (which had been carried during the Revolutionary War), and for those old veterans I mentioned above.

The public sat in rows facing the podium. A preacher mounted it and recited a prayer calling upon heaven to bless America. The assembly responded with "amen," whereupon a young man, who had meanwhile joined the preacher, read the Declaration of Independence, as is customary. It was truly an impressive spectacle. People sat plunged in silence until they heard the eloquent words of Congress recounting England's injustices and tyranny. At that, a murmur of indignation and anger ran through the audience. When Congress pled the righteousness of its cause and expressed the noble resolve to free America or die fighting, it seemed that an electric current was making hearts vibrate.

I assure you that it was not a theatrical performance. In the recitation of these well-kept promises of independence, in this return of an entire people to memories of its national birth, in this uniting of the present generation with one whose exalted passions it shared for a moment—in all this there was something deeply felt and truly great.

Matters should have rested there, but after the declaration of rights was read, a lawyer subjected us to a rhetorical harangue pompously parading all of world history to its consummation in the United States, seated at the center of the universe. It sounded just like a piece of humbug in some farce. One hears the French equivalent at the funerals of our "great men."

I left, cursing the speechifier whose gab and fatuous national pride had dampened the vivid impressions the rest of the ceremony had made on me.

We were set on spending a few days in Albany because this city is the capital of the state of New York where various administrative agencies are located, and where the legislature meets. We wanted to collect valuable information about the extent of central government in this state. Offices and records were all open to us; but we're still looking for "government." It really doesn't exist. The legislature manages everything that concerns the general public; municipalities take care of the rest. As I see it, the virtue of this arrangement is that it allows each locality to take a vigilant interest in its own affairs and generates political activity. But the drawback, even in America, is that it thwarts the administration of uniform measures and gives a character of volatility to the most useful enterprises. You cannot conceive how unstable they are.

We were especially well qualified to reflect upon the absence of centralization as it affects prisons: no fixity; nothing firm in their discipline; men succeed one another and systems follow suit; the mode of administration changes with each administrator because there is no central authority imposing a common code. This country must thank the Lord for being so situated that it needs neither a standing army nor a police force, nor a skillful and sustained foreign policy. If ever one of these three should become necessary, one can predict, without needing a crystal ball, that the United States will lose its freedom or its balance of powers.

Our journey thus far has taken us across a very curious land, which I shall describe to you one day at leisure. We have recently traveled through a region inhabited by the famous Iroquois Confederation, about which so much has been bruited in the world. All that remains of it today are a few savages in tatters, who inspire more pity than fear. The rest died or crossed Lake Ontario and faded into the wilderness.

Adieu, my dear friend, I embrace you with all my heart.

Our virtue still holds sway but we have begun to eye women with an impudence unseemly in young men who represent the penal system.

Adieu, salutations to all our colleagues.

P.S. Don't forget to keep my letters.

Tocqueville to his mother, Auburn, New York, July 17, 1831

Here I am almost eighty leagues farther from you than a fortnight ago, my dear Mama; I detest the thought that letters take three days more to reach us. Letters being an integral part of our existence now, we are highly sensitive to the least delay. Would you believe that we have not yet received mail sent on June 1? It's been more than three weeks since we've seen anything in your hand; I assure you that we are very far from numbing ourselves to this silence.

We left New York on June 28. Our voyage began on a distinctly sour note. The steamboat we boarded that evening was to sail up the North River and stop at West Point. West Point, which figured importantly in the American war, is not only a historical landmark of note but one of the country's most picturesque sites. We counted on arriving at night and spending a day there. Well, in mid-voyage we learned that our boat would go straight to Albany. We were thus in the position of a man who, having taken the wrong diligence, travels to Rouen rather than Compiègne, except of course that one can get off a diligence en route. We could only resign ourselves to our fate. And West Point was not the only omission. As the boat sailed at night and reached the city of Albany at five in the morning, all the spectacular scenery of the river passed us by.

There our misfortunes ended, and the trip became most agreeable. We remained three or four days in Albany, to cull the statistical documents we needed from the central government of the state of New York. I think we'll need a crate for all the notes, books, and pamphlets swamping us. We attended the July 4 ceremony in Albany. July 4 is the anniversary of the Declaration of Independence, and Americans hold a parade and religious ceremony to commemorate the event. Shall I describe this parade, which we followed for two hours under a splendid sun? I'd rather describe our visit with the Quaking Shakers.

The Shakers are a kind of religious community of men and women who farm in common, take a vow of celibacy, and have no private property. One of their establishments lies in the middle of the woods three leagues from Albany. We arrived there on Sunday, at around ten, and immediately went to the temple, which is just a large room, very neat, with no altar or anything to suggest the idea of religious observance. After half an hour, two groups of Shakers, male and female, entered the room by different doors. Men formed up at one end, women at the other. The men wore what looked rather like the stock costume of our playhouse peasants: white shirts with flowing sleeves; gray, wide-brimmed felt hats; loose-fitting vests with pockets. Their attire was all purple, but for the shirts, and almost new. The women wore white. They ranged from very old to very young, from ugly to comely. The very old sat up front, the young behind them; and men arrayed themselves likewise. These groups faced each other wordlessly, waiting for inspiration; when, after five minutes of total silence, one man felt the spirit rise in him, he stood and gave a long, rambling talk about the religious and moral obligations of Shakers. The groups then launched into an ear-splitting rendition of the shrillest song I've ever heard. Especially fervent members nodded the beat, which gave them somewhat the appearance of those porcelain Chinese figures with tilted heads on our grandmothers' mantelpieces. Until then the ceremony was no more exotic than a Jewish Sabbath. But once the singing was over, the two groups merged into one line. Five men and as many woman backed up against the wall and began to sing something in a lively, impetuous rhythm. At this, men and women, young and old, began to caper breathlessly. The sight of old folks with white hair keeping up with the others despite the heat and their exhaustion might have been droll if it weren't pitiful. From time to time, the dancers clapped their hands. Picture Frenchmen romping in the Dunkirk Carillon[4] and you will get a good idea of this event. When the dance stopped momentarily, one member of the congregation improvised as best he could a short religious speech; the dancing then resumed, only to stop time and again for more sermonizing. Among Shakers, there is no priesthood: anyone can say what he or she thinks appropriate. After almost two hours of this frightful exercise, they placed themselves two by two in a circle, men and women together. They then pressed their elbows to their sides, extended their forearms and let their hands dangle, like the

4. Dating to the fifteenth century, when the belfry of Saint-Éloi in Dunkirk acquired its bells, the "Dunkirk Carillon" was the most boisterous of French country dances.

front paws of trained dogs forced to walk on their hind legs. In this posture they intoned an air more lugubrious than all the others, began to walk all around the room, and continued thus for a good quarter hour. One of them made a little speech explaining that the Shaker sect was the only path to salvation and admonishing us to convert, whereupon the community withdrew in perfect order and silence. I suppose the poor devils had to rest. But just imagine, dear Mama, what queer byways the human mind can take when left to its own compass! There was a young American Protestant with us, who said afterward: "Two more spectacles like that one and I'll become a Catholic."

We quit Albany on one of this country's diligences, which are called *Stages*. They are carriages suspended on nothing but leather straps and driven at a fast trot on roads as deplorable as those in Lower Brittany. One feels quite rattled after a few miles. But the new scenery took our minds off our physical discomfort. It was our first venture into America's hinterland; until then we had seen only the seacoast and the banks of the Hudson. Everything here was quite different. I believe that in one of my letters I complained of finding almost no more woodland in America; I must now make honorable amends. Not only does one find wood and woods in America, but the whole country is still a vast forest with man-made clearings here and there. From atop a church steeple, one sees trees as far as the eye can reach swaying in the wind like waves of the sea: everything bespeaks newness. Settlers establish farms by cutting down trees to within three feet of the ground. Soil is tilled between the stumps and eventually crops grow up around them. They pock the fields of grain. What is more, wild plants continue to germinate in soil cultivated this way, with the result that every plot is a confusion of wheat stalks, saplings, tall grass, and creepers. Men forever struggle against the forest in a contest from which they don't always emerge the victor.

But if the country is new, one observes at every turn that those who have come to inhabit it are of old stock. When, after traveling on a rough road and crossing a kind of wilderness, one reaches a farmhouse, one is amazed at encountering more evidence of civilization than one would find in any French village. The farmer is neatly dressed; his dwelling is perfectly clean; there is usually a newspaper near to hand; and his first subject of conversation is politics. I can't remember where it was—in which obscure, unknown corner of the universe—that one such farmer asked us in what condition we had left France; how we viewed the relative strength of parties; and so forth. A thousand questions, to which I replied as best I could while laughing to myself over the incongruity of the questioner and the place of our interview. The territory we have just crossed was formerly inhabited by the Confederation of Iroquois, about which so much has been heard in the world. We met the last of them during our passage; they go begging and are as inoffensive as their forefathers were fearsome.

We occupy rooms in a magnificent hotel at Auburn, a town of two thousand souls, all of whose houses are well-stocked shops. Auburn, where, twenty years ago, people were frequently off hunting bear and deer, is now the hub of intense commercial traffic. I'm almost accustomed to this phenomenon of society growing like rank vegetation. I surprise myself speaking as Americans do and calling some establishment very old when it's been in existence for thirty years.

Adieu, dear mother, and all my love. Embrace my father for me and the good abbé. Pass this letter on to Édouard's household and tell them that I shall write soon. Give my news to Hippolyte. We are leading a life so fraught, so ridden with tasks, that I can't really produce more than one letter at a time.

Beaumont to Ernest de Chabrol, July 24

. . . The evening of our arrival at Buffalo, we witnessed a curious spectacle, which moved us to pity.

The government of the United States has purchased land hereabouts belonging to the Indians and pays for it at fixed intervals. There is a tribe near Buffalo who visited this city to collect the money due on the very day I passed through. It seems that the Indians spend it as soon as they receive it. If they limited their purchases to clothes and agricultural tools, all would be well. The problem is, they squander much of it on whiskey and other strong liquors. The streets of Buffalo were full of drunken Indians when we arrived. We stopped near one who was dead to the world and perfectly motionless. An Indian woman—his wife, we were told—approached him, vigorously shook his head, knocked it against the ground, and, when the poor man gave no sign of life, wailed and laughed like an idiot. Further on we saw another woman, this one intoxicated, being carried back to her forest encampment by two or three tribesmen. In general, these people are quite ugly, the women particularly: their mouths are wide, their complexions dark and coppery, their hair is long and dirty. The faces have a savage cast: nothing in their bearing speaks of nobility or dignity. The taste for strong liquors has besotted them. Their character has been extinguished by contact with Europeans. Hitherto there was something beautiful in their nakedness and noble in their savage life; since leaving the forest, they have acquired from civilization nothing but its vices and nothing from Europe but its rags. They go barefoot, wear shabby garments, and usually carry a woolen blanket on their backs, even in summer.

The government of the United States is quickly advancing the destruction of this race, which ruled over American soil. It would cost too much in men and money to annihilate them by means of war. A little patience and much perfidy will be a surer and more economical method. Thus, one lives beside Indians on ostensibly good terms, but no pretext is lost for pushing them ever farther west. Treaties are drawn up with them, the interpretation of which is the right of the mightier. Indians bring the skins of wild animals and other useful goods to trading posts; in exchange they are given the stuff of their undoing—whiskey. More of them die of drink than in battle. . . .

Tocqueville to his sister-in-law Émilie, Batavia, New York, July 25, 1831

I am in so sentimental a mood today, dear sister, that at the drop of a pin I would write you an idyll. Rest assured I won't do anything of the sort, but I want at least to describe our recent visit to Oneida Lake. If it doesn't make you dream for a week, by which I mean daydream, I shall no longer recognize you.

You should know then (since one must begin at the beginning) that about forty years ago, a Frenchman whose name no one could recall but who belonged to a rich and noble family, fetched up in America, after fleeing from the revolutionary turmoil of his native land. Our émigré was young and in good health; he never had stomach trouble (note this point).[5] He also came with a wife whom he loved dearly. He was, however, penniless. A friend loaned him some money, enough to buy necessities and to help him establish himself in a region where land would be cheap.

In those days the west of New York state was still a forested

5. As noted earlier, Tocqueville was a martyr to his stomach.

expanse whose only inhabitants were Indians of the Iroquois Confederation. The émigré thought that this would answer his purpose. He conferred with his young wife, who courageously insisted on following him into the wilderness.

So our young couple set out, stayed the course, and at length reached the shores of Oneida Lake. For a little gunpowder and lead they purchased from the Indians an island in the middle of the lake. Never before had a European, nor perhaps any human, entertained the notion of making this his residence. To do so meant felling huge, hundred-year-old trees, clearing land dense with brambles and roots, building a cabin, and scraping together a meager livelihood. For people who had enjoyed all the amenities of polite society, the first year was one of unspeakable hardship. The second proved easier. Little by little—if one may believe the story—they came to embrace their lot as providential and to live more contentedly than ever, with each other and in the world.

The book from which I gathered this information said nothing more about them, and matters would have rested there, no doubt, had our itinerary not led us to within four leagues of Oneida Lake. It was, if I recall correctly, July 9. We mounted horses to go in search of our compatriots and for several hours rode through one of those deep American forests I hope to describe to you one day. At last, unexpectedly, we came upon a fisherman's cabin situated on the lakeshore.

Picture a lake several leagues long, surrounded by trees whose roots bathe in the calm, limpid water. There isn't a sail in sight, nor a house, nor wisps of smoke rising from the woodland. All is as perfectly tranquil as the world must have been at its creation. We spied our island a mile offshore. From afar, it looked like one impenetrable thicket with no trace of cleared land. I was beginning to fear that our informant had woven a tale for the fun of it when, at the fisherman's cabin, we met his wife. We asked her if the island had a name. She replied that locals called it "the Frenchman's island." We asked why, and she explained that many years before a Frenchman and his wife had settled there. "Bad idea," she added, "since the market was so far away they couldn't sell their produce. They stuck it out nonetheless and were still around when we ourselves came to live here, twenty-two years ago. The Frenchman's wife died that year. In the meantime her husband as well has vanished and no one knows how he crossed the lake or where he has disappeared to. At some point I decided to go see the island for myself. I still remember their little cabin; it was built at one end, under the branches of a big apple tree. The French had planted grape vines all around, and a multitude of flowers, to what purpose I'm not sure. It was sad seeing how the fields had already gone to weed. I haven't returned since."

You will readily believe me, dear sister, when I tell you that, despite her tale, we wanted to visit the island; but making our desire understood by the good woman was more difficult. She opened wide her bleary little eyes and assured us again that if we had any notion of settling there we would be storing up disappointment, since the island was still far removed from any market. Seeing that our resolve was firm, she pointed to her husband's dugout (he was ill at the time) and allowed us to use it. We proceeded to row like the devil and raised half a dozen blisters on each hand before reaching the island.

Advancing farther was no easy matter, for, in order to hide more completely from the world, our Frenchman had taken care not to clear the shoreline. We therefore had to pierce a fortress of vegetation through which a wild boar would have had trouble crashing. Once inside, we beheld a curious, sad spectacle: the whole center of the island bore distinct traces of human labor; it was straightaway apparent that trees had been deliberately uprooted. But time had all but effaced these vestiges of an incomplete civilization. The forest had quickly sent its shoots into the heart of the Frenchman's fields. Vines and parasites had laid hold of the soil and begun to tie together the saplings growing round about.

It was amidst this chaos that we spent two hours vainly searching for our man's house. No more remained of it than of his lawns and flowers. We were about to leave when Beaumont spied the apple tree our elderly hostess had mentioned. Next to it, an enormous grape vine, which we mistook at first for ivy, wound upward to the treetops. We then realized that we were standing where the house had stood, and in fact, after clearing the plants that covered the ground up to that point, we found its remnants.

All you people, dear sister, imagine that because one wears a square bonnet[6] and sentences a man to the galleys, one is merely a reasoning machine, a kind of syllogism incarnate. Well, I am pleased to tell you that you are quite wrong, that when a magistrate begins to seek counsel elsewhere than in the law, there's no telling how far astray he will go.

We left the Frenchman's island with heavy hearts and bemoaning the fate of a man we had never seen, whose name we didn't know. Can one think of an odyssey comparable to this poor devil's? Men treated him as a leper, driving him out of society, he made the best of his expulsion and created a world unto himself where he dwelled, serene and happy, long enough to have been completely forgotten by his European friends; his wife then died, leaving him bereft, an alien in the wild no less than in civilization. And yet, despite it all (I say this to you confidentially lest our parents, who are excessively reasonable by nature, think us mad), is there not something seductive in the idea of being cut off from

6. Of medieval provenance, the "bonnet carré," or square bonnet, was worn by French magistrates.

the entire world, in the hidden life these two poor souls led for so many years?[7] Unfortunately there are no physicians in the wilderness, and one had best steer clear of it if one doesn't have an iron constitution.

Upon leaving Oneida Lake, we made our way to the prison at Auburn. That is what I call a come-down; but, as the saying goes, variety is the spice of life. After immersion in the penitentiary system we went to Canandaigua and the country house of a congressman named Spencer.[8] Let me tell you, dear sister, we spent the most agreeable week there. Canandaigua is situated on the shore of a charming lake (yet another lake! you exclaim). There is nothing wild about this one; on the contrary, everything around it calls to mind the advantages of civilized life. Our host is a man of sparkling intelligence, whose conversation brightened our stay. Aside from a well-furnished library, he has two delightful daughters, with whom—in common parlance—we "clicked." Although they know not a word of French, they possess, among other

7. This Rousseauian tale of exile and martyrdom must have resonated in Tocqueville's mind with accounts he had heard of his mother's family living in internal exile at Malesherbes during the Terror. He had learned about the "île du français" in childhood from a book by Joseph Camp, who plagiarized it from a novel by Sophie de la Roche. The true story, on which these authors based it, was less pathetic. A young squire from near French Flanders, having squandered his inheritance, traveled to America in 1786 with his wife. He couldn't find purchase there. Ten years later, after residing on the island in question and elsewhere, he returned to France. Tocqueville gives a longer account of this episode in "Voyage au lac Onéida."

8. At the time of this encounter, John Canfield Spencer, who had been a congressman, was a member of the New York Assembly. He was known as an authority in the field of public law. During the 1840s, he served in John Tyler's administration, first as secretary of war, then as secretary of the treasury. He published the first American edition of *Democracy in America.*

attractions, four blue eyes (two each) the likes of which I am quite sure you have never seen on your side of the ocean. I would describe them at greater length if I weren't afraid of sounding mawkish. Suffice it to say that we looked at those eyes even more readily than at the father's books. After communing over our discovery, Beaumont and I, wise as you know us to be, decided that we had better decamp—a resolution we made good the very next morning by crossing the lake (not swimming it, as Mentor and Telemachus might have done, but aboard a steamboat, which is much surer and more commodious). Here we are today in Batavia, a bit disgruntled at no longer being in Canandaigua, but, all in all, glad that we left.

You see, dear sister, that I've kept my word. I've sent you a letter brimming with sentiment, from date to signature.

Embrace all our relatives for me and rest assured that, despite the rivers and woods and lakes and even the blue eyes of Miss Spencer, I am itching to rejoin all of you. My mind is quite taken up with that happy prospect.

Beaumont to Ernest de Chabrol, aboard *The Superior*, Lake Huron, August 2

. . . Upon disembarking at Detroit, we paid a visit to an old Catholic priest, Monsieur Richard, whom we were told is a very nice man, capable of giving us many valuable documents about Michigan. We found him in his presbytery, teaching a dozen children. He speaks French very well, having been born at Saintonge and left France when the French Revolution began to persecute Catholic clergy. He made up his mind to come to Detroit. Since then, he has not budged or relaxed his efforts to *convert the heathens*; here, as at home, French clergy are bent upon proselytizing. The good-hearted soul, who assigns more importance to this than to any other task, touted his successes, which bored us a little, since we kept posing questions he didn't answer. We were very pleased, however, with his courteous behavior. The remarkable thing about him is that he was elected to Congress by Protestants, despite his Catholic ministry. At first this struck us as most surprising, but where religion is concerned, people judge differently here than in France. There isn't the same prevalent hostility among sects, and one's opinion of an individual is not colored by what one knows about his habits of worship. It astonishes me that Protestants voted for Monsieur Richard despite his freewheeling attacks upon them; he is a relentless warrior. "Their sects pullulate," he says. "At present there are 450 of them. They believe in *nothing at all;* they are neither Episcopal nor Methodist nor Presbyterian. They are *nothingists."* He thinks, as I do, that this multiplicity of cults will eventually lead to natural religion— which is to say the absence of any institutional creed—or to Catholicism.

After gathering information from two or three other people, we decided to take the Saginaw road. Saginaw is situated a few leagues from the bay bearing its name and forming part of Lake Huron. Off we went—it was July 26, if I remember correctly—on the very lean hacks we had hired, with rifles and game bags slung over our shoulders, straw hats on our heads, short tunics, and saddlebags. I must mention this; having been forewarned that Saginaw and environs are infested by gnats or mosquitoes, we visited a milliner in Detroit to buy mosquito nets. While she was fetching them, I happened to set eyes on a small engraving displayed in her shop: it represented a very well-dressed lady, with the caption: "Mode de Longchamp 1831." What do you know, inhabitants of Michigan paying attention to the latest styles from Paris! The truth is, in this remote American village, Paris is reputed to be the font of fashion; French fashion is closely followed.

The anecdote may lead you to believe that Detroit is quite civilized. But virgin forests and its inhabitants are right next door. The woods begin half a league out of town and they never end. I'll tell you a story that illustrates well what life is like here; last year a bear brought to bay by dogs at the edge of the forest shuffled across Detroit, down the entire length of the main street, for the amusement of Americans, who probably never cracked a smile, even on this occasion.

Enough digressing. I must hurry back to the Saginaw road, where our poor nags await me.

Our first day out was rough going. We had to reach the Flint River by way of Pontiac—a distance of eighteen leagues. We found a well-laid road in the middle of the woods and a few houses scattered here and there. I must bring up the subject of bears once again, to let you know that some forest dwellers use them as guard dogs; I saw a few tethered near doorways.

We dined at an inn where the talk was of a rattlesnake killed the day before. The path cleared through the forest is a monotony of level terrain, but the landscape changes radically after Pontiac, with small valleys cradling a multitude of charming little lakes. No longer are the woods thick and impenetrable; they are full of glades and resemble plantations of tall trees designed for a pleasant stroll.

A league from Pontiac we stopped at the home of M. Williams, the local most knowledgeable about Indians, about trade with them, and the roads one takes to reach them. He urged us to hire a guide for the journey to Saginaw and told us that we could safely trust an Indian. Since a guide was not yet necessary, we went our way.

Barely half a league farther on we saw an Indian walking through the forest like a deer, eating wild fruit. A moment later, another Indian appeared before us; he carried a rifle, he was half naked, his face was set in the hard, fierce expression typical of Indians. Had it not been for M. Williams's praise of them, we would certainly have taken this one for a thief. He glowered at us with eyes that had no hint of leniency in them. We replied with amiable smiles, whereupon his expression suddenly changed. It became completely gracious, but it was only a momentary flash. He put his severe face back on, as if regretting his smile. We decided to continue our journey. Much to our surprise the Indian ran after us and stayed close on our heels. When our horses walked slowly, he stopped; when we trotted, he galloped and let no space come between him and the last horse's tail. Despite M. Williams's assurances, this behavior unsettled us. We halted, he halted. I flashed another benevolent smile, he replied with one even more good-natured. What did he want? I offered him some whisky; he took a swig and seemed to find it very much to his liking. But he continued to dog us. I stopped yet again. Hanging from his neck were two birds he had killed; I wondered whether he might be hoping to sell them. I told him by signs that I would buy them for two shillings (twenty-five sous) and showed him the coins. He accepted my offer with alacrity, but when we set off again, there he was, on our tail as before. He must have run two leagues all together. At length we passed a group of Indians— men, women, children—scattered in the woods beside the road. Our man then separated from us and rejoined his companions, without addressing a word to us or even looking our way. I still don't know what he had in mind by accompanying us as he did.

The Indians whom he joined were twenty-five or thirty in number. They sat on the ground eating roast meat; quarters of bucks and does hung in front of the fires around which they had disposed themselves, and the heads of those poor animals lay beside them, still throbbing.

These Indians were returning from Canada, where they had

gone to receive presents that the English give them every year. The gifts consist of blankets, rifles, ammunition for hunting, etc. The motive for English generosity is transparent: it fosters friendly relations with the natural enemies of Americans. At the same time, it is a means of arming them, which would be most helpful to the English should war erupt with the United States.

I am keenly interested in everything that concerns these savage people. I don't know what to make of their earthly condition. Do they live, as one ought to, in accordance with the simple laws of nature? Have they fallen into a state of degradation that runs contrary to the destiny of man? Or, finally, are they at the beginning of their civilization? If the last case be true, one would have to say that theirs has been a long childhood, as their origins are lost in the night of time.

It seems certain to me that they do not form a race distinct from the European; the shape of their bodies and faces, the nature of their physiognomies exhibit no marked difference from ours. One could not say as much of negroes who seem, on close scrutiny, to have a constitution all their own.

How did these Indians enter the forests of America? Did they come from Europe on a land bridge? Or was there a discrete creation for the hemisphere in which I now find myself? These last questions are a little theoretical. But I would love to know the answer. At this moment I am reading a very good work by Mac-Culloch and a rather interesting travel book by MacKennery.[9] All in all I take more interest in practical questions than in the purely speculative and believe that one is better off knowing what is than laboriously trying to find out what was.

9. *Researches Philosophical and Antiquarian Concerning the Aboriginal History of America*, by James H. MacCullogh (Baltimore, 1829), and *Sketches of a Tour to the Lakes*, by Thomas MacKenney (Baltimore, 1827).

The study of savage people is not vain and frivolous. Nothing brings to light the nature of civilized societies better than delving into those that are not. One can judge astutely only by comparison. I sometimes wonder whether these Indians, whom Europeans scorn, deserve to be called savages. Those whom I've seen on the way to Saginaw live peacefully in their forests. All who have relations with them note their honesty, their good faith, their generosity. Europeans who trade with them are vastly superior to them in the ways of deception and always get the upper hand.

Not a day passes that they aren't expelled from the American soil they once possessed. Beside the Flint River trail I saw poor Indians gleaning leftovers from a harvested field that belonged to them a few years ago. True, they overindulge in strong spirits; but as between the buyer who receives these spirits ignorant of their danger and the purveyor who sells them knowing full well how lethal they are, who is the more barbarous? Rattlesnakes abound in the neighborhood of Saginaw. Indians treat snakebites with an infallible remedy. I asked whether they demanded payment for their medicine; I was told that they are happiest when saving someone's life and never want recompense. I should like to know whether those men are more barbarous than Monsieur Dupuytren and others.[10] Moreover, these Indians, viewed contemptuously by Europeans, return their scorn in full measure; they consider themselves superior to all other peoples; they believe nothing lower than working for *money* and regard the idle life, to which they owe their independence, as the only one worthy of man.

10. Guillaume Dupuytren (1777–1835) was France's foremost surgeon during the golden age of medical science in Paris, and a man of consuming ambition.

Their society has none of the civil and political institutions that encumber ours. Almost all of our laws were drafted to protect private property; this is the basis of European societies and doesn't exist among Indians, who believe that all of nature belongs to all men: the forests being vast enough to house everyone, there is no need to divide them. They commit so few crimes that there is no need for tribunals; men as just as this can dispense with justice. Almost their only crime is homicide, committed out of vengeance or in a state of intoxication. The friends or relatives of the victim are entitled to kill the murderer, but the latter is usually allowed to redeem his life with a sum of money, amounting to 150 francs more or less. Their religion is quite simple; they worship the great Manitou, creator of all things; they believe that there is an afterlife in which the good become denizens of superb forests stocked with enough does and bucks for an eternal hunt, and the wicked are exiled to sterile land devoid of game.

The Indians are happy in their uncouthness and ignorance. All who know them claim that they are strangers to all manner of cares and pains. When they bag lots of game, they wolf it down; when the hunt is unsuccessful they fast uncomplainingly and wait for a better day.

After this long digression on Indians, I'm not quite sure where on the Saginaw trail I left my narrative, so I'll skip ahead to Pontiac, which is halfway between Detroit and the Flint River. Just before Pontiac I killed a little blue bird of a kind I had painted at the inn, while the horses were resting. One wouldn't call my paintings pretty, but painting entertains me greatly.

There was nothing especially remarkable about the remainder of our journey, up to the Flint River. What surprised me is the wide, straight road in a countryside without dwellings and inhabitants (one can sometimes travel ten leagues and see not a single house). But this system of laying out roads before there is anyone to use them makes perfect sense: that is why Michigan and all the other American states are being so quickly populated. The highways do not increase the population, but they give those who wish to settle in a region the means of getting there; already this year, since April, the population of Michigan has increased by three or four thousand.

America doesn't populate itself by any other means: I haven't met a single person born on the soil he inhabits. This immigrant society resembles no other. They are all people without a country, whom material interest alone has displaced. They come in search of cheap land, where an acre sells for six francs. Since their own establishment in a new territory is itself a risky venture, they bring their urban métiers with them. Thus, every farmer is also a trader or a craftsman. One occupation that derives from the nature of things is that of innkeeper. Individuals who have struck root here all house the new arrivals, and don't do it gratis. It will be a source of income for years to come. The hostelries in which travelers coming on foot or on horse find shelter bear no resemblance whatever to our inns and taverns. The occupants are literate; their language is not that of the lowest class; in every single one of these log cabins newspapers are read and tea is taken twice a day. There is no lower class, but neither is there an upper. There is only a uniform society, headless and tailless, topless and bottomless. Nothing in it is abject, and nothing refined. It is, I believe, the happiest of societies, but, in my view, not the most agreeable.

We were drawing near Flint River, revolving these and other thoughts, when night overtook us in the middle of the woods. The moon did its utmost to light our way, but we were uncertain which way was ours. Having reached a river, we imagined that it was the Flint. We spied some houses a hundred feet away.

Tocqueville dismounted and ran through the woods to find out what he could. He soon realized that they were houses still under construction and empty. He shouted the bad news to me. I shouted back that he should forge ahead. Our voices echoed though a forest usually steeped in silence, and, after a laborious march, he on foot, I with two horses, we met up again, but none the wiser as to how or when we might reach our destination.

Apart from our anxieties, what a beautiful night it was! More than once I stopped to contemplate the sky. I can't do justice to the spectacle of moonlight filtering through the dense forest.

After tramping for about an hour through clearings which we took to be the trail, I saw a light. I dismounted and walked straight toward it. I soon got close enough to make out a doorless, almost roofless wooden house. Someone was moving inside but not showing himself and trying, as it seemed to me, to cover the light. Speaking in my softest, most humble voice, lest the inhabitants mistake me for a thief, I asked directions to the residence of M. Todd[11] (which was the name of the person with whom we wished to stay at Flint). A half-dressed woman then appeared, carrying a torch, who told me in the most obliging way that M. Todd's house was in the neighborhood, quite near (this poor woman was all alone, exposed to all the elements in this shanty). I didn't have time to commiserate with her and rejoined Tocqueville, though not before getting mired in a bog from which I thought for a minute I'd never escape. We finally found shelter with M. Todd and by eleven had turned in for the night, I on a bed, he on the floor.

The next morning, at five, we set out again. M. Todd procured us an Indian guide, who crossed the Flint River running

11. Major John Todd, the first American to settle in Flint, operated an inn with his wife. Beaumont consistently misspells the name "Todds."

and leaping like a roe-buck and we barely able to keep pace, even on trotting horses.

The landscape changed here: until then we had traveled through woodland, but woods that bore the mark of European axes; the trail and strips of land twenty or thirty feet wide on either side were denuded of trees. At intervals one encountered a field, a little log cabin. One recognized the presence all around of civilized man and wherever the original forest had not disappeared, stumps and half-burned trees testified to attempts at destroying it. Past the Flint River, one saw nothing comparable. The virgin forest displays itself in all its primitive beauty. There are trees of immense height and girth. I measured a pine twenty feet around and an oak eighteen feet in circumference. The ax has not been laid to any of them; those lying on the ground had been cut down by the wind or felled by old age. The road to Saginaw winds past these majestic trees, alike the standing and the fallen. One well-beaten little path is an obstacle course of dead trees, which horses must either clear or face a detour through thick undergrowth. That is how we traveled all day long on the 27th. From time to time we spotted a few Indians picking fruit in the forest. In one particularly remote locale, I saw a woman all by herself seated at the foot of an oak. She was very ugly and scantily clad. Thus far, I cannot imagine where M. de Chateaubriand found the model for his Atala.[12] I've met a few rather handsome Indian males, but the women are frightful and repellent.

Hours in the saddle made us hungry. But we couldn't eat until we found water and didn't know when we'd next encounter a river or stream. Our guide spoke not a word of English; we not a word

12. Atala is the titular heroine of a novel by Chateaubriand. She and Chactas are Indian lovers whose passion goes unconsummated. *Atala* was published in 1801, and, along with *René*, became a favorite of young French Romantics.

of Indian. I ultimately made my quandary understood with exuberant gestures. A few minutes later, he had me halt and led me to a spring but a few feet off the trail. After four or five more hours of riding, I asked him, again in sign language, how far we were from Saginaw. He drew a line on the ground, with Flint and Saginaw at either end, and indicated that we were one-third of the way there.

Knowing that I had a mind to shoot birds, he pointed them out to me when I couldn't spot any: that is how I brought down a very fine raptor. We hunted on horseback and our imperturbable mounts were not in the least gun-shy. Lots of game appeared—deer, pheasants, partridges—but we didn't do much killing.

Out of weariness we slowed our horses to a walk from time to time; when we did so the Indian would turn around, shout "Saginaw! Saginaw!" point to the sun, which was just beginning to sink, and race ahead.

The distractions of the hunt had cost us time. Also, when a beautiful wildflower caught my eye, I would sometimes stop to pick it.

At one point we left the trail for the heart of the forest. I told Tocqueville that this transition astonished me. In due course we reached a place which we've since learned is the site of a small Indian village, beside a river (the Cash River) whose steep banks are exceptionally picturesque. Here our guide suddenly halted, pointed to the sun, which was then only a few hours from setting, made it clear, with signs, that Saginaw was far distant, and that we had to camp right there on the riverbank, at the risk of being devoured by mosquitoes, which attack in blinding swarms wherever there is lots of moisture. The situation was critical. I signaled our discontent to the Indian; he replied by trying to make me understand that if we continued our journey, we ran the risk of being caught in the forest at night. The inducement was whisky.

We carried a little wickerwork bottle of it and noticed that it excited more interest in the savage than any of our other accoutrements; I indicated to him that if he led us to Saginaw that evening, I would give him the bottle. After a moment's hesitation, he took to his heels shouting, "On to Saginaw!"

Night soon caught us up, but at nine-thirty p.m. our faithful Phoebe[13] rescued us, lighting up the banks of the Saginaw. That wasn't the end of our ordeal; we had to cross a river as wide as the Seine, with no bridge. Our Indian let loose several piercing cries and a moment later a little canoe came into view, paddled by someone whom we would have taken for a savage, judging by his face, if we hadn't heard him utter several words of French. He had us board his small craft, an Indian dugout. I confess that this apparently fragile means of navigation left me wondering whether we would have to swim for it at some point. Getting our horses across posed the biggest problem, or so we thought. But without further ado our Indian pulled them forward by their bridle straps. The boatman began to paddle and we glided onto the river in a mere nutshell, escorted by our poor horses swimming after us despite their extreme fatigue. Fortunately the night was very beautiful and the moon so bright that anyone on the banks could have observed the whole extraordinary spectacle of our passage.

We had good lodgings at Saginaw. I expected some kind of town and was rather taken aback to find a mere cluster of five or six houses. All its American inhabitants had come for the sole purpose of trading with Indians. We spent our day there coaxing them to describe their relations with the savages. They didn't know what to make of our presence: some thought we wanted land on which to settle, others seeing me paint birds thought we

13. Goddess of the moon in Greek mythology.

had come as naturalists. Among them were several Canadians obviously delighted with our company. "You come from old France," they said. That is what they call France, Canada being new France. In the evening we paddled a canoe out onto the Saginaw. I have never seen a lovelier river: its waters are almost frothing and its banks covered with woods and meadows. We were alone, Tocqueville and I, in our little boat; the weather was idyllic, a cloudless sky, a setting sun and a completely silent nature. At some remove from Saginaw lies Pointe Verte (Green Point); there the river forms a kind of bay brimming into a forest of very tall trees. We entered it. The water's surface was mirror smooth. Perfect serenity reigned over nature; the slightest noise echoed through the forests; we fired a gun and the report was incredible. During our brief sojourn at Saginaw, I saw two hummingbirds. Rattlesnakes abound. "They kill their man every time," one Canadian told us while tramping through the grass with us. And Saginaw is also famous for its countless mosquitoes; we couldn't sleep there—I thought they would drive me mad. I found time to paint a bluebird.

We returned from Saginaw the way we came. But we dared to dispense with a guide and never needed one. As on our first foray, we ate meals in the middle of the forest. Nothing of great interest occurred. We did stop over at Pontiac to collect documents that explain the manner in which newcomers settle the region, the quantity of provisions they must bring, their method of clearing the forest and tilling the soil, the cost of labor and of various goods, etc.

We have precise data about these several issues. It isn't a case of pure curiosity. I am convinced that there are thousands of people in France who would be interested in coming to America and buying good land on the cheap, but most are uninformed. We might be doing our country a service by bringing to light what exists out there. The usual difficulty for immigrants in a new land is one of language, but this would not apply in Michigan, where a quarter of the population speaks French.

I was back in Detroit on August 1. Tocqueville and I planned to make for Buffalo when we learned that a large steamship, *The Superior*, with two hundred passengers aboard, had docked in Detroit, en route from Buffalo to Green Bay at the far reaches of Lake Michigan, by way of Saut-Sainte-Marie, which separates lakes Huron and Superior, and of Michillimachinac, situated between lakes Michigan and Huron.[14] Nothing equals the beauty of the Great Lakes. The territories I've just described are almost unknown, and here, for the first time, a large vessel full of "fashionable" travelers was venturing into the wilderness. At first we said: "We shall not go"; then we succumbed to temptation.

Tocqueville to abbé Lesueur, Detroit, Michigan, August 3, 1831

You will perhaps be surprised, my good friend, by a letter dated Detroit. There are several reasons for our having come this way. We were very keen to see a region in which man has only recently conquered the wilderness. At Buffalo, we learned that we could witness such a spectacle in the territory of Michigan. We found a steamboat that shuttles every day between Buffalo and Detroit, cities situated about a hundred leagues apart, and generally makes the crossing in two days and one night. So we embarked for Detroit instead of heading straightaway for Niagara Falls, as we originally intended to do. We sailed the length of Lake Erie, which is so like the ocean that I felt a little seasick our first day out. The day after our arrival in Detroit, we hired horses and

14. I have retained Beaumont's spelling of Sault Sainte Marie and Michilimackinac (now known as Mackinac Island).

rode to a place called Pontiac, twenty-five miles northwest of Detroit.[15]

I am forced to stop here as I am coming to the bottom of the page and would rather not continue on another for fear of costing you a fortune in postage.[16] We returned from Saginaw without incident. Tomorrow we leave for Buffalo, where I hope finally to collect our mail. I'm dying to see all of your scripts. If time allows, I shall write an account of this little voyage and read it to you upon my return. It would have been altogether agreeable were it not for mosquitoes. You can't imagine how these little beasts torment one in the backwoods. It is indescribable. Adieu. I must conclude. I embrace you as I love you, with all my heart.

Beaumont to his brother Achille, August 11

. . . The day we planned to leave Detroit for New York state, we learned that a superb steamship, *The Superior*, was in port, bound north on an excursion covering the length and breadth of the Great Lakes. Papers had been advertising it as an event certain to excite curiosity seekers. We visited the vessel. It was already almost booked up with English and Americans intent only on whiling away the time. Our captain assured me that the voyage would last no more than a week or ten days. Never before had a large vessel entered this remote backcountry, and the venture promised to be something more than a mere lark for those of

15. Tocqueville wrote a long account of their trek through the Michigan forest, called "Quinze jours dans le désert" [A Fortnight in the Wilderness], but gave no details in his surviving correspondence.

16. Until January 1849, when the Second Republic introduced postal reforms, charges were paid by the recipient, not the sender, based on weight and distance. Introduced as well was France's first stamp (called a "mobile" stamp).

us eager to record the new world from close up. In short, we reserved places, were assigned two rather uncomfortable beds in the *gentlemen's cabin*, stowed our baggage, and an hour later found ourselves sailing on a river, the Saint-Clair, that leads to a lake of the same name, which in turn empties into Lake Huron. But before showing you the sights, I shall introduce our fellow travelers.

We are about two hundred altogether, each with his own bed. This gives you an idea of the boat's dimensions: it is one huge ambulatory, or floating, house, more fantastic in its way than Venetian residences *built on pilings.* About most passengers I can say nothing. We have a small circle of acquaintances, which includes: first, a very good English chap named M. Vigne—an intrepid voyager, who was in Russia last year and told me yesterday that he hopes to be in Egypt next spring;[17] secondly, M. Mullon, a Catholic priest from Cincinnati (Ohio), who has come to Michilimackinac for the express purpose of publicly wrangling with a Presbyterian minister over some religious point of controversy. M. Mullon is a tall, gaunt man whose Catholic zeal verges on intolerance. The religious spirit in this region bears no resemblance to what it is in the state of New York and especially in the big cities. In New York, in Albany, the various sects live side by side peacefully and even, I understand, offer one another a helping hand. Here there is no such concord. "These Presbyterians are vipers," M. Mullon said to me. "You crush their heads and they raise themselves on their tails." Catholicism is apparently making great strides in the American West. There are already twelve bishops assigned to the major cities of New York, Philadelphia, Boston, New Orleans, Cincinnati, etc. Local clergy choose them and submit their names to the pope, papal authority

17. Godfrey Vigne wrote *Six Months in America*, published in Philadelphia by Thomas Ash in 1833.

being as iron-hard here as in Rome itself. You can infer that government is completely uninvolved in the election of bishops. From what one knows about the nature of American government, this is as it should be: it concerns itself no more with religious matters and the ministers of different persuasions than the latter do with it. All the Catholic priests I have met in this country consider the complete separation of church and state a great boon. I am tempted to embrace their view; the alliance of the state and religion in France has been subversive of the latter. When the government it walked arm in arm with was strong enough to support it, it stood on its feet. But when government was strongest, so paradoxically was opposition from parties bent on overturning it and incriminating its loyal helpmate. The brush that tarred the clergy tarred the creed. Assailing priests as champions of a world order they spurned, innovators convinced themselves, or persuaded the public, that the religion of which they were mere officiants was itself a foe. I cannot otherwise explain to my satisfaction the fury with which certain parties in France belabor a form of worship entirely outside political passions. Aside from M. Mullon, we have two other ecclesiastics, a Presbyterian minister and an Episcopalian.

Since most passengers on the steamboat are Presbyterian, the Presbyterian presided at Sunday worship. It took place in the gentlemen's cabin. Episcopalians aboard didn't quibble over doctrinal differences and adjusted very well to the prayer service of their Protestant colleagues, which is generally the case among Protestant sects. This may be a matter of tolerance; if so, I wager it doesn't run deep. As for M. Mullon, indifference is not his strong suit. He dropped by the gentlemen's cabin but fled like an escapee from hell when he saw what he saw. For myself, I was seated near my bed at the beginning of the service and stayed put, listening or sleeping as the preacher's voice rose and fell.

Among the men with whom we regularly mingle, there are three or four young Americans, very good chaps, though more or less vacuous; they seem bored to tears—and understandably so. Every American is a businessman devoted to commerce and industry; he is unfit for any kind of intellectual work. One told me that all he saw during our voyage were large expanses of water. To be sure, water is the background: except for a few hours on land, we were always cruising lakes that look like small seas. But there is more to be seen, if one is in the least disposed to observe, than a liquid surface.

The female contingent isn't much more richly endowed than the male. There are more ladies, but very few have any real substance. Miss Clemens is a very cultivated Englishwoman with an ardent, highly colored imagination, an abundance of enthusiasm, and, I believe, a very sensitive soul. She would be charming if she were ten years younger. She has told me stories half of which are concocted, I suspect. She couldn't be nicer, but as she clings to you once she has attached herself, her company becomes tiresome. These formerly pretty women who cannot get it into their heads that the bloom has come off are bewitched. We do have some young ladies aboard, among them the daughters of M. MacComb [Macomb], a major general in the American army; I particularly note the very nice and rather pretty Mathilda. Accompanying them is an uncle who at first extended us a thousand courtesies but during the past two days has kept his distance, for some reason. Miss Thomson is a petite wasp-waisted woman, as light as a butterfly, as pretty as a cherub, and as stupid as a goose, etc. We have been living amidst this society, which you see is not scintillating, since August 1. We didn't know a soul at first; now we're on terms with everyone. On August 2 we reached Fort Gratiot, at the junction of Lake Huron and the Saint-Clair river. Our arrival was an occasion for picturesque revels. The sun had just set; storm clouds covered the sky; lightning streaked across every quadrant. We were dancing on the bridge to the accompaniment of violins and English horns. Lake Huron's immense waters unfurled before us like those of the ocean. No sooner had the ball ended than the orchestra struck up "La Marseillaise." What I find appealing in the music was dampened by the memories it evoked; I heard it for the first time exactly a year ago, sung in Paris on the place Vendôme and in the courtyard of the Palais-Royal. Then and there, it echoed the cannons of July. But who could have predicted that one year later I would be hearing it on Lake Huron?

We were supposed to have a brief stopover at Fort Gratiot. The weather was so foul and the wind so contrary that we dropped anchor. It stayed foul for two days, confining us to a place devoid of interest.

We left Fort Gratiot on August 4 and arrived at Saut-Sainte-Marie the next day.

As Saut-Sainte-Marie is situated between lakes Huron and Superior, one must cross all of Lake Huron to reach it. In fair weather the voyage is delightful: you can't imagine the limpidity of these waters—however deep they are, one can almost see the bottom. Where the lake narrows, one encounters a multitude of islands large and small studding the approaches to Sainte-Marie. It makes a lovely panorama; one's perspective constantly changes, and if the view were not scenic enough to hold one's attention and interest, there is the ever-present element of danger. Danger isn't the right word; one simply risks running aground and lingering for a week until another vessel comes to the rescue. This almost happened to us. A few inches more and we would have been stuck.

My impressions of the moment fade quickly. I regret not being able to convey what I felt in the presence of vast wildernesses that framed so incongruously our civilized society in its floating house. We traveled a hundred leagues on Lake Huron and the bay next to Saut-Sainte-Marie and saw nothing of humanity but a few canoes filled with wild Indians. Hearing our boat and our music, they emerged from their forests and paddled up for a closer look. I can easily understand their stupefaction; even for a European, large steam-driven vessels are unquestionably one of the marvels of modern industry. To several of these admirers we threw bottles of whisky, which were received with the most lively exhibitions of joy and gratitude. Dropping some pieces of bread into their canoe evoked the same response.

The farther north one goes, the more Indians one sees, or, to put it more accurately, savages abound where Europeans don't yet. Toward Saut-Sainte-Marie there are territories in which the Indians will remain for quite some time. The land is barren and too rocky for raising crops. Otherwise, Europeans have only to appear and the Indian flees. This has nothing to do with *feelings*; he flees because the game he needs for his subsistence have already fled.

Many people believe that a few Indian tribes wandering in the northern forests are the nomadic remnants of an otherwise extinct race. They are mistaken. There are still three or four million savages in the north of the United States alone. It is difficult to draw a true picture of their manners and character from those one meets near cities: civilization has rubbed off on the latter, varnishing the original image. One hears that savages who live at a complete remove from Europeans are most remarkable.

Since it was late when we reached Saut-Sainte-Marie, passengers stayed put until the next morning. We docked at a lovely spot and enjoyed dancing and music all evening long, with the forest echoing the English horns note for note. Out of curiosity, I, too, wanted to harmonize with the virgin forests of America, so at midnight I took my flute, stood outside, and played variations on "Di tanti palpiti."[18] The beauty of such a night is beyond compare. Stars glittered in the sky; their reflections glittered in the water; here and there along the banks burned the campfires of Indians, who must have been startled by the unaccountable sound of Rossini and Auber.

On August 6, early in the morning, we entered the village called Saut-Sainte-Marie. It was given this name because the river flowing nearby, between lakes Superior and Huron, plunges so rapidly among rock falls that it appears to *leap* (sauter) from one place to another. Sainte-Marie, along with the other European establishments on this side, was founded by the French; one notes that Sainte-Marie is on the left bank of the river and that the right or Canadian bank formerly belonged to France. Everyone in Sainte-Marie speaks French; there are as many Indians there as Canadians and they regularly interbreed. This conglomeration is not disagreeable. It has the effect of softening the fierce cast of Indian faces. I have yet to meet a white man endowed with the savage's natural vivacity, but hardness and severity detract from it. The fire in his eyes is beautiful when, without ceasing to be intensely alive, it loses something of its primitive character: this is what the mixture of Indian and European stock accomplishes. Canadians call those who spring from it *métiches* (métis). I have seen young métiche girls of exceptional beauty.

We had no sooner arrived at Sainte-Marie than we set off for Lake Superior in a small boat. Miss Clemens, Miss Thomson, Mathilda, and a few other ladies came with us. Our destination was a place called Pointe-aux-Pins, two leagues upriver, where Lake Superior begins.

Although this lake looks just like all the others, I believe that

18. "Di tanti palpiti," meaning "For all these heartbeats," are the words by which an aria is known in Rossini's opera *Tancredi*.

its waters are the purest. Besides its immensity, it has tides in common with the sea. I was enchanted by this excursion; the boatmen who led us were delightfully buoyant Canadians; while rowing, they never stopped singing old French songs some of whose verses were very droll. Even on slight acquaintance with Canadians, I conclude that national character, particularly the French, is deep-rooted; they haven't lost one iota of French gaiety, which differs so strikingly from the glacial sang-froid of Americans. It is also true that Canadian French are gayer than we are now in France, the reason being simply that their situation has changed less than ours. Our Revolution added darker colors to our national character; and unlike us, they don't dwell on political matters that concern themselves alone. Considering only the *ancient character* of the nation, they are, I believe, more French than we are.

We wandered around Pointe-aux-Pins for an hour or two. I was introduced to an Indian chief who swooned with admiration over my percussion cap rifle. I fired it at his behest. He was so pleased that he gave me a turtle shell as a token of gratitude.

I did a drawing of Lake Superior. We then returned on the Sainte-Marie river, bravely shooting the Saut rapids. It wasn't at all dangerous because our nimble boatmen are on wonderfully familiar terms with the river and its pitfalls. Even so, the boat moves so swiftly and one is surrounded by so many rocks, the slightest contact with which would smash us to bits, that one can't help quaking. We shouldn't have feared for ourselves since we had ladies aboard; and they themselves set us an example of courage, uttering not a single scream. We spent only a few hours at Sainte-Marie. That same day, August 6, at three p.m., we steamed north toward an island with the prodigious name of Michilimackinac, situated between lakes Huron and Michigan. We saw nothing remarkable during this lap of the voyage. You need only picture eternal expanses of water in the midst of forests, which dominate the landscape so completely that one seldom sees the color of earth. It becomes a monotonous spectacle. To avoid tedium, one must busy oneself with other things than gazing. I read a bit, I write a lot. Writing letters is pleasurable, unlike reading them, I fear. As you see, mine are long and scribbled; they probably have the additional defect of being incoherent—it is terribly difficult to isolate oneself in the midst of a crowd such as this, and one is constantly interrupted. When I find a pretty bird, I paint it; but that, too, is difficult to do from a moving platform.

The other day I was on deck, seated next to my box of colors, when a little lady came up to me and said, "Oh, Monsieur! Draw my portrait." I excused myself. "I shall pay you well," she replied. I told her that I didn't want her money, whereupon she said, "In that case, I shall give you something else." It was all I could do to make her understand that I paint for pleasure and would be incapable of drawing a miniature.

I was hardly free of her when another woman approached me with a similar request, then a third, who commissioned me as follows: "If you paint the steamboat, put me in it. But wait, I'm wearing a very ugly dress; I'll have to go to my cabin and change into a prettier one."

I recounted these scenes to members of our group; they had a good laugh.

Speaking of painting, the Englishman whom I told you about, M. Vigne, paints rather well. What recommends him above all are his admirable colors, of which I availed myself, with his kind permission, to paint a *bluebird*. It bears no resemblance whatever to my previous efforts.

We arrived at Michilimackinac on August 7. This little island is the most picturesque spot I've seen in this region where, by and large, the land is very flat and unevennesses of terrain quite rare (I speak of the countryside that fringes the Great Lakes). Michilimackinac, on the contrary, has a rock-bound coast. Defending it is a fort lightly fortified by the hand of man, whose natural position gives it a great strategic advantage. Its garrison consists of one hundred American troops. The same elements to be found at Sainte-Marie inhabit this island, but its population of four hundred is four times more numerous. Their only endeavors are in commerce and industry. Everyone speaks French, and living on the island are a number of rich, distinguished residents, among them Monsieur and Madame Abbot, who welcomed us most warmly, although Tocqueville and I presented ourselves without a sponsor. The only things that seem to stir this little island are religion and the thirst for riches. Like all Americans, they are absolutely passionate about enriching themselves, but unlike many Americans, they are possessed of a religious zeal that fosters deep sectarian hostility. Catholics and Presbyterians stand jaw to jaw, with the former outnumbering the latter. Our priest on the steamboat, M. Mullon, was headed for Michilimackinac. We spent the whole of the 7th there. I saw few Indians; a large group had been present several days earlier, but were already far away. They cover immense distances in diminutive canoes reminiscent of the little boat you—our very own Columbus—made twenty years ago and sailed across the Ocean of Beaumont-la-Chartre, i.e., the fountain in the lower garden. We spent the day viewing two of the island's natural curiosities. The first is an arch naturally carved into a very high rock; some call it *The Pierced Rock,* others *The Giant's Arch.* I observed this most extraordinary formation from every angle while climbing to the top of it with Tocqueville and two of our companions. Nothing could be easier, provided one doesn't get flustered. Our guide unfortunately did. The poor devil had a dizzy spell and all his limbs began to shake. He saved himself by sliding very slowly down the hill. In order to site our lofty vantage point, I and an Englishman got into a small boat, rowed a short distance, and sketched the Giant's Arch.

No less curious is something located in the middle of the island: a rock shaped like a regular pyramid fifty feet high, but untouched by human hands; it has grooves and crevasses in which the Indians used to deposit the bones of their dead. I found a fragment and it's one of the *treasures* I shall bring back to my country.

We left Michilimackinac during the night of the 7th–8th and arrived on the morning of the 9th at Green Bay (Baie Verte). You'll find it tucked in one of the corners of Lake Michigan. We resumed our voyage the next day, the 10th. I spent my time there in a rather original way. Many of the Indian huts were on the riverbank; I went from one to another, by myself, and conversed as best I could with the savages I found at home. Some know a little French; every one of them knows how to say "bonjour," which is an opening. Moreover, they like the French very much. When I found Indians who didn't understand anything, I spoke by signs. To ingratiate myself thoroughly, all I had to do was show them my album. One rather pretty young Indian woman gave me a collar of pearls and seashells for a drawing I had done of an American green woodpecker. Now if that isn't commerce I don't know what is. The industrial spirit of America must be rubbing off on me. In my defense, I present the anecdote of ladies asking me to do their portraits; it proves that I still possess good faith and generosity, that I'm not *mercantile* to the core.

In the hut of one of my savages I amused myself by painting the face of a little Indian: I placed a bird on one cheek, a galloping horse on the other, and a cat on his cheek. His playmates were greatly taken with my masterpieces. As you know, Indians customarily paint their faces, but since their painting is tasteless and crude, they were charmed by colors arranged somewhat methodically. I learned more about the mores of Indians in half a day spent among them than I would have from a thousand volumes. I will not undertake a full description. Suffice it to say here that, all in all, they appear to be excellent people. I would call them diamonds in the rough who, being unpolished, seem inferior to less precious stones embellished by art. During my expedition among the savages, Tocqueville went off hunting and nearly drowned. He is very near-sighted and when he encounters a river doesn't hesitate to swim across if he believes it to be very narrow. In this case he miscalculated. The river was so wide that he found himself out of breath before reaching the far bank. These are dangers to which we inept swimmers never expose ourselves.

The land around Green Bay is so flat that there isn't any view, except of Fort Howard, which is occupied by several American regiments. All the military stations in these remote territories have only one purpose, which is to keep the Indians in check and drive them farther and farther back. To accomplish this, the American army is not hard pressed. The Indians are generally resigned to their fate, acknowledging the superiority of Europeans, their enemies. Recently, there was an uprising of Indians on the banks of the Mississippi, but it didn't amount to much.

The American army has only six thousand regulars, but this number more than suffices for what is asked of them. All officers are chosen from among graduates of the military academy at West Point, unlike the noncommissioned officers. Why is this? Because soldiers are volunteers—and consequently, not men of any social standing—who join the army because they don't know what else to do with their lives. What a fate for an officer, being assigned to a garrison at Green Bay or the Prairie du Chien, which is even more remote! I should mention that they are better paid than in France.

We left Green Bay on August 10 and returned to Michilimack-inac, on our way back to Detroit. As chance would have it, we arrived the very day M. Mullon delivered his argument against Presbyterians. Tocqueville and I went to hear him at the Catholic Church, where many people were assembled, the religious quarrel having become a sensational event. M. Mullon spoke with great fervor and much talent, but it seemed to me that he treated his adversaries with a most unevangelical degree of violence and severity. One must at least admire his zeal, if not his moderation, for the fact is that he traveled two hundred leagues to make his argument and will be traveling as many to go home.

On the 12th we left Michilimackinac once again and are now on Lake Huron, where I continue the letter I began the day before yesterday. Tomorrow we arrive at Detroit, where I shall post my letter in great haste, hoping that it reaches New York before the departure of the August 20 packet. Detroit is only a brief halt. Our destination is Buffalo.

Tocqueville to his father, On Lakes Erie, Huron, and Michigan, August 14, 1831

In my last letter home, dear father, I told you that I was going to leave for Buffalo, and would continue from there to Boston by way of Canada. That was, indeed, our intention. But fate inter-cepted us. On our way to the post office, we learned of the arrival from Buffalo of a large vessel chartered to loop around the Great Lakes before returning to its home port, all this comfortably and in just under a fortnight. We succumbed to temptation. Instead of leaving the next day for Buffalo, we set sail for Lake Superior, thus adding about fifteen hundred miles or five hundred French leagues to our original itinerary. . . .

We quickly steamed across Lake Saint-Clair and up a river of the same name. After adverse winds and a shortage of wood halted us for a day at the entrance to Lake Huron, we at last entered this enormous body of water, which resembles the sea in all respects save one: it is so wondrously limpid that one can see objects thirty feet below the surface. Two days and one night later, cruising at a constant three leagues an hour, we were still on Lake Huron. Come early morning of the third day we discovered for the first time a place inhabited by Whites, the village of Sault-Sainte-Marie, situated on a river bearing that name and joining Lake Superior to Lake Huron. There we dropped anchor and went ashore. In the immense expanse of shoreline we had just surveyed there is nothing strikingly picturesque. It consists of forested plains. The ensemble, however, makes a deep and lasting impression. This lake without sails, this shore devoid of any trace of human passage, the endless woods bordering it, are the stuff of poetry. They are also, I swear, the grandest spectacle I have ever seen. What is now one vast forest will one day become a country supremely rich and powerful, and it doesn't take prophetic vision to foresee this. Nature has provided everything needed for success: fertile land, incomparable waterways. The only thing lacking is civilized man, and he's at the door.

August 15

Back to Sault-Sainte-Marie. Since the river isn't navigable north of it, our vessel stopped there. But we ourselves forged ahead. Indians have taught Europeans how to make bark canoes light enough for two men to carry on their shoulders. I shall bring home a strip or panel, and you will agree, I'm sure, that the man who first paddled off in something so flimsy must have been stout-hearted indeed. Savages can turn out a canoe in just five days. The sight of this nutshell bobbing among the reefs of the Sainte-Marie river and darting through the rapids is terrifying, though in point of fact it's not at all dangerous; more than once I have had women companions who sat beside me with perfect aplomb. On this occasion the boatmen hoisted the canoes onto their backs; they were floated again beyond the rapids and we slept inside them. The entire population of Sainte-Marie is French, but of another age, cheerful and high-spirited as their fathers were. While paddling, they sang airs all but forgotten in France. It's as if we had discovered a hundred-year-old mummy preserved for the edification of our mirthless contemporaries.

Three leagues upstream of Sault-Sainte-Marie, we disembarked at a promontory called the Cape of Oaks. There we finally beheld Lake Superior, stretching out as far as the eye could reach. There is no settlement yet on its shores, and the rapids have thus far prevented any vessels from crossing it; then . . . But wait; if I recount everything in such detail, there will be no end to it. I must be brief, for we are approaching Detroit and time is short. Having conversed at length with Indians who inhabit the region, we returned to the boat. From Sainte-Marie we continued south to Michilimackinac, an island situated at the entrance to Lake Michigan, and thence to Green Bay, which lies sixty leagues farther on.[19] After several jaunts up the Fox River (or rivière du Renard), here we are, with game bagged en route. I doubt there is a single person in France who has left footsteps where we walked. The Canadians assured us that they have encountered no French voyagers before us. If I can ever manage to draw for readers what

19. Green Bay was an important trading post, with six hundred inhabitants and a base for religious missionaries—Catholic, Presbyterian, Episcopalian—embroiled in a notoriously fierce rivalry for the Indian soul.

I have seen and experienced during this rapid excursion, the picture may command attention. I have already tried and am discouraged. My impressions tumble out helter-skelter. I'd rather be recounting them at the fireside. . . .

Tocqueville to Ernest de Chabrol, Buffalo, August 17, 1831

Life takes odd turns, my dear friend! We went to Buffalo to see Niagara Falls. A vessel was leaving on a two-day voyage across Lake Erie to Detroit. We could hardly miss a chance to see one of the frontier provinces separating the United States from the vast wilderness beyond. Ten days would suffice, we thought: like La Fontaine's pigeon, we were wrong.[20]

We crossed the lake, hiked through Michigan territory, and, after ten days, returned to Detroit with plans to sail for Buffalo the next day. But when we approached the shore we caught sight of a large steamboat preparing to depart and learned that its destinations were Lake Superior and Green Bay on Lake Michigan. This tour takes place only once a year; almost all the regions visited are terra incognita, and the vessel completes its excursion in twelve days. We hurried back to our inn, paid the bill, packed our belongings on the run. We shipped out and added—would you believe it?—a good five hundred leagues to our voyage. That is the distance between Paris and Cadiz.

Here we are at last, back where we started, and, I pray, done with knocking about. Not that this jaunt was a waste of time. It fired our curiosity and even supplied us with valuable documents. The territory of Michigan was almost entirely wilderness twenty

20. Tocqueville is referring to La Fontaine's fable "Les Deux pigeons," in which the pigeon eager to travel says: "Trois jours au plus rendront mon âme satisfaite" [It will take three days at most to satisfy my soul].

years ago. Since then, immigration has reached it with the force of a tidal wave. It was ideal for studying the manner in which an American province is settled and the character of those who undertake this painful and productive enterprise. I would like to make this the subject of my letter, scanting many others. My time is so limited I can't report on everything I see.

The United States doesn't allow individuals to purchase land from the Indian nations; it does it itself and then sells it cheap. In Detroit I visited the public bureau responsible for the sale of land, or "Land Office," and was given the following information:

Since the spring thaw, that is, since last May, when the lake became navigable, until July 1, approximately five thousand "new settlers" (that's the English term; we have no exact equivalent) have arrived in Michigan. As you can imagine, this figure startled me, all the more because I subscribed to the opinion, generally held in France, that all these "new settlers" were European.

The land agent informed me that of the five thousand, barely two hundred are emigrants from Europe. Even that is a higher proportion than elsewhere. "What possesses such a large number of Americans to leave their birthplace and come live in a wilderness?" I asked. "The explanation is quite simple," he answered. "As the law requires fathers to distribute property equally among their children, each generation is poorer than its predecessor. When the small landowner in our populated states realizes how difficult it is to earn a livelihood, he sells his field, moves with his entire family to the frontier, uses his small capital to buy a large tract, and enriches himself in a few years. If his heirs don't find this fortune adequate, they go off to build a new one in a more remote wilderness. Thank God, we have land enough for expanding as far as the Pacific Ocean."

Don't you agree, my dear friend, that there is a whole book contained in this brief reply? How can one imagine revolutions taking place where the needs and passions of men find an outlet in this westward expansion? And how can one compare the political institutions of such people to those of any other nation?

I pursued my enquiry and learned that the immense peninsula of Michigan is divided into acres (the acre being almost as large as our arpent);[21] one selects one's acres on a map and pays ten American shillings for each one, about seven and a half francs.

We have since surveyed a great many of these "new settlements" and taken great pains to inform ourselves as to the manner in which people establish themselves there.

Here's how it's done. The initial expenses (and I would like this emphasized in Europe) are still quite considerable. To clear the necessary terrain one needs five or six hundred francs. With this sum, a portion of which serves to purchase a six-month supply of wheat and salt pork, the pioneer ventures forth. He usually brings along some cattle, which forage in the woods and cost nothing to feed.

The first order of business is to cut down trees and build a crude cabin called a "log house." He clears a little field around this dwelling, then another, and another. He wages war against the forest in a thousand different ways, and isn't always equal to his enemy. In my next letter I shall try to describe the external appearance of these new "settlements" and portray its inhabitants, but I'm short of time and paper.

I've just read the papers: the latest news from France leaves me frightened and anxious. Unless I'm badly mistaken, our country was or still is in violent crisis. I infer this from a great many observations and remarks made here and there. I am sick with worry; I found your packet of May 27 in Buffalo; those of the 1st,

---

21. An arpent was a French measure of area equaling approximately 3,400 square meters, or about four-fifths of an acre.

10th, and 30th of June await me in Albany, where I arrive shortly. I pray that I shall find good news!

I am deeply grateful to you, dear friend, for your diligence in writing to me; I cherish your letters.

I thank you for looking after our neighbor, whom I still love with all my heart. Her letters tell me that you have made a fast friend of her.

Tocqueville to Mary Mottley, August 20, 1831

. . . Do you know what my first thought was on waking up this morning, Marie? I thought that today would be a happy day for me, since it is your birthday. Oh, I shall never forget August 20. It will never dawn without my remembering that on this day was born the person to whom I owe the happiest hours I've ever known, those moments the soul can never forget, those one recollects with pride. I shall always remember, Marie, that on this day she was born who would prove to be such a tender friend, such a sweet consolation for all the sorrows and vexations that torment the life of a man. Ah! I shall never cease to thank God for at least one thing, I'm sure, and that is for bringing you into the world. . . .[22]

Tocqueville to his mother, On Lake Ontario, August 21, 1831

When I was on Lake Ontario, dear mother, I wrote a letter to my father, who must have told you about the voyage we improvised during the first fortnight of this month. At Buffalo, your letters of last May 27 awaited us and, despite their date, gave us

22. This letter is a fragment, copied by Marie after her husband's death. She destroyed most of his letters to her.

indescribable pleasure. I had gone so long without seeing anything of my family's script. I can tell you how touched I am, dear mother, at receiving mail from you in each delivery. I am aware that writing tires you, which makes your letters all the more precious to me. Also, thank the entire household on my behalf.

After an hour in Buffalo, we set out for Niagara. We could already hear the falls two leagues before reaching them. They sounded like distant thunder, and in fact Niagara is an Indian word that means "thunder of the waters." I find the expression wonderfully apt. (Indian languages are full of images far more poetic than our own.) We advanced toward the noise, unable to imagine how close we were to its source.

Indeed, nothing prepares one for the spectacle. A large river (which is only Lake Erie brimming over) slowly flows across flatland. The terrain remains featureless right up to the cataract itself. We arrived toward dusk and postponed our first visit until morning. August 18 dawned a splendid day and we set out early. I will unavoidably wax pathetic in describing what we witnessed. I believe that the falls surpass everything said and written about them at home; they surpass anything one's imagination conjures up beforehand. The river divides as it nears the abyss and forms two falls separated by a small island. The broader is shaped like a horseshoe a quarter of a league in width, which is to say more than two times wider than the Seine. When the river arrives, it spills over the edge to a depth of 149 feet. Vapor rises from the bottom like a cloud, with an enormous rainbow framed against it. One can clamber quite easily to the tip of a rocky spur that juts toward the falls. Nothing equals the sublimity of the view one has out there, especially at night, when the bottom of the abyss disappears and the rainbow is moonlit. I had never seen a nocturnal rainbow. It is much the same as the diurnal, but perfectly white. It arched from one bank to the other. About the cataract: walking behind that curtain of water strikes one at first as a dangerous maneuver, but it turns out not to be. We took perhaps a hundred steps before the cliff wall bellied in front of us. Now and again a sun- or moonbeam penetrates the deep, dreadful darkness of the place, everything suddenly becomes visible, and one feels that the whole river is crashing down on one's head. It's hard to convey the exact impression produced by this shaft of light; after allowing you to glimpse the vast chaos all around, it delivers you again to the shadows and din of the waterfall. We remained at Niagara for a full day. Yesterday we set sail on Lake Ontario.

This account of the wonder that filled us at Niagara may lead you to a false conclusion about our state of mind. Far from being tranquil and happy, I have fallen prey to deeper melancholy. At Buffalo, I found news of Europe and France in various newspapers. From the many small circumstances they report, I form the picture of a country in crisis and of civil war itself looming near, with all the danger that that presents for those I hold dearest. . . . These images interpose themselves between me and everything I set eyes upon, and I cannot, without a profound sense of something very like shame, stand in awe of these American falls, knowing that the fate of so many people hangs in the balance.

Beaumont to his father, August 21

. . . We had scarcely docked at Buffalo than we left for Niagara, accompanied by M. Vigne, an Englishman, and an Englishwoman named Miss Clemens. I believe I spoke to Achille about these two individuals, who were among our fellow passengers on the excursion to Green Bay: M. Vigne is a most congenial man, who travels for pleasure and instruction; Miss Clemens is the dearest soul on earth, but surpassingly tedious. A romantic to the core, she subsists on fictions, emotions, and moonlight; when she sees something that pleases her, she acclaims it: with her, there is no such thing as admiration without ecstasy. If she were twenty, she would be winsome, but she's at least forty, which makes her ridiculous. My politeness was my ruination—she thought I was wooing her—and on the steamboat, ingenious maneuvers were required to escape the charms of her conversation. If she didn't expect me to hear her recite verse, she wanted me to join her in admiring a lovely view. I developed a variety of pretexts. Alas, none of them worked after Buffalo. "I will show you my favorite resort," she said to us, "and I shall do the honors." I daresay the lady spends half her life beside the cataract; one might call her "the madwoman of Niagara." Perhaps she should arrange to live under the falls! The shower might be therapeutic. In any event, we set out with her—by now our old traveling companion. It took three hours to reach the spot nearest the falls, which is called Niagara Falls. You should know that Niagara is an Indian word meaning "thundering waters." The name fits well, for we could hear it from one and a half leagues away and its low rumble sounded just like distant thunder. I won't inflict a description on you. How does one follow M. de Chateaubriand? Even though the picture he paints seems quite inadequate to me, I don't think one can do better. Anyway, the subject surpasses all description. It is certainly one of the most marvelous and gigantic works of creation; nowhere does nature present such a sublime, imposing aspect. M. de Chateaubriand said that the cataract was "a column of water from the Flood," and in all that he wrote about Niagara only this image does justice to the immensity of the thing. . . .

As you know, Niagara marks the border between Canada and the United States, the right bank belonging to the latter, the left to England. We reconnoitered both, in order to survey all the fields of view. I made a sketch that will, I hope, help you picture it. Miss Clemens bored us silly during our sojourn in her domain: she was forever proposing walks, boat rides, etc. One day, when M. Vigne, Tocqueville, and I set out, with rifles slung over our shoulders, to see an especially picturesque site called the Whirpall [Whirlpool], she stubbornly ran after us, ignoring all our efforts to make her stay behind. Since reason would not prevail, we thought to convince her with arguments of another kind and started walking at a brisk pace. It was perhaps the warmest day of the year; it was noon; we were apoplectically hot. No matter. The need to avoid a sentimental old lady gave spring to our legs, to mine above all—I outpaced everyone, having already endured the assaults of the enemy. We really looked like prey pursued by an ardent bloodhound; we were all out of breath, we leapt over barriers like stags.

In similar circumstances, I believe I would have hurdled the reservoir of Beaumont-la-Chartre twenty times over. But our fair Englishwoman, like a pack of dogs expecting their reward in meat from the hunt, easily cleared every obstacle; after an hour or more, despite all our efforts, we had no more than fifty steps on her. We halted in despair. Eventually we saw what we had come to see and made for home with our intrepid Dulcinea. The contest began all over again but this time with better results; we gave her the slip and bolted like escaped convicts. Upon our return, we felt somewhat ashamed of our rudeness. While we were consoling ourselves over a good meal, a note arrived in which Miss Clemens asked to be forgiven for having lost us en route. We were strongly inclined not to pardon her, but agreed that she might profit from the lesson. Had I known what a nuisance she was to make of herself the following day, I would certainly not have let her off so lightly. This poor woman has showered me with gifts and I blush at the thought of how ungrateful I've been. She gave me a very good work on the art of perspective, a lovely album containing a poem of Thomas Moore, various biographical sketches of great Englishmen, and some very tender, remarkably well-turned verses of her own composition. I would blame myself for having accepted all that if it had been in my power to refuse it, but I declare that no power on earth could have withstood the will of Miss Clemens violently exercising itself upon me. Tocqueville as well was obliged to accept a rather pretty Christmas-gift book.

Beaumont to his father, September 5

My last letter was dispatched from Montreal on the day I arrived. We barely touched ground in that city. It is large, and situated on an island in the middle of the Saint Lawrence. Its population numbers twenty-five to thirty thousand, which makes it Canada's largest city, though not its capital.

We had a letter of introduction to the head of the Montreal seminary, a very amiable, distinguished graduate of Saint-Sulpice, who came here four years ago. He was an excellent host and supplied us with much precious information about Canada. We found this country terribly exciting. Of its 900,000 inhabitants, more than 800,000 are French; subjected to English domination by the shameful treaty of 1763, which ceded Canada to England, Canadians have always been a people apart, entirely distinct from the English seeking to introduce themselves among them. They preserve their language, their mores, and their nationality. The English government is mild, not the least tyrannical; its wrong was its original conquest. The conquered will remember their defeat long after the conqueror no longer remembers his victory.

In Canada there are seeds of discontent, of malaise, of hostility toward England. People of the humbler sort are not clearly aware of what they feel; but the enlightened class, which is not yet numerous, directs them and provides a rationale for their passions.

One cannot imagine a more felicitous population than that of the Canadian hinterland. Informing the character of all its villages is a moral purity that European city dwellers, if one described it to them, would dismiss as make-believe. Crime and acts of indecency are simply unknown. Parishes have only one public functionary, the priest; his moral custodianship is all the police that's needed. Everyone is Catholic. Some traces of feudalism survive: all the lands are divided into manorial domains and each tenant-farmer pays rent to the lord. This rent is minimal, typically five or six francs for a tract measuring ninety arpents. The lord has a bench reserved for him at church; otherwise, he is a lord in name only and enjoys absolutely no special privileges. The priest receives a tithe of the harvest, consisting of the twenty-sixth part. This scheme works to the advantage of the inhabitants, who pay no taxes. We visited several of them. The ease and well-being that permeate their dwellings and surroundings speak of great happiness. But their happiness may not last long. Every year, England, Ireland, and Scotland disgorge boatloads of adventurers seeking cheap land in America. The English government, which has a stake in building up Canada's English population, directs them this way, so that Canadians, if they don't take care, will find themselves engulfed by a *foreign majority,* and drowned. What aggravates the danger is the fact that wealthy people in Canada are almost all English; the English control major commerce and industry; they fill the country's two big cities, Quebec and Montreal. They do their utmost to crush the Canadian population, whose poverty they scorn and whose happiness they do not comprehend.

This influx from Great Britain will continue so long as Europe is at peace. Canadians are already vexed by it; efforts are already being made, through educational improvement, to give them the means of better understanding their political interests. The clergy has closed ranks against the government; it is a curious spectacle, country priests not unlike the curate of Marçon or of Beaumont-la-Chartre embracing liberalism and playing the demagogue. It all seems bound to end in a violent struggle. But it is difficult to foresee which of the two populations, English or Canadian, will gain the upper hand.

We left Montreal on August 24 and embarked on the *John-Molson,* a magnificent steamboat, which took us to Quebec in less than twenty-four hours (a distance of about sixty leagues).

I cannot imagine a more beautiful river than the Saint Lawrence. In fact, it's the biggest one known to mankind: ten leagues beyond Quebec it widens to seven leagues and remains that wide for fifty leagues, expanding still farther before merging with the sea. Quebec is very picturesquely situated, at Cap Diamant. Its French founders built powerful fortifications on which the English government nonetheless continues to work relentlessly. Quebec is the capital of Canada and the seat of English administration. Garrisoned there is a numerous armed force, maintained at the expense of England. Canada costs England six million a year, but the colony is worth it, being, notably, a year-round source of wood for the construction of vessels.

While land that yields rich harvests is normally banal, and scenic countryside unprofitable, the banks of the Saint Lawrence embody a contradiction. They are exceptionally fertile, yet present the grandest, most magnificent spectacle imaginable. To the right and left are plains covered with crops, in the middle of which the river channels its vast waters. Beyond it all, where the farming ends, high mountains cast a shadow upon the scene.

In Quebec, we got in touch with all the prominent men of the region, who received us with open arms; they were delighted to see Frenchmen from old France. One of them, M. Neilson, took a particular interest in us, became our guide, and very obligingly showed us everything worth seeing. With him and my friend Tocqueville I visited a large parish three leagues from Quebec called Beaumont, the center of a manorial domain founded in Louis XIV's time by a Monsieur de Beaumont. He came from France, but it is not known from which province. The story of this Beaumont would have interested me a great deal more if I hadn't remembered that back then the Beaumont clan to which I have the honor of belonging still bore such common names as Bonnin or Bonninière; in spite of that, I was given the royal treatment.

No less interesting was our excursion to where the Montmorency River cascades into the Saint Lawrence, from a height of 240 feet. It's beautiful, but not comparable to Niagara. An analogy might be the difference between a stream and a river, between the pretty and the magnificent. I saw many other things in Quebec, among them a convent whose sisterhood includes very distinguished women all of whom have relatives in France. I met a judge, Monsieur Taschereau, whose family comes from Touraine; he claims to be a relative of our Taschereau de La Chartre. He is the only Canadian in Quebec entrusted with a public office by the English authorities, a lucky thing for him, as it pays 25,000 francs a year. I dined with him at the home of one of his relatives, in whom I found the French gaiety and customs of yore. Since I've been in America, I haven't heard laughter except in Canada; at dessert, everyone must sing his favorite song. Bonhomie and cordiality are everywhere evident among Canadians.

Religion has a powerful hold over society. The Catholic clergy is universally respected; there isn't a philosopher who is not at the same time a religious man, or who dares to appear irreligious. One day I went strolling with one of Quebec's *democrats:* whenever we passed a church, he made the sign of the cross.

Tocqueville to abbé Lesueur, September 7, 1831, Albany

You can't imagine, my good friend, how pleased I was when, upon arriving here, I found a sheaf of letters dated June 20 and 30. I was distraught over public affairs and over you. The letters informed me that you had indeed been ailing and were still not altogether well. Now I'll be on tenterhooks until I read the letters of July 10 and 20. I know for a fact that they are in America, but they were forwarded to Boston, where we shall arrive in two days. Only then will I have subsequent bulletins about your health. I am terribly anxious to know the latest.

It gives me enormous pleasure, my good friend, to be back in touch with you at last. Until now, only one of us was talking. Now it is a conversation. All the details I've received about the reception of my last letter please me inordinately. Continue to supply me with as many particulars as you can. Don't worry how small they are; at a distance of two thousand leagues, minutiae bulk large. . . .

We have just completed a far-flung tour in the west and north of America. The last fortnight was spent visiting Canada. When I last wrote to you I didn't think we would shape our course in that direction. The lack of political news had become so insufferable that we planned to make straight for Albany. Fortunately, we received news of France en route and decided that we could afford a week sailing down the Saint Lawrence. We now pat ourselves on the back for having done so. Apart from everything else, the region we have just covered is very picturesque. A little past Quebec, the Saint Lawrence, the world's broadest river, measures seven leagues across and stays that wide for quite some distance before expanding to fifteen, twenty, thirty leagues and finally merging with the ocean. It's as if the English Channel were streaming inland and parting the continent. One should not wonder at its immensity, considering that it alone drains the Great Lakes, from Superior to Ontario. The lakes hang together like a bunch of grapes that burst through their skin into the valley of Canada.

But what interested us most keenly were Canada's inhabitants. I am astonished that this land is so little known in France. Six months ago I believed, as everyone does, that Canada had become completely English. My fixed point of reference was the 1763 census, which reported the French population to be only sixty thousand. But since then population has been on the increase as rapidly as in the United States, and today there are six hundred thousand French descendants in Lower Canada alone. I assure you, there can be no doubt about their origins. They are as French as you and I. They resemble us far more closely than Americans of the United States resemble the English. I can't tell you how comforting it was to be in the bosom of this community. I felt at home, and we were received everywhere as compatriots—as children of what they call "old France." The epithet does not fit, in my opinion: old France now lies on this side of the ocean, new France on the other. We rediscovered old French habits and mores, especially in the countryside, where houses cluster around churches surmounted by the Gallic cock and the lily-wreathed cross. Canadian landowners, unlike English or American, prefer not to live isolated from one another. By and large, the peasant is rich, pays no taxes whatever, and dwells in a well-built house—solid outside, neat and clean within. Parents and children—the former typically vigorous, the latter cheerful and robust—gather four times a day for meals at a round table. The ritual after supper is to sing old French songs and recount the valiant deeds of Canada's original Frenchmen—feats of swordsmanship under Montcalm or during the wars with the English. On Sundays, there is frolicking and dancing after the religious service, with the parish priest himself participating in communal festivities (so long as they don't degenerate into licentiousness). He is the arbiter of games, the people's friend, their adviser. The English, far from considering him an advocate of the powers-that-be, treat him as a demagogue. When it comes to resisting oppression, he is unyielding, and the people know that they have in him a pillar of strength. Religion for Canadians is therefore a matter of political passion as well as principle. Clergy are the upper class because opinion and custom want them to stand at the head of society, not because the laws require it. I've met several of these ecclesiastics and they are, indeed, the country's most distinguished men. Generally amiable, good-humored, and well-bred, they call to mind our old French curates.

Along with religious ideas, morals have remained strong. In all of these villages, reputation holds almost absolute sway. A thief is never denounced; the moment he falls under suspicion he is compelled to leave the community. And there is no rarer presence than that of a fallen woman. However different French and Canadian peasants, they both cherish equality and independence, and cordially detest everything reminiscent of lords and feudal rights.

Isn't it tempting to surmise that the national character of a people is determined more by the blood that flows through it than by political institutions or the nature of the country? French have been living here in the midst of an English population for eighty years—subject to the laws of England and more completely cut off from the mother country than if they inhabited the poles. Well, what do you know! They are still French, feature for feature, and not only the older people, but everyone, even little moppets spinning their tops. Like us, they are lively, brisk, intelligent, scoffing, hot-headed, loquacious, and terribly difficult to manage when their passions are enflamed. They make good warriors and love noise more than money. Living beside them, also native born, are Englishmen as phlegmatic and rational as those living on the banks of the Thames—people who abide by precedents, who believe in first things first; estimable citizens who think that war is the greatest scourge, but who would wage it as bravely as others because they reckon that some things are more intolerable than death.[23]

Adieu, my good friend. I love you and embrace you, my father and mother as well, with all my heart.

Tocqueville to his sister-in-law Émilie, Albany, September 7, 1831

What has happened since I've come to America, my dear little sister, is the opposite of what should have taken place; while you have often sent me the most agreeable, most amusing letters, I have answered only twice, if I'm not mistaken. I can assure you with absolute sincerity, however, that I am remiss through no fault of my own; our lives, especially during the past two months, have been incredibly peripatetic. And every ten days, willy-nilly, I've had to reassure the family at great length that all is well. I would hope, however, that you are not discouraged by my negligence. Your letters give me great pleasure; they speak of a friendship that is dear and precious to me. Moreover, there are a great many small family details that you alone can relate.

You are at last settled at Nacqueville, God be praised! I was on

23. Following "more intolerable than death" is a partially illegible sentence, the end of which reads: "practical and careful who don't give thought to anything beyond physical well-being and, as for all the rest, is tempted to say, like the mathematician: 'What does that prove?' "

tenterhooks thinking of you in Paris. I heard, however, that in the end you had adjusted to life there. Our parents tell me that you have put flesh on your bones and that your face has regained its beautiful color. There will be more of both, I'm sure, now that you're back home in Normandy. Remain there as long as you can, dear sister; my advice is egotistical since I myself am away from Paris and will be none the poorer for your absence. Still, it is good advice. And I know that you are inclined to follow it, unlike your husband perhaps, who is sometimes given to wanting his own way.

I have just returned from an immense journey through the interior of the continent; step by step, and guided serendipitously, we at last reached Lake Superior, more than four hundred leagues from New York. We saw millions of acres of woods to which no one has ever laid an ax and numbers of Indian nations. Apropos, do you know what Atala, or her kinswoman, looked like? I shall draw a portrait of her that you can compare to Monsieur de Chateaubriand's. Atala is a very dark Indian, café-au-lait colored, whose wiry, glossy tresses fall straight as arrows to her lower back. She normally has a large, rather thick, and more or less aquiline nose, a wide mouth armed with sparkling teeth, and two black eyes, which, in broad daylight, resemble those of a cat at night. Don't assume that she disdains artifice because she is endowed with so much natural beauty. Far from it. First she draws a dark stripe around her eyes, then, underneath it, stripes of so many different colors—red, blue, green—that her face looks like a rainbow. Then she suspends from her ears a kind of Chinese carillon weighing half a pound. The most stylish insert through their nostrils a large tin ring that dangles over their mouths, to very pleasing effect. They also wear a necklace of wide plaques engraved with various wild animals. A linen-like tunic falling slightly below the knees is their ordinary dress; almost always draped over it is a blanket on which they lie at night. Wait, I haven't finished my portrait. The custom among women of the forests is to have their feet pointing inward. I don't know if inward is more unnatural than outward, but our European eyes can't easily adjust to this form of beauty. It is achieved by binding the feet of female infants. By age twenty, a woman walks pigeon-toed, and the more pigeon-toed her walk the more *fashionable* she is thought to be. All I know is, I wouldn't accept a king's ransom to fill the role of Chactas. Indian men look better than the women. They are strapping fellows, built like stags and just as agile. They charm you when they smile but grimace diabolically when mad. We didn't see as many of them as we would have liked; the forests are emptying with incredible rapidity.

We came back by way of Canada. If you ever go to America, dear sister, it is there that you must base yourself. You will rediscover your dear South Normans in every last trait. Monsieur Gisles, Madame Noel—I see all those people on the streets of Quebec. The best specimens of the region could pass for your cousins from (where are they from again?). And peasants assured us that there was never any need to go to town because the "creatures" assumed responsibility for weaving and making their clothes.[24]

Adieu, my good and dear sister, I beg you always, in whatever circumstance, to count upon my most zealous friendship.

24. "Créatures" is apparently a reference to their womenfolk, not pejorative. One definition provided by the nineteenth-century French lexicographer Émile Littré is "une bonne femme," meaning a simple, ordinary housewife.

NEW ENGLAND

From Albany the two traveled east to Boston, where they were grandly received in Brahmin society, and after several weeks returned to New York by way of Hartford and the penitentiary at Wethersfield.

Tocqueville to his brother Édouard, Boston, September 10, 1831

I learned of Bébé's death yesterday evening, my good friend. I was already worried, because the last batch of letters included none from him. Knowing his punctuality and affection, I suspected that he was more seriously ill than you allowed; and on the way to Boston I told Beaumont again and again how much I feared that news of some great misfortune awaited me. Yesterday, although it was very late, I fetched my letters at the post office. When I opened the parcel and didn't see his script, I guessed the terrible truth. Never in my life have I felt so painfully disconsolate. I have no words for it. The announcement stunned me. I loved our good old friend as I loved our father; he was indeed another father to us in his concern for our well-being, his tenderness, his attentions—all because he willed a paternal bond.

Now he has left us forever, and I couldn't receive his last blessings. It's easy to say that one must accustom oneself in advance to the idea of separation from an eighty-year-old man; no, my dear friend, one doesn't get used to the idea of suddenly seeing the mainstay of one's childhood disappear, the friend—the incomparable friend—of a lifetime. I hope eventually to recover from this blow, but there will always be a void that neither time nor friendship nor the future—whatever rewards the future may hold in store—can fill. Irreplaceable is the loss of something few people are privileged to enjoy here below—a being all of whose thoughts, all of whose affections were vested in us; whose life revolved around us alone. I have never encountered or heard of such devotion. Ah! If only you knew, my poor Édouard, how impatiently I looked forward to our reunion! With what happiness I imagined his joy at holding me in his arms again. In my last letter, I told him—as if he could still hear me—that the prospect of my return was exhilarating. Instead, I shall behold an empty bedchamber; there will be nothing but ashes in my heart when I embrace all of you. No, I cannot yet imagine being separated from him forever. Last night I seemed to see him in front of me with that kind, tender expression he always wore for us. But I shall never hear his voice again; his counsel and his example are all I have left. Oh, dear friend, I wanted to write calmly, but these cruel ideas have prevailed, and the page in front of me is a blur. The thought of eternal separation weighs upon my soul. I can't crawl out from under it. It colors everything of the world around me.

Do not, however, fear for my health. I'm well, truly I am, and the absolute necessity of keeping busy will, I hope, pull me from this slough. The one idea that sustains me is that our abbé was perhaps fortunate to have quit the world as matters in it stand today. He departed for a better place, leaving us tranquil, if not happy. Who can predict the fate reserved for his adopted family at the brink of a revolutionary decade? Perhaps he would have been tested in ways he couldn't have endured. Then too, dear friend, I have never been as certain of a person's eternal happiness as I am of his. I have read much about the immortality of the soul; never have I been so convinced of it as I am now. That he who lived only to do good could possibly suffer the same fate as great criminals is something against which my heart and my reason violently rebel. Yesterday evening, I prayed to him, as I would to a saint; I hope he heard my voice and understood that his good offices have not been altogether lost on me.

My greatest consolation at this moment, dear Édouard, is the thought that we never gave him grief. He must have realized throughout his life the strength of our attachment. He often told me so. It was the only thing that lent charm to his old age. In that sense we were each other's debtors, but the greater debt was mine and yours. With what unselfishness this poor friend sacrificed his happiness for ours! Despite the gloomy presentiments that certainly haunted him at our last encounter, he assured me—to make the leave-taking less painful—that he had every hope of seeing me again. His last letters were written in that same vein. I had almost managed to believe it. We deceived ourselves: I shall never see him again. Thank Papa and Mama for the tender care they gave him, especially Mama, who is so much in need of support herself. Since, as ill luck would have it, neither of us was beside him when he breathed his last, I am at least comforted by the knowledge that he did not want for attention and proofs of friendship at the end.

September 12

I've been here [in Boston] for two days now and managed at times to lose myself in my normal pursuits. But when, inevitably, emotions troop home, the experience is harrowing. I can't describe it. We all have different ways of grieving.

If I could, I would flee the entire world . . . I haven't yet breathed a word of these thoughts to Beaumont. I would like to be alone, entirely alone. And yet, unburdening myself to you, who share my sorrow, makes me happy. The happiness is sad, but it's happiness all the same. I know you understand what I'm going through, as you've endured the same. Were we not tied to our poor friend by the same bonds? How many proofs of unconditional friendship did we receive from him, you and I alike? Who took greater interest than he in your felicities and disappointments? And when you fell sick, what were his ministrations! It was the same for each of us. I remember that during my illness it was on his face that I sought to construe the message of hope or fear, placing greater trust in him than in myself. Do you remember, dear Édouard, when we returned from Italy [in May 1827], how happy he was to see us again? I can still see him, with tears of happiness in his eyes, unable to express his joy otherwise. One of the greatest satisfactions I could have had in this world would have been to afford him another such moment. But God did not wish it.

. . . Well, my good friend, what can I say? There's a frightful taste of dust in my mouth, a profound sorrow that robs me of the courage to do anything whatever and results in my throwing myself up into work that interests me the most, like a convict into his labor. I see all objects in a somber light. Everything around me has changed, as have I.

However, I don't want to end this letter without speaking about you. I am very happy that Alexandrine is with child.[1] I am greatly relieved to learn that she is making progress. I hope that her health becomes still more robust. Kiss her for me.

I feel closer than ever to all of you since this misfortune has befallen us. It has been borne in on me that true happiness lies in family affections. A few days from now, when I hope to have

1. Alexandrine was pregnant with her and Édouard's second child, Bernard-Hubert de Tocqueville.

recovered some peace of mind, I shall write my father a long letter on a great many matters of fact. Adieu, I embrace you with all my heart.

Beaumont to his brother Jules, September 16

We left Albany on September 6 for Boston. We traveled about ten leagues and after several hours arrived at Stockbridge, where we intended to visit Mademoiselle Sedgwick, the renowned author of several American novels. She had invited us to come see her in the country, but due to an unfortunate contretemps we didn't find her there: she had left the very morning of our arrival and was not to return until the following day. Her brothers and sisters received us most hospitably, but this did not answer our objective, which was to see someone whose works have made her celebrated. We could have set things right by tarrying at Stockbridge, but we were too eager to reach Boston and knew that letters awaited us. We therefore went on our way and in a day and a half crossed all of Massachusetts.

The state is extraordinarily picturesque, in stark contrast to the whole western part of New York. While the former is mountainous, the latter is unrelievedly flat—between Buffalo and Albany hills and hollows are rare sights. We were struck by the appearance of wealth and prosperity in Massachusetts. Everything testifies to a happy population. Nature is no longer the wilderness one encounters throughout the western states. No trace of the virgin forest remains. Massachusetts, which, as you know, once bore the name New England, is obviously old—old by standards in America, where two centuries are a veritable antiquity, and where most cities have sprung up during the past ten or twenty years. In Massachusetts one sees neither tree trunks in the fields nor log cabins. Fields are carefully enclosed; crops are varied and the inhabitants obviously use the earth to best advantage, plowing furrows close together. The growth in population in no way threatens American society. Every year, people leave this region in numbers for western New York state to buy cheap land and establish new settlements. Fifty leagues away they find all the acres they want at ten shillings apiece (six or seven francs). Overpopulation is thus never to be feared. True poverty is unknown. . . .

I don't understand why the health of these Americans, who appear so happy, is so frail; the women in particular are very thin and generally afflicted with lung disease. One wonders whether it has to do with the changeable climate, with its extremes of hot and cold, or whether one must attribute it to the way women live. Here one never sees them working the earth and doing country tasks. The result is that their labors are all domestic and confined to care of the household. This withdrawn life may be unhealthy. Since I've been in America (Canada excepted) I haven't seen anyone who bears the least resemblance to our peasant women.

Boston has sixty thousand inhabitants. Its port is magnificent. It lies in the middle of an island, access to which from every direction is by roads built over water. One notes much less commercial traffic than in New York, but the general demeanor of the city is far more attractive. Being on level ground, New York presents itself to the spectator, wherever he stands, only as a single row of houses. Boston, on the contrary, is hilly and from a certain distance offers charming views. Its many private dwellings combine taste and elegance. As for public edifices, the only one I find somewhat remarkable is the State House.

We have lodgings in the city's best inn (the Hemont Hotel).[2] Everything here is on the grand scale. There are 150 foreigners

2. The Tremont Hotel.

resident. We are splendidly served, at no greater cost than elsewhere. From the moment we arrived, we sought to contact the city's leading lights. The first day our quest came to nothing: we met no one. Having no letters of recommendation for Boston, we found ourselves in an awkward situation. Thrust upon each other after these fruitless efforts, Tocqueville and I fell prey to sad reflections; "Is it possible that we owe the warm welcome we have received until now to the few scraps of paper we carried with us? Is it that now, reduced to our own intrinsic value, we don't deserve the least consideration? So much for our amour-propre. We had begun to regard ourselves as men of distinction, but when we have only our personal merit to recommend us, we aren't given the time of day!" and other complaints of the same kind.

Our fear was exaggerated and our imagination darkened the picture. To be sure, people did not embrace two young men arriving without recommendations, but when word got out of who we are, of our social position, we were treated extremely well. As for our merit, it will undoubtedly be recognized in due course.

Our impression is that Bostonians do not throw themselves at foreigners as exuberantly as New Yorkers; but there is more true politeness. Businessmen do not make up the whole of society. Attention is paid here to the fine arts and literature. There are people engaged in neither commerce nor industry who, with inherited money, spend their lives enjoying the amenities of an advanced civilization. This class is agreeable, if not numerous. It is by nature rather changeable, because the equal division of estates prevents a fortune from remaining for long in the same family. But new ones are constantly emerging. Besides, the law that governs inheritance is far from being as democratic here as it is at home. In France, equal division among all parties is enforced, while here a paterfamilias has the right to bequeath all his property, real estate and chattels alike, to only one of his children, and, when he does so, his will is upheld. This right, which renders paternal authority much more effective than it is among us, exercises great moral influence upon the entire society, not to mention the fact that it works against the extreme parceling up of property.

The other day we dined at the home of M. Sears,[3] a millionaire five or six times over, whose townhouse is a kind of palace exuding luxury. He treated us splendidly. I've never attended *a more sumptuous dinner.* Among the table ornaments was a very pretty young woman who is, I believe, his niece. We conversed at length, but as I have no idea whether I'll see her again, the feelings aroused are all for nothing. I could say as much about every beauty I encounter. We meet with quite a few in society and get all stirred up three or four times a week, on an average; but the faces are always new, and I believe, God forgive me, that we always tell them the same thing, at the risk of complimenting a dusky woman on her alabaster complexion and a blond on the dark gloss of her hair. But all that is trivial and occupies a very small place in the life of two political men entirely taken up with speculations of the highest order.

We have already attended two balls and are preparing for a third this evening. The toilette of women is exactly as it is in France; French fashion holds sway in the United States, and its slightest changes are carefully noted. Many ladies questioned me on the subject; if they had consulted me about the penal system, I could not have replied with more perfect aplomb, speaking about hair ribbons as knowledgeably as a Michalon or an Alcibiade.[4]

Music is cultivated here somewhat more successfully than

3. David Sears, a prominent philanthropist and merchant who developed a substantial part of Brookline, Massachusetts. His mansion on Beacon Hill now houses the Somerset Club.
4. Michalon and Alcibiade were two fashionable coiffeurs in Paris.

in New York; but the great majority have no innate feeling for music. There is a picture museum, but since I have not yet visited it, you will forgive me for not saying anything further about it.

On the 12th of this month I attended a rather curious ceremony. Bostonians celebrated the consecration of two flags they are sending to the Poles.[5] The militia and the regular troops came together; the authorities, the learned societies, etc. assembled and walked in procession to a place called *Faneuil House* [Faneuil Hall] where deliberative bodies usually hold their political sessions. Of course we joined the procession in our capacity of distinguished foreigners. Upon entering the hall we saw an enormous gallery packed with very well-dressed ladies, and not a man among them; this separation of men and women is customary at all public gatherings in the United States. The ceremony opened with a prayer for Poles delivered by a Congregationalist minister. The man of God excoriated despotism and oppression with all his thunder, and spoke pompously in praise of insurrection and liberty. The two flags were then unfurled, on which various inscriptions were embroidered, among others Poniatowski's last words: "It is better to die gloriously than to surrender."[6] There was loud applause from the public, especially when it heard the name La Fayette, who will receive the flags and forward them to their destination. The ceremony concluded with the singing of odes, of hymns, etc.

5. In 1830 and 1831 there were expressions of solidarity here and throughout Europe with Poles whose armed rebellion against the Russian Empire in November 1830 had been crushed by the tsar's army.

6. Prince Josef Anton Poniatowski was the nephew of Poland's last king, Stanislaw II. He fought the Russians first in the campaign preceding the Polish partition of 1792, then in the insurrection led by Thaddeus Kosciusko, and finally as a general in the *grande armée* during Napoleon's 1812 campaign. His last words were uttered at the battle of Leipzig, where he covered the retreat of French troops. Cut off from aid, he plunged his horse into the Pleisse River and was drowned.

Many people in attendance found all the patriotic bluster ridiculous. How will these flags from Boston serve the brave Poles? This demonstration of enthusiasm for their cause would have some bearing on reality if money were sent along with the fine phrases. In fact, there was barely enough to cover the cost of the ceremony. I met any number of sensible people who took a dim view of this foolishness but couldn't prevail against the youths who organized the event and set everything in motion.

The news we receive is so implausible that I am loath to comment on the subject, except to say that Europe seems to me a volcano about to erupt. While the political world engenders revolutions in Europe, here physical nature is prey to frightful convulsions. All the talk is about enormous hurricanes and appalling devastations; New Orleans, the Antilles, have been the theater of these calamities.

I'm running out of room. I don't want to end my letter without telling you something about the penal system; you wouldn't guess that that is why we're here in Boston, but we seriously devoted three days to it and haven't finished our research. We've consulted the best authorities in the field: Messieurs Dwight, Clay, Gray, etc. We visited two very well maintained prisons, organized according to the new model, whose basic principle is solitary confinement. The advantages of this system are widely recognized and have been adopted by almost every state of the Union. Not for a moment do I doubt its superiority. The only obstacle to its introduction in France will be its cost. Such establishments are easily constructed by a nation with nothing to weigh upon its budget but the expenses of internal administration. Our situation is quite different; I believe that we should aim for incremental improvements. And when it comes to building a prison, it will cost no more to build it one way or another.

We shall come home rich in documents and observations. We

shall be incontestably *the universe's foremost penitentiarists.* May we find a government intact, to which we can report on our mission!

Tocqueville to Ernest de Chabrol, Boston, September 17, 1831

. . . All the news from Europe has combined with the irreparable loss [of the abbé Lesueur] . . . to shroud my mind in such sadness and discouragement as estrange me from my surroundings; I look at what I see without intelligence or interest.

I believe that only in a happy or at least tranquil frame of mind can one apply oneself to theoretical subjects, and right now current events are overwhelming me: I cannot bring myself to ponder the institutions, mores, and laws of a foreign country when my own is in such a critical state. Nor can I entertain myself with conjectures as to what America will become four centuries hence when, for all I know, France is embroiled in a civil war or in conflict with another nation. In short, my regrets, my hopes, and my fears are over there with you. Only my body is in America.

A vessel that left England last August 6 has just brought news that Laffitte came up just five votes short of being elected president and that the well-known republican, Salverte, was elected one of the vice presidents.[7] Casimir Perier withdrew, but it is said that a ministry of centrist legislators has succeeded him.

What does all that mean? In the general picture there is something incoherent and absurd, confounding the imagination. One thing seems clear to me, however: affairs are getting steadily worse. Whichever ministry succeeds C. Perier will be dragged into war.

If the Chamber has an extreme left majority, it will turn every-

7. Jacques Laffitte, a former regent of the Bank of France, played an important part in putting Louis-Philippe on the throne in 1830 and served the king as a minister without portfolio. Eusèbe de Salverte was a liberal member of the legislature elected from Paris.

thing upside down. If, as I believe will be the case, parties balance one another, it will be just moderate enough to give the nation its fill of moderation, without being wise enough, or strong enough to make order prevail. It will be pulled to the right and left according to the passions of the moment, without wielding power or enjoying consideration; and it will end up wretchedly by passing an electoral law more democratic that the one that brought it into existence.

I confess that this electoral result, which I didn't anticipate, leads me to envisage the future—the near future, not the distant one—through very dark lenses. . . .

Beaumont to his brother Achille, September 25

Tocqueville and I are still in Boston. We have a rolling fire of engagements and are constantly on the move. This is unquestionably the most interesting city we've seen until now. As we meet people of every walk, from all nations and of every view, we do our utmost to get to the heart of things. . . . Every minute of our day is accounted for; we are flooded with invitations; we almost never dine at our hotel and have attended a ball or a political meeting every evening. We have encountered men of truly wide-ranging knowledge, among others a German, M. Lieber, whose radical political views earned him expulsion from Germany. It took time in America to temper his republicanism. Now that he has seen for himself the differences between America and Europe, he regards as *ideologues* those who would impose the American form of government upon us. He devotes his exile to compiling a work entitled *The Encyclopedia Americana*. Seven volumes have already appeared. This book, which is held in high esteem, has been bought by a publisher for a trifling 100,000 francs. He gave us a copy.

Occasionally I also see M. Sparks,[8] an American at work on a history of the United States. He has culled historical documents from all over the world, among them, letters of men and women who have figured in political life over the past thirty years. He showed them to me; there is Washington's correspondence, many letters of Madame de Staël, of Louis-Philippe (written during the emigration), of La Fayette, etc. The latter sent a truly curious letter from prison in Olmutz, condemning the "new infamies of Monsieur d'Orléans" and referring to the "horrible assassination" of Louis XVI by the Convention in '93.

Poor La Fayette! Here he is considered a simpleton; the English word applied to him is "visionary." The same people who have a low opinion of his political sense deck him with laurels and continually profess their admiration.

Tocqueville to his mother, Boston, September 27, 1831

I received, three days apart, dear Mama, the mails of July 30 and August 10. I deeply appreciate the pains you take writing to me; I never dared count on such an abundant correspondence; and when I think of the effort a letter costs you, yours, I assure you, become all the more precious. I must say, however, that opening the thick sheaf from France without seeing our good friend's script is terribly painful. I can't get used to it. Every packet brought me evidence of his tenderness, in letters so imbued with charm that one would want to preserve them, even if they were addressed to someone else! Their absence chills my heart. I've

8. Jared Sparks, with whom Tocqueville frequently corresponded during his stay in America, was a Unitarian pastor and editor of the *North American Review* in the 1820s. He later published *The Life and Writings of George Washington* in twelve volumes and, in 1849, succeeded Edward Everett as president of Harvard University.

already asked others to thank you, dear Mama, but I want to do so now for all the care you gave him in his final hours; I'm more touched than if I had received it myself. Our old friend will have seen how dear he was to us; and dying will have been made easier. I deeply regret that I wasn't near him, that I didn't receive his last blessing. Denied that consolation, I have been swept up, every day, into work that distances my mind from the loss we suffered and prevents me from revisiting, as I should—as I want to—the memory of his affection and his examples. I hope, however, that if he sees what is happening inside us—and I don't doubt that he does—he realizes that I am not ungrateful. So long as I live he will have a secure place in my soul.

I fear, dear Mama, that you and other members of the family exaggerate the advantages to be gained from this voyage. One thing it will clearly do, as I see it, is give me experience and furnish me, on most of the subjects troubling France, ideas that may one day be of practical use. But will I ever write anything about this country? The truth of the matter is, I have absolutely no idea. Everything I see, everything I hear, everything I perceive—perceive still from afar—is a tangle in my mind and I scarcely know whether I shall ever have the time or power to sort things out. Portraying a society as vast and heterogeneous as this one would be an immense labor. Meanwhile, I continue quite relentlessly to cull all kinds of documents.

We depart today for Hartford, in Connecticut. We shall be in Philadelphia toward October 6.

Adieu, my dear Mama. I think of all of you incessantly. I embrace you, my father, my brothers and my sisters, both of whom have sent me the most affectionate letters. I am including a letter for my uncle Rosambo.[9]

9. Louis Le Peletier de Rosambo (1777–1856), Madame Louise de Tocqueville's brother. Alexis was close to him.

Tocqueville to Ernest de Chabrol, Hartford, October 7, 1831

. . . Our sojourn in Boston was extremely useful; we met a multitude of distinguished men and found precious documents. But it is constantly borne in on us that the greatest obstacle to learning is not knowing.

About any number of points, we don't know what questions to ask because we don't know how France works, and the mind is stymied if it has no basis for making comparisons. . . . What strikes the traveler most in this country, whether or not he is disposed to reflect upon it, is the spectacle of a society that walks on its own, without benefit of a guide or a crutch, thanks to the cooperation of individual wills. Racking one's brains in an effort to locate the government makes no sense; government is imperceptible, and the truth of the matter is that, in a manner of speaking, it doesn't exist.[10]

You may gather that to understand this state of affairs one must carefully disassemble the social body, examine each component, and see how it operates within its sphere of action so that the whole forms a nation. To carry out this project, one must have reflected much more than I have ever done, for lack of time, on the principles that regulate in general the administration of a country.

At least I would like to know *the facts* of government in France. As I just said, government is so negligible here that I am having

10. Tocqueville noted in his journal on October 1 that he had questioned John Quincy Adams about the "lack of government" in the United States and the phenomenon of "Conventions" (two of which, the Free Trade Convention and Friends of Domestic Industry, were soon to be held). Adams replied that he found the assemblies dangerous because they usurp the place of political bodies and threaten to impede their action.

difficulty understanding how it can be so consequential in France. The twelve hundred employees of the ministry of the interior seem inexplicable to me. I know that you have never given any more thought to administrative matters than I have. I am therefore not asking you for general principles, but perhaps you could obtain precious practical information for me. . . .

Tocqueville to his father, Hartford, October 7, 1831

We left Boston three days ago, dear Papa, and are now in Hartford. It is a small town, the capital of the state of Connecticut, on the banks of a river bearing that name. Its greatest merit, from our viewpoint, is the fact that it lies a stone's throw from one of America's most famous prisons, Wethersfield. As we have been favored with superb autumn weather, we come and go on foot, which is virtuous and economical.

Wethersfield's balance sheet is the strongest argument for the discipline of American prisons. Before reform, it cost the state thirty thousand francs annually; today it shows a profit of forty thousand. These are not theories but figures proven and supported by documents. It is probable, however, that upon our return you will find us less *clear-cut* on the subject of the American prison system than when we left France. We are not exceptions to the rule that people speak with greatest assurance and certitude about that which they know imperfectly. Now that we have a better grasp of our subject, we are sure of only two things, the first being that the American system is more economical than ours, the second that men who enter it are never worse when they emerge. But are they truly reformed? You sitting there in the corner of your fireplace can answer that question as well as I. All I can say for sure is that I would not trust my purse to these gentlemen.

You could, dear Papa, do me a great favor—one that will not,

I think, require a very considerable sacrifice of the leisure you now enjoy. It has to do with something that especially interests me in the United States, the internal administration of each state and of the Union as a whole. I am trying to understand as best I can the way in which administrative responsibilities are apportioned among town councils, larger provincial bodies, and the central government. I am stymied in this research by one problem. I have no basis of comparison for discerning the idiosyncratic features and measuring the importance of a given fact. To judge America rightly, nothing would be more useful than a knowledge of France. In the latter I am totally deficient. I know, generally speaking, that our government meddles in almost everything; the term "centralization" has been dinned into me a hundred times, with no elaboration. I have had neither the time nor the occasion to study any part of France's intricate administrative machinery. On the other hand you, to satisfy your intellect and out of sheer necessity, have wrapped your mind around it, dear Papa. You have seen the administration at work in matters large and small, and I believe that your familiarity is such that you will be able, without inconveniencing yourself, to furnish me the documents I need.

I would like to know what we have in the way of internal administration: what, first of all, are the accepted principles of a general nature; secondly, how are they applied, that is, what is the township's portion of independence, what can it do and not do; what functions lie within the competence of district and departmental councils; and finally, in precisely what do the prefect and the central government have a hand. If you can break down for me this word "centralization" you would be rendering me an immense service not only for the present, but also for the future.

As you see, that is a factual task. If, in a second part, you could append some political observations, the whole would be far more useful. Thus, I would like to know your opinion as to where the line should be drawn against action by the central government; what kind of independence can be prescribed for townships; the utility of administrative tribunals; how much power can safely be vested in departmental assemblies. The problem is that (assuming you accept this modest assignment) you will have to send me the results without delay, for time is flying and our sojourn is short. Put the memoir in an envelope addressed to me, and send it to Monsieur Prime with a cover letter requesting that it be forwarded as economically as possible. I recommend that you do this because postal rates are ruinous in the United States and a bulky package would reach me as well on a public coach as by official post. In comparison, transatlantic rates, even for the bulkiest letters, are negligible.

Apropos of transatlantic, I note with great pleasure that you have been sending all my letters in each mail; I was afraid that you intended to do the opposite and would have been terribly vexed. Letters are half our existence here; not receiving them punctually would be an intolerable deprivation. I assure you that there is no expense I regret less than payment for mail received. I only regret not having to pay more often. Packets are now hopelessly slow; I have heard nothing of the one that left France forty-eight days ago; its immediate predecessor took forty-nine days to cross.

I've fallen behind in my correspondence with Hippolyte, Émilie, and Alexandrine but can't catch up right now. Beg them on my behalf, dear Papa, not to be annoyed. We have so much to do that life proceeds in *spurts.* Every day brings a new task. If we stopped for a minute, we would be buried in the accumulation. As for America, I won't know what to make of it until I've left. One must give up the idea of understanding anything in depth when one impression follows on the heels of another. A few general ideas survive the phantasmagoria, a few large results, which may, later on, shed light on details, when one has time to study them.

You are undoubtedly wondering, dear Papa, why my script is shaky and even less legible than usual; the reason is, I'm on a restless steamboat. Today we left Hartford at noon and are sailing down the Connecticut River; tomorrow, at six in the morning, we arrive in New York. We shall remain there for only two days and hurry down to Philadelphia.

We are very eager to visit this second city. A remarkable event is now unfolding there: all the parties that champion free trade have sent delegates to what the Americans call a *convention*. It is a large assembly which, outside the precinct of state powers, discusses one or another of the questions most apt to stir political passions in this country, addresses pertinent articles of the Constitution, and, under the pretext of drafting a petition to Congress, really plays the role of Congress. We are very curious to see the inner workings of this convention. In so doing, we shall be observing one of the more extreme consequences of the dogma of popular sovereignty.

Adieu, dear Papa, I embrace you warmly, and my mother, my brothers, and sisters.

P.S. I am sending you a report for the attorney general. I would appreciate your reading it and having d'Aunay do the same before forwarding it to its addressee.

Beaumont to his mother, October 7, written from Hartford

To return to my account of our life in Boston, people live well there, the one drawback being that they drink too much. It was all we could do to avoid toasts made in our honor. Dinner is customarily served at two or three and lasts until late afternoon because here, as in England, guests remain at table after the meal, drinking and conversing. One can, however, excuse oneself at six without giving offense, which is what we always did because we were expected elsewhere. Elsewhere would generally be a tearoom where, beginning at six-thirty or seven, we sat for an hour or two with acquaintances digesting our meal. We would then return to our hotel and change into evening dress. We attended balls or dance soirées every evening and sometimes two or three in succession.

Among the people whose society proved most interesting and pleasurable were M. Webster, America's preeminent orator, and M. Adams,[11] the former president, a man of wit and intriguing conversation, who impresses one as a kind of dethroned king. Also interesting to us was M. Channing,[12] a highly meritorious writer. We have been given a whole collection of books, pamphlets, and memoirs. It amused us that we never left an author's house empty-handed. Whenever we were presented to one, we guessed that a few compliments would be bait enough to land his latest work, and we never guessed wrong.

Tocqueville to the comtesse de Grancey,[13] New York, October 10, 1831

I cannot tell you, my dear cousin, how touched I was by the letters you and your mother sent me. Words of friendship do the

11. Daniel Webster, who in 1831 was a senator from Massachusetts, and John Quincy Adams, sixth president of the United States, who had been defeated in his bid for reelection in 1828 by Andrew Jackson. Two years later Adams won a seat in the House of Representatives.

12. William Ellery Channing, Unitarian minister of the First Federal Church in Boston. A famous pulpit orator, he professed a Christian humanism that influenced the Transcendentalist movement.

13. Eugénie, comtesse de Grancey, was the daughter of the marquise de Cordoue, née Montboisier, a granddaughter of Malesherbes and first cousin of Alexis de Tocqueville's mother.

most good when one is grief-stricken. Under any other circumstance I would have felt ashamed of lagging behind you in our correspondence, but I confess that [shame] was completely dispelled by the pleasure of your writing, and by my gratitude for all the nice things you had to say. I thank you, dear friend, for your help. You know our domestic life well enough to calculate the degree of our misfortune. Many people believe that we suffered an ordinary bereavement, but you know that we are mourning the loss of someone who was a father to us in his tenderness and care. It was on his knee that we learned moral discernment; it was he who gave us that childhood education whose lasting effect has been to make us honorable men, if not distinguished ones. I confess that this sorrowful event has seriously dulled the daily interest I was taking in my voyage. The objects around me are still the same, but they appear in a different light. There are indeed moments when I would like to find myself back in Europe, and yet I assure you that the prospect of a return is now tinged with bitterness.

You are undoubtedly already acquainted with most of the details of our voyage, dear cousin. We have been treated impeccably in this country, [although] the informality and impertinent manners of *men of consequence* take some getting used to. I must confess that we exploit to the utmost a very natural misconception into which all Americans blunder. The United States has no literature, no eloquence, no wars, no plagues, no fine arts, few major crimes—none of those things that command attention in Europe. Here people savor the blandest happiness imaginable. Political life consists in discussing whether a bridge needs to be built or a road repaired. A fine prison therefore looms as large as the pyramid of Cheops. . . . And we who are regarded in some sense as the penal system incarnate, . . . because the French government commissioned us to visit American prisons—how can we be anything but men of the first rank? What is greater than a prison? If we told Americans that only a handful of people in France have ever heard of a penal system, and that the French government is so innocent of the far-sighted views imputed to it that it probably doesn't know that it has two commissioners traveling in America, they would no doubt be astonished. But you will agree that veracity consists not in saying all that is true but in not saying what is false. I shall admit, moreover, that *Glory* has its drawbacks; the penal system being a French invention, we must, willy-nilly, turn it to good account every day. . . . Wherever we go in polite society, our hostess or her daughter, next to whom one or the other of us is purposely seated, would consider it a lapse of savoir-vivre not to talk to us about gallows and lock-ups. Only after exhausting a subject known to be of vital interest to us, about which it is presumed we have something to say, does one try to steer conversations toward more vulgar subjects.

You cannot imagine, dear cousin, the whirlwind in which we've been spinning since our arrival here. One scarcely has the time to collect one's wits: ideas, impressions, faces fly past us in unbelievably swift succession. We are swept along by a current in which one cannot hold still for a moment. This manner of observing things on the run does not suit a man as inattentive as myself. Most of the time I remember what I had to ask someone just after I've seen him for the last time. But I must confess that this feverish state has its charms. The monotony of Versailles was killing me. Isn't the great point of this life to forget as far as possible that one exists? Well, I challenge anyone to imagine an existence (ministers' lives excepted) that draws a man out of himself more completely than ours. Apropos of ministers, . . . I believe that what kills them once they've left office is that, having long been strangers to themselves, they cannot get used to living constantly in their own company.

This has been a long digression from America. I left off, I believe, when we arrived at New York. After six weeks in that city we felt the need to talk about things other than prisons and resolved to slip away for an extended tour of the West. We wanted to see the *wilderness* and *Indians.* But you wouldn't believe how hard it is now to find these two things in America. We walked for more than a hundred leagues in the state of New York following the track of . . . savages without encountering any. We were told that the Indians had still been there ten years ago, eight years ago, two years ago, but European civilization is advancing like a forest fire and driving them before it. At last we arrived at Buffalo, on the shore of the Great Lakes, without having seen a single one. How could we return to France without an image of a savage in the virgin forest? It was unthinkable. As luck would have it, a steamboat bound for the shores of Lake *Michigan* and the entrance to Lake *Superior* was departing Buffalo at just that moment. We made up our minds to seize the opportunity, and thereupon added a mere five hundred leagues to our voyage. This time, as it turned out, we were completely satisfied; we cruised along vast shores, where white people haven't yet cut down a single tree, and we visited any number of Indian nations. I hope one day to be able to relate the many incidents that occurred during this great voyage, but today I must restrict myself.

They are a most peculiar people, these Indians! They think that when a man has a blanket to cover himself with, a weapon with which to kill game, and a beautiful sky overhead, he has all that good fortune can provide. He despises the yearnings and seekings of our civilization. It is absolutely impossible to bend him to any of our ways. He and his fellows are the proudest creatures in creation. He smiles with pity at all the measures we take to protect ourselves against fatigue and bad weather; rolled up in his blanket under a tree, he believes himself superior to the president of the United States and the governor of Canada. Of all my European accoutrements, the only item that Indians envied was my double-barreled gun; this weapon made much the same impression on them as the penal system on Americans. I remember an old chief whom we met on the banks of Lake Superior seated near his fire in a state of immobility befitting someone of his rank. I sat down next to him and we chatted amicably, thanks to a French Canadian interpreter. He examined my rifle and observed that it was not made like his. I then told him that my gun did not fear rain and could shoot in the water. He wouldn't believe me; but I fired it in front of him after submerging it in a nearby stream. This demonstration left the Indian agog; he examined the weapon once again and declared emphatically: "The brothers of the Canadians are great warriors!" As we were parting, I noticed two long hawk feathers on his head. I asked him what this ornament signified. He flashed an agreeable smile, displaying two rows of teeth that would have terrified a wolf, replied that he had killed two Sioux (the name of an enemy tribe), and that these feathers were the tokens of his double victory. "Would you be willing to surrender one to me?" I asked. "I would wear it in my country and proclaim that I received it from a great chief." I seem to have struck a sensitive chord, for my man stood up, detached one of the feathers, and presented it to me with a grand, slightly comical gesture. Then he . . . extended a large bony hand, and shook mine so hard that I had trouble freeing myself from his grip. As for Indian women, I shall say only that one must read *Atala* before coming to America. In order to be considered perfect, an Indian woman must have a chocolate complexion, the small eyes of a feral cat, and a mouth that slits her face more or less from ear to ear. So much for nature; then there's art, and she is not without devices. While European women rouge their cheeks, she takes greater pains, drawing blue, black, and white lines on hers.

Moreover, here as in France there are those geniuses of fashion who dare to innovate. Thus, I remember having met a young Indian woman whose face was painted half black and half red, right up to the rim of her eyes. But I think that this was an infelicitous experiment. I needn't tell you that people, however great their prestige, don't always succeed in having the singularities they invent adopted. What is more generally done—one might even call it a classic style in the toilette of Indian women—is piercing the septum between the nostrils and introducing a large ring. I find this abominable. And yet I very humbly ask you to explain to me why piercing ears is more natural than piercing the nose. There is one last respect in which the beauties of Lake Superior are different from ours. You know that among us feet are tortured into pointing outward. Would you believe it, Indian women undergo the same torture to produce the opposite effect? to have their feet point inward? They are decidedly poor, pitiful savages.

In any event, I seized the opportunity to buy slippers from them, called moccasins, which they wear on important occasions. If these objects pique your curiosity I will be more than happy to offer them to you. Each of these moccasins is large enough to house two of your feet, if I remember your dimensions correctly. I do not pretend, therefore, that they will serve any practical purpose. You must pardon the enormity of my letter, dear cousin. You see that I never know how to do the proportionate thing. First I don't write, then I write too much. I hope, however, that you will blame my silence on the penal system, and my loquacity on the pleasure it gives me to converse with you after a long hiatus. I am calling upon the generous side of your nature. Allow me to protest once again my very lively and sincere affection.

Tocqueville to the vicomte Ernest de Blosseville,[14] New York, October 10, 1831

Relying heavily on your good will, sir, I would like to ask of you a favor that, although not difficult for you, will catch you in the midst of your many occupations. You know that, quite apart from prisons, we are paying close attention to everything connected with judicial institutions. First we examined regular courts, then special courts; up to now we have nowhere found a trace of administrative judges resembling in the least our prefectural councils and Council of State.[15] Administrative matters do indeed exist. But by whom are they adjudicated? How does one dispense with properly constituted administrative tribunals? What are the political consequences of this scheme? These are questions that remain opaque for us.

I confess that what hinders me the most in trying to figure out how things work in America is my almost complete ignorance of French institutions. You know that in our country administrative law and civil law are two separate worlds, neither friendly nor hostile enough to know each other well. I have always lived in one and know nothing of what occurs in the other. To acquire

14. Blosseville was a member of the legislature, the Chamber of Deputies. Tocqueville had met him in 1830, when Blosseville was serving the prefecture of Seine-et-Oise as a counselor. He had written *L'Histoire de la colonisation pénale et des établissements de l'Angleterre en Australie* [On Penal Colonization and English Establishments in Australia], the first volume of which appeared in 1831. Five years earlier he had been asked by the French government for advice on the feasibility of establishing a French penal colony in western New Holland (Australia).

15. The Council of State (Conseil d'État) is an organ of French government that provides the executive branch with legal advice, and functions as the administrative court of last resort.

the general notions I sorely lack in this respect, I thought that I could do no better than appeal to you.

Am I being presumptuous in asking you to trace briefly the constitution of our administrative tribunals and the principal rules of their competence? To importune you further, I would like your thoughts about the usefulness of these tribunals, the political influence they can exert. What I want, in a word, is information not found in books, whose greatest value consists in its being furnished by a man of your judgment and scope.

I need not add that if you are curious to have *factual* documents about America, I would be happy to furnish them; in any event, I would try my best to do so. As for the present, do not take it amiss if I tell you nothing about the United States. Since our arrival, we have seen so many men and things that whenever we wish to speak about America, we are immediately confounded by a swarm of ideas and memories.

Please accept, sir, my respectful wishes. Beaumont has asked to be remembered to you.

To M. Bouchitté,[16] New York, October 11, 1831

In your last letter, my dear friend, you wanted me to describe the state of public instruction in the United States. Before answering, I must remind you again that you must not place absolute faith in what I say. There are twenty-four states in the Union, and their different positions, not to mention their vanity, tend to produce singular discrepancies of law. I shall therefore tell you only about

16. Louis Bouchitté was a former professor of history at the collège de Versailles and an inspector of schools in the Paris region. He had written philosophical treatises on the relationship between fine arts, morality, and religion. He and Tocqueville met at Versailles in the 1820s and maintained their friendship until Bouchitté's death in 1857.

those states I have seen. But they are the most powerful, enlight-ened ones.

The general rule, in matters of public instruction, is that every-one is free to found a school and to direct it as he or she sees fit. It is just another industry, whose *consumers* are the judges and with which the state does not interfere in any way. You will want to know if this unlimited freedom produces bad results. I believe just the opposite. But note that none of the antireligious passions that torment us have gained the upper hand here. Therefore, the great-est danger associated with freedom of education in France does not exist in America. Left to follow their natural bent, men always prefer moral and religious schools to all others. A remarkable fact is that in this America where no state religion holds sway, educa-tion is almost entirely the province of the clergy, or rather, of *cler-gies:* they absolutely dominate and direct the instruction of youth.

I told you that complete freedom of education is the general rule, but an exception is made for schools founded by the state itself; or rather, in this case, the state assumes the right of individ-uals, which is that of directing the schools it founds, however it wishes to do so. This has far-reaching effects, as you will see for yourself: in all of New England and in the state of New York, for example, the law compels every commune (their commune, called a *township,* being an aggregate of three or four thousand souls) to maintain a free school, or one that charges minimal tuition; fur-ther, the state has *a school fund* whose purpose is to encourage com-munes and to assist them in fulfilling their obligation. If they flout the law, they are penalized. There is much to say about this system; my only observation is that the state exerts, directly or indirectly, a right of surveillance and direction over its schools. In the state of New York there exists a commissioner responsible for inspecting all the schools every year, examining the masters, the schoolchildren, the schoolbooks, and submitting a report to the legislature. This seemed too governmental in the New England states, which vested these powers in local committees elected annually. Their reports are published, but there is no unity imposed upon public instruction. There you have the American system in a nutshell, as much as I was able to make of it. In point of fact the state plays the biggest part in the direction of public instruction. But it supervises only its own establishments; it has no all-encompassing right.

The effort made in this country to disseminate learning is truly prodigious. The universal and sincere faith professed in the efficacy of knowledge strikes me as one of America's most remarkable features, all the more because for me this is still an open question. But it is absolutely in the American grain, whatever people's political or religious beliefs may be. Catholics, Unitarians, deists, all march together. The result is one of those quiet but irresistible movements born of a common and universal impulse; there has never been a people as enlightened as that living in the north of the United States. . . . But does this redound to the advantage of morality? I'm not yet convinced of it. We could spend a year and a day discussing this question, and I am pressed for time. Adieu.

FROM PHILADELPHIA TO NEW ORLEANS

This leg of the journey lasted from October 12, 1831, to January 3, 1832. Tocqueville and Beaumont spent several weeks in Philadelphia, with an excursion to Baltimore, before heading west again, this time across Pennsylvania's Allegheny Mountains and down the Ohio River to Louisville, whence they continued overland to Memphis. There, before boarding a paddle steamer bound for New Orleans, they witnessed the deplorable spectacle of Choctaw Indians exiled from their native lands being transported across the Mississippi.

Beaumont to his father, October 16

We arrived at Philadelphia on the 12th. This city of about 200,000 souls resembles none that we've seen until now. It is laid out with a regularity one is tempted to call too perfect. All the streets are aligned with geometric precision and all cross the entire city in one direction or the other. All the buildings are clean, carefully maintained, and look like new. It is a charming city, a place fit for people who don't own a carriage, since every street has wide sidewalks. Its one defect, I repeat, is its monotonous beauty. As for its inhabitants, my acquaintance with them is slight. We brought a multitude of letters of introduction and promptly had many delivered to their addresses but are yet to enjoy much society for having been taken captive, upon our arrival, by men associated with the penal system. Nowhere do prisons—the running of them, the theories underpinning them, and everything else relevant to incarceration—occupy more of civic consciousness than in Philadelphia. The society of prisons lost no time appointing a commission to furnish us all the documents we may need.

The day after our arrival, we had to digest a big dinner at which we were surrounded by all of the region's philanthropists. I believe that philanthropic theories, the wise application of which we saw in other states, are abused in Philadelphia. The prison is truly a palace. Its construction is insanely expensive, with each inmate enjoying all the conveniences of life in his own cell, and each cell costing two or three thousand francs! I wonder how we'd manage in France if we had to build such prisons for thirty-two thousand convicts. (That is the number of prisoners the country had at last count.) Though we are both equally struck by the defects of such a system, it behooves us to continue our examination as probingly and attentively as we would if we had some hope of profiting from it. The Philadelphians are well-intentioned people who ascribe immense importance to their experiment. . . .

As for our evenings, here is how we have spent them so far. The first day, we went to the theater. Some actors from New Orleans were performing a French play, *Napoléon à Schoenbrunn et à Sainte-Hélène* [by Charles Dupeuty]. It was strange for us to see on an American stage a play we saw in Paris at the Porte-Saint-Martin, but apart from curiosity there was nothing else to arrest us: the theater itself is frightful and the actors detestable. The next day we were invited to a musical soirée at the home of

M. Walsh, a very distinguished Philadelphian. The singing was *adequate*, which is to say that no Americans, male or female, participated in it: it featured an Italian man and French women. The Americans, who are frigid by nature, wondered whether the Italian, gesticulating and striking histrionic poses as he sang, was possibly a lunatic. The concert ended with several waltzes and quadrilles. We spent the following evening at the philosophical society of Philadelphia, under the auspices of M. Duponceau,[1] a very erudite ex-Frenchman, who is the president of this society. I was thoroughly bored and found no one I had any desire to see again. Yesterday, we dined at the home of M. de Choiseul,[2] ex-prefect of Corsica and [Jean-Benôit] Lantivy's successor, now French consul in Charleston, who happens just now to be in Philadelphia with his family. Madame is a good sort and the two daughters are pleasant, attractive young women. He himself seems to be a very nice fellow, but the man is an incredible numbskull and we sometimes look at each other amazed that anyone as stupid as he could have been given responsibility for administering all of Corsica. . . .

1. Born in 1760, Pierre-Étienne du Ponceau (or Duponceau) accompanied Baron Friedrich von Steuben to America at age seventeen as his secretary and became his aide-de-camp when the baron joined the revolutionary army. He settled in Philadelphia, opened a law practice, and became an authority in international law. He wrote prolifically about problems of philology.

2. Comte Xavier de Choiseul administered Corsica for only several weeks, having been appointed prefect in April 1830 by the Bourbon regime and transferred to a minor diplomatic post after the Revolution of July 1830. A later reports suggests that Choiseul did not forcefully make his presence felt in Charleston: "M. de Choiseul resides in North Carolina and comes from time to time to Charleston. There he stays at a hotel. The consulate, on the fourth floor of an apartment building, has no seal, very little furniture, and no office equipment."

Tocqueville to his sister-in-law Alexandrine, Philadelphia, October 18, 1831

It must be said, dear sister, that you are singular people, over there in Europe. About six weeks ago, it was thought, imagined, or at least hoped—according to my informant—that you were preparing to give me a nephew.[3] I rejoiced but didn't yet dare communicate my joy for fear that my letter might cause you pain if the announcement proved false. I have been waiting impatiently for confirmation of the news; more than a month has elapsed, and the matter is so hushed up one would think you were carrying the heir to the Chinese Empire. In the last mail, August 20, neither my father nor my mother, nor Hippolyte nor—wonder of wonders—Édouard, had one word to say. Since my mind is not inclined to think the worst, I suppose that this silence means that hopes are confirmed; but why not say so explicitly? When one is present at events, one always imagines that what one knows and sees is known and seen by absentees; in fact one should realize that with the latter one must start from scratch and work on the assumption that one's correspondent always needs new details. The fact that everyone is telling me how much more satisfied you are with your state of health leads me to believe, however, that the outcome one hoped for two months ago has come to pass. I know that you do not do things by halves. Despite my reasoning I await the next mail impatiently. When will it arrive? God only knows. The Atlantic crossings are now extremely slow: the August 29 packet was fifty-nine days at sea, the one that left on September 1 has yet to make port and nothing augurs its imminent arrival as the wind has been blowing westerly for several days.

3. Édouard and Alexandrine's second child, Hubert, was not born until February 1832.

We left New York a week ago and have set up here. Philadelphia is a huge city: your map will convince you of it, as it
occupies all the land between two rivers, the Delaware and the
Schuylkill. Its houses, which follow the English model in having
no carriage entrances, are all made of brick, and the streets are
drawn in a straight line. This regularity is tedious, but most con-
venient. Philadelphia is, I believe, the only city in the world where
streets are distinguished from one another by number rather than
name. The layout is so regular that, starting with street no. 1 at
the Delaware, one advances from number to number clear across
to the Schuylkill. I am living on street no. 3. Don't you agree that
it took a people uniquely bereft of imagination to invent such a
scheme? Europeans, without fail, attach an idea to every external
object: a saint, a famous man, an event. But these people know
only arithmetic.

Otherwise, I must say nothing disparaging about them, for
they continue to treat us wonderfully well; Philadelphia above all
is besotted with the penal system and, since the penal system is our
stock-in-trade, we are courted by one faction and another. There are
two types of men here prodigiously interested in prisons but viewing the matter from different angles: the theoreticians and the
pragmatists, those who write and those who act. Each rival hopes
to take us captive. A week before our arrival, the warden of the
prison presented his card to the French consul, requesting that he
be notified the instant we arrived, while the society founded to
examine penal theories convened at the same time and appointed a
commission to help us in our research. On one and the same day
we received an invitation to dinner from the warden and a letter
from a Quaker (the man of theory par excellence) who, without
using the honorific "Sir" and addressing us in the familiar "thou,"
pressed us to sup with him and several of his friends. It being our
business to hear everyone out without taking anyone at his word,

we cut excellent figures in the eyes of both parties and accept from all hands the books and meals they thrust upon us.

At heart they are all very good men, but the political rivalries —above all those that beset small towns—preoccupy them almost as much as if they were French. Someone said to me the other day: "The last elections resulted in prison directorships being taken away from very capable men." I asked him what elections had to do with prisons. "Not much," he answered, "but in that domain as in all others the victors get the spoils." You will agree that one need not travel two thousand leagues to see things of that sort.

Tell Édouard, dear sister, that I can't write to him today, but that I wish right away to compliment him on the charming verses he sent me; they are good from beginning to end and some better than that. I am trying to assemble for him the documents he has requested about banks. This country is, I believe, most instructive in that regard: there are thousands of banks, paper is everywhere replacing coin.

Since I am assigning you tasks, here is another one: tell my father that his anxiety about letters being opened is baseless. I have received them *all,* and all well sealed. What is there to fear about a piece of paper sent to America? I also beg you to tell him that, upon reflection, I believe it prudent to send me some money before my departure from this region; we are almost certain to have enough, but if the least mishap throws us off course, we would find ourselves in dire straits.

I learned with infinite pleasure that Monsieur O. [Ollivier] had at last returned to the bosom of his family. Please give him my news and assurance of my very warm attachment.

I have received reports about Denise. I can't wait to renew my acquaintance with her; my only concern is that she doesn't yet have teeth.

With that I must leave you, but not before embracing you very tenderly. Do the same on my behalf to father, mother, brothers, and sisters.

I don't know why Schérer thought that we wanted to go to Cuba. We never had any such intention; the voyage from New Orleans to Havana is very easy, but we would need three weeks and we can't spare even one for an object of curiosity.

I received from Monsieur de Belisle a charming letter to which I shall reply by the next mail.

Tocqueville to Ernest de Chabrol, Philadelphia, October 18, 1831

. . . The news from France seems a little more favorable now than a month ago. I've just found some French newspapers. I closely read the parliamentary debates. I have the impression that this legislature is inexperienced, but that its majority is far from being revolutionary. My hope is that we won't have too much to complain about if the great crises are at an end. As far as I can tell, parliament doesn't have one new man of any talent.

It is odd that a time of revolution should be so unproductive. I take consolation in this, mind you; the long-standing members will, as a result, retain a useful influence. What worries me is the attitude of the royalists; they are holding fire for the moment, but it's clear to me that the trouble brewing internally is far from dying down. If we should enter into conflict with a foreign power, civil war would break out, I'm sure of it.

Acting in concert with one's country's foes is, however, a pitiful expedient. I tell you that the thought of it makes me deeply sad, for myself and for France. Bound to the royalists as I am by a few common principles and a thousand family ties, I find myself in a way chained to a party whose conduct often strikes me as dishonorable and almost always extravagant. I can't help taking their faults deeply to heart, even as I condemn them with all my might.

The more I examine myself, dear friend, the more I think that I was not made to live in revolutionary times. If it had only been a matter of working for society, I would perhaps have been able to render service, but I could not march behind a party standard, no matter which one. Parties are always composed of passionate, credulous people who act out of conviction, and of rogues who follow them out of self-interest. Having a cool mind and some scruples, I don't conform to one type or the other.

What you said about finding it painful to leave Versailles for your holiday pleased me. I find it the easier to believe knowing as I do that your departure left one person bereft.

Every mail delivery brings me charming letters from Marie; they are the source of my greatest pleasure in this country. I've already told her so, but tell it to her again, on my behalf. . . .

Tocqueville to Eugène Stöffels, Philadelphia, October 18, 1831

. . . It was while traversing one of those forests [in Michigan] with Beaumont, led by an Indian guide, that I suddenly remembered that it was July 28!!![4] I can't tell you, my dear friend, how this memory affected me. I buried my face in my hands and for a moment was transported back to those scenes of civil war we witnessed together. Never perhaps has the past beset my imagination so forcefully. The sentiments, the passions that agitated me at that time, from my mother's living room to the little house in

4. The Revolution of 1830 began on July 28.

Saint-Cloud: it all seized my memory with unbelievable violence.[5] And when, afterward, I looked around me, contemplating a foreign scene—the darkness of the forest, the litter of fallen trees, the savage faces of our guides—I doubted for a moment that I was the same man whose memory had just recaptured these events. In any case, it seemed to me that more than a year had elapsed, and the truth is that I still can't believe it. The nocturnal tocsin, the rifle-fire in the streets, our leaving Paris, our armed patrols in Versailles, the nights spent in a guardhouse, it all still seems like a dream, the memory of someone else's life, not mine. . . .

I hope, dear friend, that your family is well. Édouard reports that his little girl is already giving him great happiness. I believe that you have the same to say. The more I gad about, the more I am led to believe that only domestic happiness has any meaning. Will I ever attain it? Truthfully, I doubt it. Reason tells me that it should be all that the human heart requires, but my passions object. When I am agitated and wandering, the idea of internal tranquillity seduces my imagination. As soon as I return to a regular way of life, the sameness of existence kills me: I become indescribably anxious. Emotional or physical excitement is such a commanding need that I will risk my life to purchase it; deprived of it, I squirm.

In short, there is no one in the world I know less well than myself; I am a permanently insoluble problem. I have a very cool head and a reasoning—even calculating—mind; at the same time, ardent passions carry me off without convincing me, subdue my will without compromising my reason. I see the good very clearly, and spite it every day.

5. Tocqueville witnessed the flight of Charles X and his entourage from the royal residence in Saint-Cloud on July 31.

Tocqueville to Charles Stöffels,[6] Philadelphia, October 22, 1831

I have long wanted to write to you, my dear Charles, but I've been swept up in a busy life that doesn't prevent me from thinking of good friends such as yourself, but deprives me of the leisure to tell them so. However, I shouldn't want my negligence to interrupt the flow of your letters, which always give me great pleasure. And in fact you don't have the same excuses as I do not to write. I see, from the tenor of your last letter, that you were sad and dejected, prey to a thousand doubts. No doubt that melancholy mood has dissipated by now. However, I would like to talk to you about it, because your cast of mind very often exposes you to that painful state, about which I can talk knowledgeably, as I have often experienced it.

If I'm not mistaken, my dear friend, you are living in a world of fantasy. I'm not blaming you; I myself have lived in that realm for a long time and despite my best efforts am often swept back into it. When one first embarks upon life as a youth, one feels that one's lot is to enjoy complete happiness or suffer boundless misfortune. I don't believe it; one's hopes and fears are excessive. Almost no man has ever been continually happy or unhappy. Life is therefore neither very good nor very bad, but rather—forgive the expression—a mediocre hotchpotch. One mustn't fear it too much, or expect too much of it, but see it for what it is, without revulsion or ardor—as an inevitable phenomenon which one hasn't produced, which one will not end, and, above all, which one must make tolerable. Don't think that I've arrived at this wisdom without inner turmoil, or that I am always equal to it; like you, like all men, I harbor an ardent passion that impels me to-

6. Charles Stöffels, like his brother Eugène, had been Tocqueville's schoolmate and friend at the collegiate school in Metz.

ward unlimited happiness and leaves me feeling that the absence of such happiness is the greatest imaginable misfortune. But trust me when I say that this is a weak passion, which one must oppose. It is not virile, and can result in nothing manly. Life is neither all pleasure nor all pain; it is a serious responsibility of which we are duty-bound to acquit ourselves as best we can. I assure you, my dear friend, that whenever I've envisioned life this way, the thought has been a wellspring of inner strength. It has allowed me to face the future with greater serenity, has given me more courage to endure the pains, the vexations, the monotony, the vulgarity of the present, and has bridled intemperate desires of every kind. Having more moderate expectations, I am less inclined to feel discouraged and more easily reconciled to reality.

There is yet another fantasy of early youth which one must guard against. When I first began to reflect upon the world, I believed that it was full of demonstrable truths; that one had only to look hard to see them. But when I applied myself to considering matters, all I perceived was a tangle of doubts. I don't have words, my dear Charles, to express the horrible state into which this discovery cast me. I've never been more miserable; I can only compare myself to a man who, seized with vertigo, feels the floor quaking underfoot and sees the walls around him shifting. I'm still horrified when I think about that period. I daresay I wrestled mightily with doubt and in a spirit of rare desperation. And only yesterday (!) did I convince myself that the search for absolute, demonstrable truth, like the search for perfect happiness, is futile. Which isn't to say that there aren't some truths worthy of our whole-hearted conviction, but you can be sure that they are very few. For the immense majority of questions to which we need answers, all we have are likelihoods, approximations. To despair over this is to despair over being human, for therein lies one of the most inflexible laws of our nature. Does it follow that man should never act because he can never be sure of anything? That is by no means my creed. When I must determine something important, I carefully weigh the pros and cons, and, instead of despairing over the lack of absolute certainty, I soldier on as if I had no doubts at all. Experience has taught me that it is better, all things considered, to strike out vigorously in the wrong direction than to stand paralyzed by indecision or to act feebly.

One must therefore resign oneself to the elusiveness of demonstrable truth. But, you say, the doubt to which one resigns oneself will always be a painful state. True, I consider doubt one of the great banes of existence; I place it right after sickness and death. But it is because I have this opinion of it that I don't understand why so many men impose it upon themselves gratuitously. That is why I have always considered metaphysics and all the purely theoretical sciences, which serve no useful purpose in the reality of life, as a willful torment that man has consented to inflict upon himself.

I'm at the bottom of the page and must finish. I hope you don't hold it against me that I've sent you a homily rather than a description of America. Adieu. I embrace you with all my heart. Keep this letter. I shall be glad to reread it one day.

Tocqueville to his mother, Philadelphia, October 24, 1831

I have nothing new to report about myself, dear Mama. Alexandrine will no doubt have read your last letter. My situation has not changed in any way since then: our life consists of prisons, learned societies, and soirées. I continue to feel well: that's a detail you will appreciate. Autumn, here, is admirable; the sky, pure and sparkling, as on the fairest summer days. The foliage is far more varied than in Europe at this time of year, displaying every shade of green and red; America appears in all its glory.

Don't believe half the unfavorable things S.[7] told you about this country. He doesn't know it at first-hand, and what he does know comes from a certain class of Frenchmen he kept exclusive company with and who, in America as elsewhere, seem to be representative of all that is flawed in the French mind. Along with England this is the most curious and instructive of countries to visit; and unlike England, it has the unique privilege of combining childhood and manliness, which gives it the world's most extraordinary appearance.

I confess that social intercourse with the country's inhabitants is not always agreeable. A great many smoke, chew tobacco, spit in your presence. For all that, they are a race of very remarkable men. If their manners are unbuttoned, they are admirably tolerant of free-and-easy behavior in their guests. Nothing is more difficult than riling an American. Unless you plant your fist in the middle of his face, it doesn't cross his mind that you mean to offend him; he attributes everything to chance and nothing to intention. These very things, however, are what make S. deeply indignant. He would willingly allow Americans to lie and steal, to be dissolute and irreligious, but let them step on your foot without excusing themselves, and launch a gob of spit without [taking the trouble to apologize], these are insufferable abominations that dishonor a people. The fact is—and I recognize it—that, generally speaking, they lack refinement, grace, and elegance; one is constantly aware in America of an upper class that, if it existed, or were not in its infancy, could set the fashion for everyone else. But that, after all, is only a matter of superficial importance. . . . You shall see that it amounts to very little. If I write a book about America, I shall undertake to do so in France, with the documents

7. "S." refers to Édouard Schérer, Tocqueville's fellow passenger on *Le Havre.*

I've acquired. I haven't yet studied them, but by the time I leave I shall be equipped to understand them: that is the plainest result of my voyage. Otherwise, all I have are disordered, incoherent notes, disparate ideas the key to which I alone possess, isolated facts that call to mind a hundred more. What I'm bringing back of greatest interest are two slim notebooks in which I have recorded verbatim the conversations I've had with America's most remarkable men. These scraps of paper are invaluable, but only to me, who can properly interpret the innuendo of questions and answers. The few general ideas I've thus far expressed about this country are in letters to family and one or two other French correspondents. Even they were formulated on the fly, aboard vessels or in some nook where my knees served as a table. Will I ever publish anything about America? The truth is, I don't know. It seems to me that I have good ideas; but I'm not yet sure where to place them, and airing them publicly frightens me.

Adieu, dear Mama; the wind is blowing from the east, so I hope to receive your news in two days. I would never have believed myself capable of loving rain; that, however, is what's happened since I've arrived in this country, for rain here is the east wind and the east wind speeds the packet from France.

To Ernest de Chabrol, Philadelphia, October 26, 1831

. . . The most recent mail delivery brought a letter from the mother of our friend Louis de M. informing me that:

1) Paris is beset by fear of cholera, and that

2) an admirable specific has just been discovered, namely Cajeput oil, which comes straight from China.[8] The genuine article is almost impossible to obtain in Paris, and I am asked to send

---

8. The Cajeput tree is native to Australia. Its oils have many herbal uses and are held in high regard in the East.

some from America. . . . I have in fact found some here; you can imagine how much faith I place in the remedy, but a friend's wish is my command. Fortunately it is taken in very small doses. So Beaumont and I purchased about two bottles of it and have decided to send them to you for apportioning. . . .

You will therefore have to supply yourself with phials after you receive the parcel. . . . I would like my contribution divided in three: one-third for Madame de K. [Kergorlay], another for my father, and the last for your neighbor [Mary Mottley]. I need not tell you to tap some for yourself from the two bottles. . . . I can't believe it will do any good, but in love as in religion one must make allowances for superstition. . . .

There's more to the story. The merchant who sold me Cajeput oil couldn't tell me whether it is prohibited by Customs. He advised me to label the bottles *Cubebs oil,*[9] which I've done. But I remembered afterward that Cubebs is a known cure for *syphilis,* of all things. I therefore thought it ill-advised to associate you with it openly; the name *Carné* is less recognizable than yours, and the package will reach you under that alias.

Phew! I'm out of the apothecary at last and free to address Bouchitté's questions.

He asks me first of all whether, as reported, Catholicism is gaining ground in the United States. I can answer with an emphatic yes. Its growth is prodigious. Forty years ago there were thirty Catholics in New York. The chapel of the Spanish consulate could accommodate all of them. Today there are thirty thousand, and they have built six churches at their own expense. The same is true in all the large cities, even Boston, the heartland of Puritanism, which has two Catholic churches and a convent. It is

9. The Cubeb or "tailed pepper" grows in Java and Sumatra, and like the Cajeput tree, it was valued in the East for oils reputed to have therapeutic qualities.

said that this religion is spreading rapidly out west. We found it to be almost universal in Canada. Today there are seven or eight hundred thousand Catholics in the United States, ten seminaries, and a great many establishments of various kinds.

Those are the facts. Now, what are the causes? The greatest is immigration; thousands of Catholics pour into the United States every year: Irish, French, German. It is said, furthermore, that there are numerous conversions, especially in frontier settlements. I can't prove it, but I can easily believe it; Protestantism has always struck me as being to the Christian religion what the constitutional monarchy is to politics—a kind of compromise between opposite principles, a way station between two different states, a system, in short, unequal to its own consequences and unable completely to satisfy the human spirit. As you know, I've always believed that constitutional monarchies would end up as republics; and I am likewise convinced that Protestantism, once it has run its course, will become natural religion. What I am telling you here is very keenly felt by many religious souls; they recoil from the prospect of their doctrines having this outcome, and fly to Catholicism, whose principle may be highly debatable, but where everything coheres.

Note that in the United States, treating religion flippantly is unimaginable. There is more wrangling over this subject here than anywhere else in the world; far be it from Americans to exhibit the indifference that, among us, forestalls the danger of infidelity. As a result, religion is still, along with politics, the subject most on people's minds. It is obvious that cold and calculating characters, argumentative and logical personalities, incline strongly to deism, whereas ardent souls, passionate imaginations, are drawn to Catholicism. The latter will one day find itself confronting natural religion, I don't doubt it, although I have no idea when the confrontation will occur.

What remains to be examined is the political situation of Catholics. . . .

Arrayed against them are a host of religious prejudices, but I venture to say that these do not at all affect their political status; by law and in practice they are on exactly the same footing as everyone else. In society they are indistinguishable from Protestants and are appointed or elected to the same offices: the attorney general of the United States is Catholic, as are members of Congress.

So much for the way they are viewed politically. But what is their own attitude? It may surprise you to learn that the demagogues and levelers over here are Catholics. It doesn't surprise me, convinced as I am—more than ever—that the Catholic religion inherently favors absolute monarchy, or anyway the aristocratic republic. I have conversed with many a priest and sense that just beneath the surface of their democratic sentiments is great contempt for popular rule, that they want to regiment and direct society. I believe, frankly speaking, that they profess tolerance only as a last resource. Why then are Catholics democrats? Because they are poor and Protestants are rich, because in almost all the countries from which they come, the aristocracy is Protestant. I don't deny that religions have a political bias but I believe that theorizers make too much of it. Religion can sway political opinion, no doubt about it, but one's social position and material interest are what hold ultimate sway.

As for the situation of Catholics as a religious community, one notes this curious twist, that Catholicism in America is at once more rational and more dependent on the pope than in Europe. Let me explain: thanks to the extreme fragmenting of Protestant sects, Catholicism is now the most numerous communion. It is compact in all its parts and marches as one. Here it has assumed the same proud and haughty attitude it displays everywhere else; staunch in its beliefs, it keeps to itself. While all Protestant sects greet one another, Catholicism, eternally immobile, won't shake anyone's hand. And yet, it has undergone change. It has quietly surrendered all it could without subverting its identity: there are no monasteries in America, no external practices of a ridiculous kind, no obvious superstitions. Catholicism makes a point of appealing to reason. It has to some degree forsaken the bombastic style that almost always characterizes pulpit language in Europe. It *professes* religious freedom and loudly declares that it *can* and *wants* to do without the state.

Even so, Americans are, of all the world's Catholics, those most dependent on the pope. There are several explanations for this singular state of affairs. In general, American Catholics are poor. For a very long time, they could not, despite their religious fervor, afford to create seminaries; as a result, most of their priests are foreigners who, having no ties to the flock and no authority conferred by the government, which doesn't concern itself with religion, naturally find themselves in the position of representing only the pontificate. Moreover, Catholics, scattered as they are over the immense American continent, do not yet have a common bond, a focal point of social organization, a collective power of resistance. One therefore sees the paradoxical phenomenon of the pope unilaterally appointing bishops in a democratic republic, prescribing discipline, doing all he cannot do in states governed according to political principles that more closely resemble those by which he himself wields power.[10]

One last observation, most telling of all perhaps. When Catholicism was founded over here, Europeans no longer had any say in the government of the church, and the civil authority alone

10. In France, according to the terms of Napoleon's Concordat with the Vatican, which remained in effect under Louis-Philippe, the king appointed bishops and the pope endorsed the appointments.

counterbalanced the pope's power; transplanted to a country in which the state does not concern itself with religion, they submitted unconditionally, as one might expect, to the Court of Rome. I don't believe that this situation will last; the new generation of priests will be nationalist; indeed the Court of Rome is already obliged to treat them with kid gloves, and I imagine that attempts will soon be made to limit its power by law and to acquire guarantees that have not existed hitherto.

Bouchitté, in a letter written on the eve of my departure from France, asked me to inform myself about Quakers. He has what seems to be an exaggerated idea of their influence. Certainly the religious direction that America took owes something to Quaker doctrine. . . . They set the example of practical tolerance and propagated its principles. However, I doubt that their influence would have been sufficient if it had not been aided by the march of civilization and also, it must be said, by the progress of indifference. Unquestionably, their influence is almost nil today. Most Quakers sided with England during the American Revolution. This cost them followers and their popularity has continued to wane ever since. More baneful yet, Quakers are possessed by the Roman Church's mania for inquisition and regulation, without having the dogma of infallibility to bolster them: if a Quaker has a shady character, if his conduct is not exemplary, if he marries a woman of another religious faith, he is excommunicated. To be a Quaker, one must not only hew to a certain doctrine, one must use the familiar "thou" when conversing, one must abstain from certain society, one must wear garments cut and buttoned in a certain way. Quakers lose their spiritual authority in minutiae. They grow purer and sparser. . . .

P.S. I have just indirectly received news dating to September 16. I see that cholera has begun to stir universal anxiety and that cajeput is mentioned as a good remedy. . . . If cholera should in fact reach France, Marie must be evacuated. I confess that her departing, perhaps never to return, would make me abjectly sad, for I love her more than I can say. But her life is more precious to me than anything else. Her health is delicate: like me, she has long endured acutely painful stomach ailments, which would make her more vulnerable than other people. This thought distresses me. So do your best: give advice and take suitable measures. What I have vested in this is not pleasure or vanity but something real and immense, a feeling that goes to the bottom of my heart.

I confess, my dear friend, that at this moment life is weighing heavily upon me. I no longer have time today to write to Marie. But tell her that she is even more present for me than usual, that I love her with my entire soul.

I can't help saying it, though I know that words prove nothing. I wish she were in my place and I in hers; if that were not possible, I would be happy at least to stand by her in dangerous circumstances and be equally imperiled.

Beaumont to his sister-in-law Félicie, October 26

I am trying to assemble as many documents as I can about a variety of subjects. Pennsylvania has a German population with which I would like to familiarize myself. They are immigrants from different parts of Germany, who, during the past two decades, have solidified into a compact mass numbering 140,000. They speak only German, they have their own papers, published in their language, and they preserve their German ways. One can hardly imagine them ever merging with Americans, though they will have to do so sooner or later. Also in Pennsylvania is a population of an entirely different kind, whose fate is quite interesting: a population of men of color. They are no longer slaves. The Constitution regards them as equal to whites and grants them the same political rights; but laws don't changes mores. People are accustomed here to consider a negro a *slave* and to treat him accordingly. One observes with curiosity the aristocratic pride evinced by these *free men* whose government rests upon the principle of absolute equality. The white color is nobility and black the mark of slavery. One must foresee what consequences this will have. Every day the ignorance of blacks diminishes, and it is to be feared that when the day of full enlightenment comes, they will avenge themselves violently against those who now scorn them.[11]

A thousand other things draw our attention in this part of the country. Every evening I write down what I observed during the day, and my notes on Pennsylvania are copious. Something else to be noted, at least as interesting as the Germans and the negroes, are the pretty women who abound in Philadelphia, some of them quite beautiful. They dress just like French women, though less tastefully. Since no one here has a carriage, they get around on foot. One often meets them, richly adorned, during one's walks and is reminded of those *princesses of the boulevards* crowding the streets of Paris.[12]

Young women enjoy a great deal of freedom . . . I hope they will not cause me to lose my own. I'm confident that they won't, for I would sooner hang than get married in a foreign land. That aside, they are gracious and banter with perfect ease. It isn't at all unusual to spend an entire evening conversing with the same person, uninterruptedly.

11. In 1835, three years after returning from the United States, Beaumont published a novel about slavery titled *Marie.*

12. "Princesses of the boulevards" is a euphemism for prostitutes.

Tocqueville to his brother Édouard, Aboard *The Fourth of July*, November 26, 1831

I begin this letter, dear brother, aboard the steamer taking us from Pittsburgh to Cincinnati. I shan't finish and date it until I arrive at the latter city in a few days. Right now we are on the Ohio River, which is already as wide as the Seine at Paris, though still quite some distance from its junction with the Mississippi.

What I see are the world's most beautiful mountains. Unfortunately, they are covered in snow, for winter has finally reached us. We encountered it in the middle of the Alleghenies and it has stayed with us ever since. But we are fleeing it, and a week from now it will no longer present a threat. Pittsburgh is the former Fort Duquesne. There was real genius in the way Frenchmen situated their military outposts here, before the war of 1754. When the interior of the North American continent was still terra incognita to Europeans, the French established bases in the middle of the wilderness, from Canada to Louisiana—a string of small forts which, now that the country has been mapped to a fare-thee-well, are recognized as ideal sites for cities whose fortunes depend on their ability to attract commerce and command the navigation of rivers. Here, as in many other circumstances, we worked for the English, who profited from a vast scheme of our devising. If we had succeeded, the English colonies would have been hemmed in by an immense arc, with Québec and New Orleans its two extremities. The French and their Indian allies would have been at their back, and Americans of the United States would not have rebelled against the mother country. They all recognize this. There would not have been an American Revolution, and perhaps not a French one, or not the revolution that played out as it did.

The French of America possessed within themselves all the resources to be a great people. They are still the finest offspring of the European family in the New World. But, overwhelmed by numbers, they were bound to succumb. Their abandonment is one of the most dishonorable episodes of Louis XV's inglorious reign.

I have just seen in Canada a million brave, intelligent French, made to constitute one day a great French nation in America, who live rather like strangers in their own land. The conquerors control commerce, employment, wealth, power. They populate the upper classes and dominate all of society. The vanquished, wherever they don't enjoy decisive numerical superiority, are day by day losing their customs, their language, their national character. There you have the effects of conquest, or rather, of desertion.

Today the die is cast: all of North America will speak English. But aren't you struck by men's inability to foresee the ripples of a present-day event, to sense the eternal danger of regretting or rejoicing without discernment? When the Battle of the Plains of Abraham, the death of Montcalm, and the shameful treaty of 1763 placed England in possession of Canada and of a country bigger than all of Europe, which formerly belonged to France, the English exulted almost fulsomely. Neither the nation nor its greatest men suspected then that, by reason of this conquest, the colonies, no longer dependent on the mother country's support, would aspire to independence, that independence would be a fait accompli twenty years later, with England in economic tatters after a disastrous war and facing an immense new nation on the American continent, English-speaking but her natural foe, almost certainly destined to usurp her lordship of the seas.

November 30, 1831
We are arriving at Cincinnati after a painfully cold, snowy voyage.

Tocqueville to his sister-in-law Émilie, On the Ohio River, November 28, 1831

I would like to write to your husband, dear sister, but I don't know where my letter would find him. The last news from France suggests to me that he has undertaken a long voyage of necessarily indeterminate length. You know that I have never approved of such capers; they seem to me useless at best; but at a distance of two thousand leagues from one's friends, one is not well placed to offer advice—it would arrive after the event. I can therefore only confine myself, limply, to hoping that all turns out for the best.[13]

You know, dear sister, that we have revised our travel plans and will probably be back in France sometime during the month of April. I trust that you will understand all the considerations that have led us to shorten our sojourn in America and that you will not greet us with a sour face. It would be most unfair, in the first place because we have acted for the best, and secondly because we shall be so happy to see you again that a less than joyful response from you would be sheer ingratitude. The day I set foot on French soil again will be a beautiful day indeed. You who *live in the country* have no idea what it's worth; on the contrary, speaking poorly of it is one of your favorite diversions—I can attest to that, having heard you deliver long tirades against it. Well, I believe that a voyage abroad would change your opinion. I've already *knocked around* this world quite a lot. I've encountered people in different positions, but nothing of what I've seen proves to me that any other nation is fundamentally better off than we. Here, for example, I observe a marginal display of all the

13. Tocqueville is referring to plans for a royalist uprising in Brittany, associated with the clandestine return of King Charles X's exiled daughter-in-law, the duchesse de Berry.

nasty political passions that come so glaringly to light during our revolutions. But I shall stop there, for fear of *falling* into lofty political, philosophical, metaphysical, economic, and moral considerations from which I could not extract myself before putting you to sleep.

I was saying that America is not worthier than France. The example I shall adduce is *the fair sex*, to use the language of madrigals. I confess that from a certain point of view, this land is the El Dorado of husbands; one can almost certainly find perfect happiness in it, provided one totally lacks romantic imagination and asks of one's wife only that she prepare tea and raise one's children—the sovereign duties of conjugal life, as we know. In these matters, American women excel. They are reasonable people, eminently *reliable*, as they say, who confine themselves to their teapots and stay indoors once they've pronounced the famous "yes." I grant that this is an undeniable advantage. Despite it, however, I often find myself wondering whether, at bottom—note well the "at bottom"—there isn't a prodigiously close resemblance to European women. Don't regard me as a peevish philosopher disappointed in love, I beg of you, but listen to my reasons. I shall enumerate them.

My first and principal reason is that they are all, before they become wives, consummate flirts. Properly speaking, love plays no part in this, which makes for a tranquil society. I have not heard about a single suicide by drowning or hanging in the entire Union since the Declaration of Independence: people don't fight or throw fits. Young women are perfectly free to choose and their choice is always the swain whom the family notary would have recommended, if consulted. You see that I am impartial; if they are outrageously flirtatious, I note that they are *reasonably* so, as they never fail to set their cap at men who, quite apart from their social rank (an advantage often much exaggerated in Europe), are in easy circumstances. This reflects honorably upon their rectitude. But it remains to be understood how such perfect domesticity is accomplished, how these women cease to be coquettes from one day to the next. How does one explain a change so sudden and punctual? If it occurred once, randomly, I would believe in a miracle, but when it repeats itself every day, I am confounded. Might one suspect, might it not be possible to imagine, might we not have some reason to think—you see how circumspect and suitably dubitative I am—that the cure is only apparent and that the coquetry still exists, though unable to display itself? The fact is, and this has been remarked by all travelers, that married women in America are almost all weak and languishing. For myself, I am tempted to believe that they are ill from repressed coquetry. Why not? Isn't it commonplace to see men green around the gills with repressed ambition? Let it be said that this is pure conjecture and I don't attach great value to it. But even so, it's already enough to prove that, all things considered, one is better off living in France than in America.

I don't know how I can have the courage to talk such silliness with you, dear sister. One should refrain from writing frivolous letters when one is two thousand leagues from home; by the time my chuckles reach Europe, you may be in tears over something. This thought haunts me. I never laugh whole-heartedly here, always fearing that at that very moment a terrible misfortune has struck me on the other side of the world. It is also true that the world has never seen a family like ours: a collection of old crocks worse than any found in a hospital. I have yet to receive, in the past eight months, a single letter that contains this one little phrase: "Everyone is faring well." Yet I don't think they were laying it on too thick in portraying their decrepitude.

When I arrived here, dear sister, I found one of those letters only you can write, testifying so lavishly to your affection for me.

Although our friendship already goes back quite some time, that testimony gives me as much pleasure now as when I first received it. One of the things I most regret about not being in France is being unable, at difficult moments, to offer your husband my advice, and to offer all of you the services that warm friendship can render. But patience! I shall soon be home, and we must hope that we are not yet done with revolutions, so that, in another one, we may regain what we've lost. I am going to address this letter to Nacqueville once again and hope that it succeeds better than the last in reaching you. How wise of you to love Nacqueville! At the present time, one cannot do better, I believe, than to stay put there quietly and await *one's day.*

Adieu, dear sister, I embrace you with both arms and all my heart.

Tocqueville to Ernest de Chabrol, November 28, 1831

[The continuation of a letter begun on November 26, the first part of which, describing the American judicial system, with particular reference to its operation in the Pennsylvania courts, is included in the Appendix.]

Marie will tell you, my dear friend, that these lines only just missed being the last I ever addressed to you. In the evening of the day before yesterday, our vessel, driven by the current and a full head of steam, smashed like a nutshell against a rock in the middle of the Ohio. The collision, as we subsequently learned, could be heard a quarter of a league away. As soon as it happened, the cry of *we sink* [sic] rent the air, and the boat, with all its gear and passengers, began to head for eternity.

I have never heard a ghastlier sound than that of water rushing into the ship. Do not speak of the accident to my family.

My intention in taking up the letter I began two days ago was to let you know that an American will present himself to you with a letter of recommendation from me, which I've just written. I don't know the young man, but he is a friend of the famous Robert . . . , America's Grand Penitentiary, with whom we are intimately connected, as you can imagine. He is also the nephew of the richest man in Philadelphia, who has received us with open arms. I hope you extend to him the same courtesy his uncle has extended to us. I believe that he wants to obtain information about our judiciary system; you can, if it's worth your while, introduce him to jurists such as Elie, Carné, and others of our acquaintance. Do what you think best.

I am in a hurry and have only enough time to embrace you.

Tocqueville to Ernest de Chabrol, Cincinnati, December 1, 1831

I just arrived at Cincinnati, my dear friend, and found three letters from you, which gave me great pleasure.

Would you please put your neighbor [Mary Mottley] to shame for having written only *two* by informing her that you have written *three*. Among these three is one that really hurt, the one in which you complain about my correspondence flagging during the loop we made around the Great Lakes. I would do anything not to give you grief. You might deduce this from the long letters I write to you whenever the opportunity presents itself. I deny myself the pleasure of writing them only when time is *truly* short. To be sure, Marie will have received a letter from me during that interval, but I need not tell you that love is egoistic and unreasonable. Go make a woman understand that you lack the time to write to her!

So, after doing the *impossible* to send Marie a letter, I simply don't have a minute left in the day for correspondence with others.

Your grievance afflicts me all the more because soon you may once again have grounds for complaining: I doubt that I shall have time to write, much less write at length, during our three weeks on the Mississippi.

Don't hold it against me, I beg of you. Is our friendship not more than equal to these small contingencies?

I embrace you whole-heartedly.

Beaumont to his sister Eugénie, written on December 1 from Cincinnati

... The fact is that except for a small circle of literate men, whose urbane mores and old-world manners put me in mind of our most decorous salons, one can say that in Philadelphia, as in all other cities in the United States, American men are preoccupied by only one thing—business. ...

The voyage from Philadelphia to Pittsburgh was one of the most painful yet: the roads are deplorable, the carriages even worse; we traveled around the clock for three straight days. Thirty leagues west of Philadelphia, in the Allegheny Mountains,[14] we were gripped by terrible cold. We traveled almost all the rest of the way in a snowstorm worse than any that locals had seen in a long time, especially at this time of year. The Alleghenies are not very high, but they roll on endlessly; they aren't a mountain range so much as an interminable succession of hills transected by myriad valleys, all extremely picturesque. I must admit, however, that I was too cold to admire the beauty of the landscape. ...

After a hundred leagues we arrived in Pittsburgh, Pennsylvania's industrial heartland, the Birmingham of America, per-

14. Beaumont and Tocqueville consistently spell Allegheny as "Alleghany" and Mississippi with only one "p."

petually shrouded in smoke from the steam engines that drive factories. . . . After a brief stay, we embarked for Cincinnati, not in a carriage but in a steamboat. Many vessels on the Ohio regularly ply between Pittsburgh and Louisville (Louisville being farther downriver than Cincinnati, closer to the Mississippi).

The banks of the Ohio must be lovely in fine weather. This river flows quite some distance between mountains that form a spur of the Alleghenies and are lavishly picturesque. After a day's sail we had almost sighted the small town of Wheeling. A league short of it, we experienced one of our most peculiar mishaps, but I can't give you a proper account here; remind me to tell you about it when I come home.[15]

Nothing eventful marked our passage from Wheeling to Cincinnati. We descended the Ohio in a very handsome steamboat, the *New Jersey*. If you want to know what I passed en route you have only to trace the course of the Ohio in your atlas. The nicest riverbank towns are Marietta, Gallopolis [Gallipolis] (thus named

15. Beaumont means the sinking of the *Fourth of July*, described in Tocqueville's letter above. Beaumont also concealed the gravity of the accident from his family. In an obituary notice he wrote after Tocqueville's death, Beaumont recounted their mishap with dramatic flair: "Toward midnight, there was a cry of alarm in the captain's voice—'All lost!' We had struck a reef (Burlington Bar), which split open our vessel. The situation was grave, as we two hundred passengers had only two lifeboats, each with room for ten to twelve people. The water rose ever higher; it soon filled the cabins. Admirable *sang-froid* of American women. . . . The Ohio stretched more than a mile across and was sweeping chunks of ice past us in its strong current. Tocqueville and I viewed this spectacle and grasped each other's hand in farewell. . . . Suddenly the boat stopped sinking; its hull was suspended on the very reef that impaled it. . . . Out of danger, but imprisoned in the middle of the river like convicts on a hulk, we wondered what would become of us. At length another steamboat, the *William Parsons*, drew up and took us aboard."

because it was founded by Frenchmen), and Louisville. Cincinnati, where I arrived yesterday, is a city of thirty thousand souls. Where it now stands was wilderness twenty-five years ago. Its growth is phenomenal. Furthermore, Ohio and Kentucky are the two states of the Union in which growth is rampant. We're going to spend a few days here, before doing what we have yet to decide.

Tocqueville to his brother Hippolyte, Cincinnati, December 4, 1831

Upon arriving here, my dear friend, I found a letter from you, which has given me great pleasure. When you wrote it you were faring well, Émilie too, and were leaving Paris for Nacqueville. I was afraid that you might embark, instead, upon a long voyage the usefulness of which seemed questionable to me.

The newspapers of October 10 informed us that the Reform bill had been voted down. In rejecting it, the English aristocracy has acted rashly and has, I daresay, put itself in much the same position that Charles X did after choosing his ministry of August 8.[16] It is caught in a vicious circle from which I see no escape. It may have resources unknown to a foreigner.

You can tell that on my distant perch I often think about events in France. It is, indeed, the subject of almost all my thoughts. And I confess that after trying to guess what lies ahead for us and racking my poor brains over it, I usually end up lost in doubt. The one obvious fact is that we are slogging through a period of transition. But are we moving toward freedom? Or are we marching toward despotism? God only knows.

16. On August 8, 1829, Charles X appointed a stiff-necked, authoritarian administration in answer to mounting opposition. This set the stage for revolution.

This said, I am more hopeful than fearful. In the chaotic land-scape before us, I discern a signpost definitely indicating that during the past forty years we have made immense progress in our practical understanding of ideas of freedom. Like individuals, nations must learn how to comport themselves. That ours is advancing I do not doubt. There are riots in the large cities, but the mass of the population calmly obeys the laws, even though the country is ruled by a government of no account. We are harvesting the fruit of fifteen years of freedom for which we are indebted to the Restoration. Doesn't it seem remarkable to you that even as the far left is clamorously refusing to act except by lawful means, royalists are declaring that public opinion must be consulted, that it alone can fortify the throne, that it, above all, must be won? You will agree that these developments, despite the mayhem of the moment and the bout of high fever induced by the July revolution, offer reasons to hope that society will at last achieve stability. I don't know if we are made to be free, but I am certain that we are infinitely less incapable of it than we were forty years ago. Had the Restoration lasted another decade, I believe we would have been saved; the habit of legality and of constitutional forms would have pervaded manners and customs. But might it be possible now to put things back in order? Might it be possible to have another Restoration? I see many obstacles, the greatest of them being the royalist faction likely to emerge triumphant. Never will you drum it into those militant heads that there are concessions to be made, without which one cannot rule; that the legitimate monarchy will be short-lived unless it is national; that it must harness itself to ideas of freedom or be crushed by them. If ever the Bourbons remount the throne, they will want to govern by force and they will fall again. It may be possible to contemplate the advent in France of a regime strong by virtue of glorious military feats, but not one whose strength derives from its reliance on law alone. Law can buttress it if it governs capably, but cannot protect it from its failings if it proves inept.

In any event, it seems to me that the conduct of royalists is well known. I am quite happy to see them occupying the high ground of legality and working to win the majority instead of attempting to impose a minority by force. It augurs well. If they had always acted thus they would have spared themselves, and France, much grief. Furthermore, by adopting what is reasonable in ideas of freedom, they are making a tacit commitment to respect those ideas, should they ever regain power. Many royalists have been won over to that conviction, and say so, indirectly. They have acquired the habit of endorsing, of invoking public opinion—free, constitutional habits previously alien to them. This is the spectacle that reassures me about the future. I hope that we shall succeed, after so much cut and thrust, in saving ourselves from anarchy and despotism.

There you have a confused political effusion, my dear friend. The fact is, common sense cannot do justice to a subject as immense as this in a mere letter. Fortunately, I shall be able to enlarge upon it in person five months from now, or less. For now, all I can do is finish the letter, with a heartfelt embrace.

Tocqueville to his mother, Louisville, December 6, 1831

We arrived here this morning, dear Mama, and shall endeavor to resume our journey before the day is out, making for New Orleans; we are eager to reach temperate latitudes. With regard to cold, the difference between this continent and Europe is incredible. Here we are in the same latitude as Sicily, yet it's several degrees below freezing, the earth is covered with snow, the rivers are clogged with ice—it's like winter in the north of France. In such weather, our voyage becomes painful and sad, but happily, we shall have reached tropical climes in a week. I can't remember if we had already decided, when I wrote my last letter, to travel by way of Louisiana. We chose that route upon learning in Cincinnati that the roads across Kentucky at this time of year are considered impassable. Descending the Mississippi with all its twists and turns is quicker than cutting straight across the hinterland. We shall barely touch New Orleans so as to have in reserve as many days as possible for Charleston and Washington.

We are very satisfied with our recent sojourn in Cincinnati; it was terribly interesting. We had no real understanding of the western states, except for some superficial notions derived from our acquaintance with the others. What we encountered there is all the good and bad of American society set in bold relief, not unlike the letters writ large in a child's primer. Everything is jarring, outlandish; nothing has yet found a secure place; society is growing faster than man. Where Cincinnati lies was virgin forest thirty years ago. This city presents a completely novel scene; everything in it expresses hectic growth: lovely houses and cottages; freshly paved, imperfectly aligned streets encumbered with building materials; unnamed squares; unnumbered houses; in short, the sketch of a city rather than a city. But in the midst of these imperfect structures, there is the hum of life, a feverishly active population: that is Cincinnati today. It may not be thus tomorrow, for each day renders it unrecognizable to its own inhabitants. When Europeans came to America they left behind, in large part, the traditions of the past, the institutions and mores of their fatherland. They built a society analogous to the European model, but, at heart, radically different. From the bosom of this society a new host of emigrants has sprung forth during the past forty years, swarming toward the West as their fathers had done toward the New England coast, South Carolina, Virginia, and Maryland. They, too, abandoned the ideas of their fatherland and founded in the valleys of the Mississippi a new society connected to Europe only by language. Here is where one must come to witness the most singular state of things imaginable. A people absolutely without precedents, without traditions, without habits, even without foundational ideas, has cleared a new path for itself in its civil, criminal, and political legislation, and plunged ahead, indifferent to the wisdom of other peoples and all memory of the past. It is shaping its institutions the way it has built roads straight across the forests, secure in the knowledge that it will encounter no limits or impediments; a society that does not yet have any bonds, be they political, hierarchical, religious, or social; where each individual is what it pleases him to be, regardless of his neighbor; a democracy devoid of limits or measures. In the other states of the Union, wealth and birth do not confer privilege, but there are personal influences. In the West, no one has been able to acquire a reputation or had the time to establish his credit. So, with this last barrier removed, democracy displays all its distinctive attributes, its fickleness, its violent passions, its instability and anxious character. These people inhabit the most fertile region in the world; they are only a million in a state that could sustain ten times that number. Do you think they have put down roots? Not at all, they are once again on the march; every year they cross the Mississippi in strength and seize new expanses of wilderness. Here there is a notable race of men called *pioneers*, whose taste for this adventurous life rises to the level of passion. They make way for white men in America's wildernesses, forming the vanguard of the civilization that will follow, pushing back the Indian, destroying big game, probing the forests.

The nomadic families of pioneers camp in regions completely lost to view. They stay there for several years, leading lives of almost savage freedom. When the sedentary population begins to overtake them, they hitch their horses to their wagons again and roll westward with their wives and children. It's as if they have come to find ineffable charm in the perils and vexations of existence. Solitude has become as necessary to them as society to other men. They are unhappy if they aren't plowing new soil, tearing up roots, cutting down trees, fighting wild beasts and Indians: therein lies their pleasure, as pleasure for other men lies in making money hand over fist and living within four walls.

I have been so carried away by my description that I only have time and space enough to embrace you. I do that now, but not before thanking you again for being a faithful correspondent. If you could only see the pleasure your letters give me, you would not, I hope, regret the effort of writing them.

Beaumont to his mother, December 15, written from Sandy Bridge in Kentucky

Sandy Bridge is nothing but a small inn made of logs laid on top of one another and situated on the road that leads from Nashville (the capital of Tennessee) to Memphis, a small town on the banks of the Mississippi. . . . I'm writing in a room with three beds on which weary travelers, however many and of whichever sex, collapse. A fire is roaring in a fireplace not unlike those of old castles, big enough to hold ten logs, each three feet around. Despite this fire, which could roast an ox, the room is freezing. A little while ago I wanted to drink a glass of water, which had been brought to me, but, imprudently letting it stand for five minutes, I found it frozen solid. Two things explain this: first, the temperature outside is about eight degrees, and second, between the logs that make up the walls are spaces wide enough for air to enter freely. This severe cold, accompanied by half a foot of snow, is rather extraordinary considering our latitude, which is that of

Egypt. But such is America's climate: in the southern states, where one swelters during the summer, one dies of cold during the winter. . . .

My hosts are very good people, very proud, innkeepers though they are, and lazy, though poor. They are proud because they live among slaves. There isn't a landowner, however down-at-heel, who doesn't own two or three negroes. The latter are obligatory fixtures in the house of white men, like tables or armchairs. What comes of this is that men who are not black, and who are consequently free, all regard themselves as privileged beings. Here, color is a true mark of nobility. The convenience of being served by slaves renders whites indolent, and the fertility of the land, from which one reaps abundant harvests with little effort, favors this disposition. So does the weather, which turns excessively warm when spring arrives. But I believe less in the influence of climate than in that of slavery. . . . My host, a small landowner who finds work ignominious, is convinced that it should, by rights, be the exclusive domain of slaves. He has feudal mores: he spends his time hunting, horseback riding, or doing nothing. He owns a superb rifle, which he uses with great success against does, bucks, and other game; he has no difficulty bagging birds. The rifle is so heavy that it's all I can do to carry it. This morning I decided to hunt a little. I rambled through the woods for an hour or two; I saw bevies of charming birds, notably some red and yellow parrots of matchless beauty; but, armed though I was, I couldn't bring down a single one. At my side was my little republican lord. He wanted to know who owns the woods in France. What advantage an individual might derive from ownership puzzles him, because he is surrounded by woods that belong to no one, and that no one has taken the trouble to claim. When we want a fire, a big oak tree is felled in the forest, and slaves belonging to our lord of the manor quickly cut it into logs.

You're no doubt wondering why I'm staying at Sandy Bridge in this inn, not knowing for how long. I shall explain. We left Nashville with several other passengers in a small public coach that looked just like a char-à-banc. It didn't close, we rode day and night, and froze to the bone. To warm us up, fortune arranged three accidents that nearly left us stranded: first the straps under the carriage broke, then a wheel, then an axle. With the aid of several oak trees from the surrounding forest, we patched up our poor tattered cart *limping on all fours,* and arrived at Sandy Bridge. Here we must remain until our vehicle is repaired. But why the devil did we come to Nashville in the first place? you ask. And what are we proposing to accomplish in Memphis?

I'll answer your questions. You will recall perhaps that in my last letter to Jules I told him I was on the Ohio River nearing Louisville. . . . It shouldn't have taken up more than two hours to travel the seven or eight leagues that remained, but we were suddenly halted by an invincible obstacle. . . . The weather had been very cold for two or three days; ice had formed with overwhelming suddenness and packed the Ohio. We passengers were put ashore with all our belongings at a small village called Westport. We couldn't find any means of transport to Louisville, but we did manage, after much investigation, to obtain a cart, on which we piled our trunks. It lumbered toward Louisville, with the driver and the two of us on foot, escorting the horses. We thus walked eight leagues in the snow, on a path that wound its way very agreeably through the woods, across an endless succession of hills and hollows. Nothing could have been more picturesque, but weary travelers don't have eyes for changes in a scenic landscape. At Louisville, we overcame one predicament only to face another. . . . If we didn't take winter quarters in Louisville, what would we do? what would become of us? where would we go?

We decided to descend the Ohio, then the Mississippi, and

make for Charleston by way of New Orleans. What with ice blocking the Ohio, all our plans were upset. To retrace our steps through all the places we had visited was an *odious* prospect; on the other hand, to wait for the Ohio to thaw was to take a big risk, though everyone assured us that the freeze wouldn't last two more days. We took a middle course, which seemed, and still does, to be the wisest: since there are steamboats regularly plying the Mississippi, we thought that if we could only reach this river, which never freezes over, we would be sure to find transportation by water. . . .

Tocqueville to his father, Memphis, December 20, 1831

The place from which I write, my dear father, may not be on your map. Memphis is a very small town on the banks of the Mississippi, at the far southwestern edge of the state of Tennessee. We've been here for several days. By what chance, you ask, are we in Memphis rather than in New Orleans? Therein lies a long, pitiful tale, which I shall attempt to relate as succinctly as possible.

I wrote my last letter to you when I was sailing down the Ohio and about to arrive at Louisville. There I expected to find a steamboat ready to make the six- or seven-day voyage to New Orleans. But during the night of December 4–5, the temperature, which was already low, fell so precipitously that the Ohio, despite its strong currents and its width, froze, trapping us in ice. You should know that Louisville is in the same latitude as Sicily. It doesn't often freeze there, to say the least, and no one could remember ever experiencing such cold before the end of January. That's what I call *dumb luck!*

In any event, we managed to get ashore, where we learned that Louisville was nine leagues distant. A local frontiersman, a big bruiser, offered to transport our trunks to the port in his cart.

Our traveling companions, who numbered ten, did the same as we, and off we went, on foot, across mountains and woods that had never, since the beginning of time, been visited by a loaded wagon. It rolled, thanks to the audacity of our driver and to some strong shoulders occasionally put to the task. But we were marching in snow knee-high. The journey became so strenuous that our companions began to drift off, one after another. We, on the other hand, persevered and finally arrived at Louisville toward nine in the evening.

The following day we learned that the Ohio was frozen solid, that we would have to establish winter quarters in Louisville or turn back. But there was another alternative. At a small town called Memphis on the banks of the Mississippi in the state of Tennessee, all steamboats plying the river replenish their store of wood. We were told that if we found our way there, we could surely resume our journey waterborne, since the Mississippi never freezes. Because this information was conveyed by eminently credible people, we acted on it straightaway and left Louisville for Memphis. These two cities lie about 150 leagues apart; we had to travel that distance on the most abominable roads, in the most infernal carriages and, above all, the most dreadful cold imaginable—the natural order seemed to have been upset for our particular discomfort. Tennessee is in about the same latitude as the Sahara Desert. Cotton is raised there, as well as other exotic plants, and when we crossed the state, it was fifteen degrees below freezing;[17] no one had ever seen anything like it. Finally arriving at Memphis, we learned that several miles upriver, the Mississippi itself was unnavigable; one could see icebound steamboats sitting as motionless as rocks.

We must now plan ahead. If, after several days, this freakish

17. Fifteen below zero Celsius is five degrees Fahrenheit.

cold doesn't let up, we shall forgo our voyage to the South and make for Washington by the shortest route possible. I will say this: apart from the frustration of having our projects more or less thwarted (through no fault of our own), we do not regret our trip through the forests of Kentucky and Tennessee. We acquainted ourselves there with a breed of humanity and a way of life completely unknown to us. The only inhabitants of that region are men called Virginians. They have preserved a moral and physical identity all their own; they are a people apart, with national prejudices and a distinctive character. There, for the first time, we had the opportunity to observe the social consequences of slavery. The right [north] bank of the Ohio is a scene of animation and industry; work is honored, no one owns slaves. But cross the river and you suddenly find yourself in another universe. Gone is the spirit of enterprise. Work is considered not only onerous but shameful: whoever engages in it degrades himself. The white man is meant to ride horseback, to hunt, to smoke all day long; using one's hands is what a slave does. South of the Ohio, whites form a veritable aristocracy that, like every other, marries low prejudices to lofty instincts. It is said—and I am much inclined to believe it—that these men are incomparably more sensitive to issues of honor than their counterparts up North. They are straightforward, hospitable, and value many things higher than money. They will end up being dominated by the North, however. The latter grows richer and more populous by the day, while the South, if it grows at all, grows poorer.

Inhabitants of Kentucky and Tennessee live scattered in vast forests and deep valleys. It was there, one evening after a long day, that we happened upon a log cabin with chinks on every side through which a big fire could be seen crackling. We knocked. Two mongrels, as tall as donkeys, rushed to the door. Their master followed, roughly shook hands with us, and invited us to enter. Picture a fireplace half the width of the room, in which a whole tree was burning; a bed; a few chairs; a six-foot-long carbine; a hunter's accoutrements hanging on the log wall and dancing in the draft. The mistress of the house sat near the fireplace, with that quiet, modest air so characteristic of American women, while four or five robust children were frolicking on the floor, in light summer clothes. Sitting on their haunches under the mantelpiece of the chimney were two or three Negroes who looked as if they had been shivering ever since Africa. Our gentleman played the host nonetheless easily and courteously for his house being a hovel. He hardly stirred, mind you, but the poor blacks served us at his behest: one presented us glasses of whisky, and another corncakes and a plate of venison. The third was sent off to fetch more wood. The first time I heard this order given, I assumed that he was going to the cellar or a woodpile; no, the blows of an ax echoing in the woods soon informed me that a tree was being felled for our benefit. That is how things are normally done here. While the slaves were thus occupied, the master, quietly seated in front of a fire that could have roasted an ox down to its bones, majestically wrapped himself in a cloud of smoke and between each puff entertained his guests with an account of his most memorable feats as a hunter.

I must recount one more little anecdote, which will tell you at what price a man's life is held here when he is unlucky enough to have black skin. About a week ago we faced the Tennessee River. The only means of crossing was a paddle steamer operated by two slaves with a horse. We ourselves made it over, but since the river was full of drift-ice the master hesitated to transport the carriage. "Rest assured," one of our traveling companions said, "that should the boat sink, we will compensate you for your horse and slaves." This argument seemed irresistible: the carriage was loaded, and sailed across.

Tocqueville to his mother, On the Mississippi, December 25, 1831

At last, at last, my dear Mama, the signal is given and here we are cruising down the Mississippi, as rapidly as possible under the combined influence of steam and a strong current. We were beginning to despair of ever escaping the wilderness. If you take the trouble to examine your map, you will see that we had reached a pretty pass. In front of us, the Mississippi half frozen and no boats launching; overhead, a Russian sky, pure and frozen. We could have retraced our steps, you say. But that option was fast disappearing. During our sojourn in Memphis, the Tennessee had frozen, and carriages could no longer cross. So there we were, in the middle of a triangle formed by the Mississippi, the Tennessee, and impenetrable backwoods to the south. We might as well have been marooned on a rock in mid-ocean, inhabiting a world made expressly for us, without newspapers, knowing nothing about the rest of mankind, and facing the prospect of a long winter. That is how we spent a week. I must say, however, that except for our anxiety, those days were not disagreeable. We were staying with good people, who did their utmost to ingratiate themselves. Only twenty paces from our house was the edge of the world's most beautiful forest, a sublime place, picturesque even under snow. We had rifles and plenty of powder and lead. A few miles from the village lived an Indian nation, the Chickasaws; once on their land, we always found a few natives happy to join us in the hunt. Hunting and warring are the sole occupations of the Indian, his pleasures as well. For large game we would have had to go too far afield. Instead, we killed a great many pretty birds of a species unknown in France. We found this highly diverting, though it didn't do us much credit in the eyes of our allies. I killed red, blue, yellow birds, including parrots with plumage more brilliant than any I had ever seen. That's how time passed, lightly at any given moment, but with the future weighing upon us. At last, one fine day, we noticed a wisp of smoke on the horizon, over the Mississippi; the wisp soon became a cloud, out of which loomed not the giant or the dwarf of fairy tales, but a large steamboat chugging up from New Orleans. It dilly-dallied in front of us for a quarter hour, as if wanting to keep its intentions secret. Would it stop, or continue on its way? Suddenly, it blew like a whale, made straight for us, smashed the ice with its heavy hull, and docked. The whole population gathered at the riverbank, which, as you know, once formed the edge of our empire. All of Memphis was astir; the bells weren't rung because there aren't any, but the assembly shouted hurrahs! and the new arrivals knelt down on the shore after the fashion of Christopher Columbus. We weren't yet saved, however, for the captain had Louisville, north of us, as his ultimate destination, while we had our sights set on New Orleans to the south. Fortunately, there were about fifteen other derelicts not wanting to make Memphis their winter quarters. We exerted collective pressure on the captain. What did he think he could accomplish up the Mississippi? He would unavoidably be halted by ice. The Tennessee, the Missouri, the Ohio were frozen. We all swore we had witnessed the situation for ourselves. The ice would not only stop his vessel but almost certainly damage it, or worse. We had only his interest in mind—his rather than ours, of course. . . . The spirit of altruism lent so much color to our argument that the man began to waver. Even so, I am convinced that he would still have gone forward, but for a felicitous event, thanks to which we have not become citizens of Memphis. As we were parleying on the riverbank, we heard an infernal racket in the nearby forest: drumbeats, the neighing of horses, the barking of dogs. At length, a large group of Indians emerged—old people, women, children, with baggage

—all led by a European, and came toward us. These Indians were Chactas (or Tchactaws), to pronounce it as Indians do.[18] Apropos, I shall tell you that Monsieur de Chateaubriand behaved a little like La Fontaine's ape; he didn't mistake the name of a port for that of a man, but he gave a man the name of a powerful nation of the American South. You would like to know, no doubt, what these Indians were doing there and how they could serve us. Patience, I beg of you; since I have time and paper today, I don't want to hurry.

You will learn that the Americans of the United States, a rational people without prejudices, known for their philanthropy, conceived the idea, like the Spanish before them, that God had bestowed upon them, as an unrestricted gift, the New World and its inhabitants.

And listen to this: it having been demonstrated that one square mile could nourish ten times more civilized men than savages, it followed logically that wherever civilized men settled, savages had to make way for them. What an excellent thing is logic. When the Indians found themselves a little too near their white brethren, the president of the United States sent them a message explaining that, in their own interest naturally, they would do well to retreat slightly westward.[19] The region they've inhabited for centuries belongs to them, no doubt: no one denies them this incontestable right. But it is, after all, uncultivated wilderness—woods, swamps, very poor land really. Beyond the Mississippi there is, on the

18. The appellation generally used today is Choctaws.
19. Tocqueville is referring to the Indian Removal Act, signed into law by Andrew Jackson in May 1830, which led to tens of thousands of Indians emigrating westward in what was described as "a trail of tears and death." It is estimated that 40 percent of the tribes died en route. The Choctaws were removed in 1831, the Chickasaws in 1837. The two nations merged for a time in Oklahoma.

contrary, splendid terrain which the European will never reach, where game have never been alarmed by the sound of a woodman's ax. Pioneers are separated from it by a hundred leagues. Throw in various gifts of inestimable value, calculated to buy the Indian's compliance: casks of whisky, glass-bead necklaces, earrings and mirrors. What clinches the argument is the insinuation that if Americans meet with a refusal, force may be applied.

What to do? The poor Indians carry their old parents in their arms; mothers hoist their children onto their shoulders; the whole nation begins to march, taking their most cherished possessions with them. They abandon forever the soil on which their forefathers lived for a millennium perhaps and settle in a wilderness where the whites will be harassing them ten years from now. Can you see what becomes of a high civilization? The Spanish are real brutes, unleashing their dogs on Indians as they would on ferocious beasts; they kill, burn, massacre, pillage the New World like an army storming a city, pitilessly and indiscriminately. But one cannot destroy everything; fury spends itself. Indian populations that survive end up mingling with their conquerors, adopting their customs, their religion; there are several provinces today in which they hold sway over those who subdued them in the past. Americans of the United States, being more humane, more moderate, more respectful of law and legality, never bloodthirsty, are more profoundly destructive of the Indian people than Spaniards. And one cannot doubt that within a century there will no longer remain on the North American continent a single Indian nation, nor even a single man belonging to the most remarkable of Indian races. . . .

But I've left my story behind. I was writing about the Chactas, I believe. The Chactas form a powerful nation occupying the border country of Alabama and Georgia. This year, after protracted negotiations, they were persuaded to leave their homeland and emigrate to the west bank of the Mississippi. Six or seven thousand Indians have already crossed the great river; those appearing in Memphis came there with the intention of following their compatriots. The government agent who accompanied them, with authority to pay their passage, hurried to the riverbank upon hearing that a steamboat had arrived. The fee he offered for their transportation sixty leagues downriver fixed the wavering mind of the captain. He gave the signal to depart. The bow was turned south and we cheerfully climbed aboard, passing passengers on their way down the gangplank who, instead of going to Louisville, found themselves—poor souls—obliged to await the spring thaw in Memphis. So goes the world.

But we hadn't yet left; we had to board our exiled tribe, its horses, and dogs. Here a truly lamentable scene unfolded. The Indians advanced mournfully toward the riverbank; first came the horses, several of which, unfamiliar as they were with the forms of civilized life, took fright and leaped into the Mississippi, from which they were rescued with difficulty. Then came the men, who, in the customary fashion, bore nothing but their weapons. The women followed, carrying children tied to their backs or swaddled in blankets; they were also loaded with bundles containing all their wealth. Last of all came the old folk. Among the latter was a woman 110 years old. I have never seen such a horrifying figure. She was naked, except for a threadbare blanket revealing, here and there, the scrawniest body imaginable. She was escorted by two or three generations of grandchildren. Having to leave one's land at that age and seek one's fortune in a foreign country— what an abomination! Amid the old people was a young woman who had broken her arm a week earlier; for lack of care, the arm had frozen beneath the fracture. She was obliged nonetheless to join the march. When everyone had passed, the dogs approached the bank but refused to go further and protested with hair-raising yelps. Their masters dragged them aboard.

This whole spectacle had an air of ruin and destruction; it spoke of final farewells and of no turning back. One felt heartsick watching it. The Indians were calm, but somber and taciturn. One of them knew English, and I asked him why the Chactas were leaving their land. "To be free," he replied. I couldn't get anything else out of him. We shall deposit them tomorrow in the backcountry of Arkansas. One must admit, it was a singular chance that placed us in Memphis as witnesses to the expulsion, one might say the dissolution, of the remnants of one of the most celebrated and oldest American nations.

But enough about the savages. It is high time I returned to civilized folk. Just one more word about the Mississippi, which, in truth, hardly deserves more than that. It is a large, yellow river, gently rolling through the emptiest of unpeopled countrysides amid the forests it floods in the spring and fertilizes with its muck. There is not a hill to be seen, only woods, more woods, yet more woods: reeds, vines; profound silence, no vestige of man, not even the smoke of an Indian camp.

THE LAST LEG: FROM NEW ORLEANS TO WASHINGTON AND NEW YORK

After a brief sojourn at New Orleans, they crossed the southern states by way of Montgomery, Augusta, and Norfolk. Tocqueville met Sam Houston, who boarded the boat where the Indians disembarked, but reserved his account of their interview, as well as his observations of life in New Orleans, for his diary.

**Tocqueville to his sister-in-law Alexandrine,
On Chesapeake Bay, January 16, 1832**

You know, dear sister, that our intention was to return to France by way of England. We anticipated an excursion no less useful than pleasurable: with what we have learned of the language and to some extent of English customs, three weeks in England, amid the political passions boiling there, would have expanded our knowledge greatly; but at Norfolk we heard reports that damnable cholera has made its appearance in the north of the country.[1] Tomorrow, in Washington, we shall know the truth; should those reports be confirmed, we will straightaway revise our plans and

1. The cholera pandemic reached Moscow in 1830, Berlin in 1831, London in February 1832, and Paris on March 26. The death toll throughout France was appalling: twenty thousand in Paris and as many in Marseille between March and October. Like many Parisians who could afford it, the Tocqueville family left the city for the suburban town of Saint-Germain-en-Laye. Several of Alexis's cousins died.

return directly to France. Two reasons explain why we won't hesitate. The first is that we don't fancy *snuffing out* en route and the second that we fear the quarantine likely to be in place along the French coast. God willing, the disease will not have already come to our country. That it will spread sooner or later seems to me inevitable, however; the only question is when.

Don't pity us too strenuously for returning to Europe just when the plague is wreaking havoc there, my dear sister. It will soon reach America, everyone here expects it. It will come from England, borne by people or by the wind. After all, it has traveled from Calcutta to the edge of northern France, and commerce with Asia is less extensive than between the United States and Europe.

In any event, inform my father of our new plans; tell him that if indeed cholera is rampant in England, it is useless to have money waiting for us at Liverpool. He should arrange an account at Le Havre, with three or four hundred francs available between March 1 and 10, which I may need to hire the diligence and perhaps pay Monsieur Hottinguer for agent and entry fees.

It's been six weeks since I've had any news of you. But I know that the mail of four deliveries awaits me at the French ambassador's residence. I look forward to collecting it with impatience and something like dread. Since the great misfortune that befell us seven months ago I cannot overcome a vague but pervasive feeling of anxiety. It becomes intense when I'm unsealing letters; I breathe freely only after quickly glancing through the first one.

We have just completed a very long, very interesting, and quite tiring voyage. Our sojourn in New Orleans, which couldn't have been more agreeable, lasted longer than originally scheduled. With precious little time to reach Washington, we decided that it made no sense to go by way of Charleston. We would have had very few days to spend there, and besides, almost all of the distinguished gentlemen we were intent on seeing have left town for the Congressional session in Washington, where we shall catch up with them. So we kept Charleston to our right, looped across Mississippi, Alabama, Georgia, and the two Carolinas and finally, yesterday, arrived at Norfolk. This morning we set sail on the Chesapeake for Washington. We berth tomorrow and shall stay three weeks. From there to New York takes two days. The voyage from New Orleans to Norfolk was very interesting but rough, as several regions in between are untamed wilderness. The odd thing is this: I have not felt better in the last five or six years than I have during the past two months. Right now I am the *sturdiest* member of the band, though I expect Beaumont to regain his advantage once we've returned to Europe. If I ever write a book about medicine, I tell you it will bear no resemblance to the usual pap. I shall contend and prove that, to keep well, one must: eat corn and pork; eat little, heartily, or not at all as the occasion warrants; sleep on the floor fully clothed; move in the course of a week from ice to heat and from heat to ice; push wagon wheels or wake up in a ditch; above all never *think.* That's the principal point; immerse oneself as much as possible in *matter;* be the closest thing to an oyster. I believe that it was Rousseau who said that the thinking man is a depraved animal; I have my own version of his dictum—the thinking man is an animal with poor digestion. So take it from me, dear sister: let us not think. Or, if we do, may it be only at our (future) dinner.

I leave you to reflect upon my last, pithy sentence and shall now prepare for bed. Papa will in all likelihood receive a long letter from me in the February 1 mail. I bid you adieu, my good little sister, with a heartfelt embrace for you and your husband.

Tocqueville to Ernest de Chabrol, Chesapeake Bay, January 16, 1832

. . . Yesterday, upon arriving at Norfolk, I learned that cholera had entered England during the month of November. It's still only a rumor, but apparently quite reliable. If it's confirmed, we shall give up the idea of returning by way of England and sail directly to France, where we would probably make port during the first half of March.

God willing, the illness will not yet have reached French shores. But my hopes exceed my expectations. I've always thought it certain that it will soon arrive, and I am more convinced of it now than ever. Cholera will circle the globe. It is the worst scourge that God has ever visited upon the world, since nothing arrests its progress, neither seasons nor climate, and it always retraces its steps.

I see from the letters I've received from your neighbor that she is very frightened. Do everything you can, my dear friend, to soothe her. In epidemics, terror sometimes makes people more vulnerable. In any event, however swiftly the illness spreads, I hope to be in France before it arrives. If so, and Marie is still there, I can almost guarantee that I shall restore her to her normally calm disposition.

I have just completed an interesting but very tiring voyage. It lasted two months, during which nuisances of one sort or another were daily events: broken and overturned carriages, bridges swept away, swollen rivers, a lack of seats. The plain fact is that crossing the immense expanse of country we've just seen, doing it so quickly and in wintertime was not a practical enterprise. But we were right to do it, since we succeeded. That's the moral of the story.

Our sojourn in New Orleans, although brief, was most curious and agreeable. Should you encounter anyone alleging that climate has no effect on the constitution of a people, assure them that they are wrong. We have seen French in Canada—they are calm, moral, pious; in Louisiana we met Frenchmen of an entirely different stripe—restless, dissolute, lax in every way. Separating them are fifteen degrees of latitude; I can't think of a better explanation for this difference.

What mores, my dear friend, are those of a southern land where slavery has been introduced! It is a scene that confounds the imagination. . . .

Tocqueville to his brother Édouard, Washington, January 20, 1832

Upon arriving here, my good friend, I received news of the death of poor Monsieur Ollivier. I had already had grave concerns about him, such that when I wrote to Alexandrine a week ago I dared not mention her father for fear that ill had befallen him. It's the kind of sad precaution one learns to take during long voyages.

This death has affected me sorely; I felt a close bond to Monsieur Ollivier. Moreover, I saw him as playing a key part in fostering your happiness. He was the soul of the household; his spirit, his fretful attentions, lent great charm to domestic life.

My first impulse, dear friend, was to write to Alexandrine and express the feelings roused in me by this sad news, but I then thought better of it. It occurred to me that my letter would arrive almost four months after the event, when the wound would no longer be raw. I was afraid of awakening her grief instead of bringing consolation. Take it upon yourself, dear friend, to explain my silence; you can easily do it without causing more pain. Tell her how fully I have participated in the misfortune that has struck us all; my condolences, issuing from your mouth, will not throw her into a deeper state of bereavement. Furthermore, I shall soon speak to her myself, probably a scant ten days after this letter reaches you: I leave on the following packet.

I must say, my dear friend, I look forward with great impatience to our reunion. I am worried about those near and dear to me in France. How death has ravaged our families during the past ten months! Hitherto, our home life has not been cheerful; now it must be positively lugubrious. I wouldn't have believed that I could ever return to my country with a soul so dark. And in what spirits will I find all of you? There isn't a word in your letters about cholera; I believe that you have made a pact of silence among yourselves, to allay our anxiety, but it can't be hushed up—there's been too much talk of it. Cholera is rapidly advancing upon France; the most civilized regions of Europe are unable to fend it off. There is no doubt whatsoever that it will visit itself upon us. It will surely circle the earth. Finding it well established in France upon my arrival would be a cruel turn of events. It would make even sadder the return I expected to be so joyful.

I leave America after employing my time here usefully and agreeably. With the southern states of the Union I have only a superficial acquaintance; to know them as well as the North, I would have had to remain another six months. Generally speaking, one needs two years to form a complete and exact picture of the United States. I hope, however, that I didn't waste my time. In my baggage are numerous documents; I conversed and mused a lot about what I saw. I believe that if I enjoy any leisure when I'm back in France I could write something tolerable about the United States. Attempting to embrace the whole would be folly. I am incapable of aiming for universal exactitude; I haven't seen enough to justify such pretensions. But I think I already know much more about this country than is ever taught in France, and certain details of the picture may be of great interest, even topical interest.

We embark, as I told you, on February 10. Our family may be inclined to take fright at the idea of an ocean passage in midwinter. Use your influence, I implore you dear friend, to dispel such unreasonable fears; in the first place, we shall probably arrive before the equinox, and besides, the voyage on American packets is without danger at any time of year. To convince yourself of it, you need only consult the record: during the past decade, a vessel of this kind sails for Liverpool every week, for Le Havre every ten days, and another for London; to date, not one has been lost. There you have an incontrovertible fact, which I hope will set everyone's mind at rest. Something you didn't suspect is that we ran an infinitely greater risk on steamboats. Thirty of them exploded or sank during our first six weeks in the United States. We disembarked from one only three hours before a mishap; another time, our boat split apart like a nutshell on rocks in the Ohio. I'll recount all that upon my return; time is short now.

I believe that your wife will have given birth by the time I see her. That dear little sister of mine, how present in my imagination she has been during the past ten months! At Le Havre I would like to find a letter, poste restante, reporting the state of everyone's health.

Adieu, my good friend, time is flying but I would as well it flew faster to bring us all together that much sooner.

Beaumont to his mother, January 20, 1832

A word about my sojourn in Washington. When we first arrived, we went to see the French minister, Monsieur Sérurier, with whom we had been corresponding for several days, and who received us most hospitably. The gentleman is a little disgruntled now with the government of Louis-Philippe, which has decided to save money at its ambassador's expense. The fact is that his income has been reduced, absurdly, to 40,000 francs, less than that of the humblest chargé d'affaires. The French minister should not find himself in such a position of inferiority, especially next to the English ambassador, who receives 150,000 francs.

Monsieur Sérurier introduced us yesterday evening to the president of the United States. The latter, General Jackson, is an old man of sixty-six, well-preserved, who seems to have remained vigorous in body and mind. He is no genius. He was formerly famous as a duelist and hothead. His great achievement is to have won the battle of New Orleans against the English in 1814. This victory made him popular and led to the presidency, illustrating once again how nations—even a nation of merchants and businessmen—are carried away by the prestige of military glory.

The president lives in a palace that would qualify as a fine mansion in Paris; the interior is decorated tastefully but simply. His salon is much less splendid than those of our ministers; he has no subaltern doing guard duty at the door, and if there are people courting his favor, they are not very persistent—he was alone when we entered, on a day set aside for receiving the public. And during our visit, only two or three people joined us. We chatted about insignificant things; he offered us a glass of Madeira and we thanked him, calling him "mister," as we would a man on the street. The French have a false idea of the presidency of the United States; it is seen as a kind of politically sovereign office comparable to our constitutional monarchies . . . but the authority of this president would be infinitely more extensive if it resembled that of our king.

Today I visited the Senate and the House of Representatives of the Union. These two political assemblies convene in the Capitol, a beautiful building, worthy of its reputation as a magnificent monument. This does not suffice for Americans, who greatly exaggerate its merits. You will often hear them ask foreigners, naively, whether anything in Europe compares with their Capitol. The tone of parliamentary discussion is grave and dignified; seldom do political passions disrupt proceedings. One of the great advantages of the government of the United States is its location in a city with twenty thousand inhabitants or so. The authors of the Constitution purposely made this the seat of supreme authority. In a populous city, with many people of the lower class, the great political bodies can never conduct free deliberations. The men I saw today deliberated all the more judiciously for doing so in a calm environment. We were introduced into the Senate and the House by Monsieur Poinsett,[2] a very distinguished man whose acquaintance we had made in Philadelphia and whom we were delighted to encounter in Washington. He has played a very important political role in this country; it was he who instigated the revolutionary uprising in Mexico. . . .

Tocqueville to his father, Washington, January 24, 1832

This letter, dear father, will perhaps be the last I write to you from America. Praise the Lord! We plan to sail on the 10th or 20th of February from New York; and thirty days being the average length of crossings, we shall arrive in France toward the 10th or 20th of March.

2. Joel Roberts Poinsett, born in 1779, a physician, botanist (who gave his name to the poinsettia), congressman, the first United States minister to Mexico, and later, secretary of war under Martin Van Buren. He co-founded the National Institute for the Promotion of Science and the Useful Arts, which prefigured the Smithsonian Institution. He had been educated in Europe and traveled to the Middle East in the first decade of the nineteenth century.

At this moment I am revolving many ideas about America. A fair number still reside in my head; I've scattered the seed of many more onto notepaper; others crop up in summaries of conversations I've had. All these raw scraps will be served up to you. You will not find them interesting in themselves but will judge whether something of value can be drawn from them. During the past six weeks of our voyage, when my body was more tired and my mind more serene than it has been for a very long time, I have given much thought to what might be written about America. Drawing a complete picture of the Union would be an utterly impractical venture for someone who has spent only one year in this immense country. I believe, moreover, that the boredom of such a book would match its instructiveness. One might, on the contrary, by being selective, present only that which is pertinent to our own political and social state. The work would thus be both of permanent interest and of moment. There you have the general idea, but will I have the time and capacity needed to furnish it? That is the question. Something else preoccupies me: I shall write what I think or write nothing at all, while bearing in mind that wisdom does not want every truth aired. I hope that we shall be able to speak about all that at our leisure two months hence.

We have been here for a week and shall stay on until February 6. Our sojourn is useful and agreeable. Gathered in Washington at this moment are all the most prominent men in the entire Union. We no longer need to elicit from them ideas about what we don't know, so we go over more or less familiar ground and concentrate on doubtful points. It's a very useful kind of counterproof. We are always treated with great respect and courtesy. Yesterday, the French minister introduced us to the president, whom we called "Mister" with perfect ease. He, in turn, greeted us in much the same way that he does his familiars, shaking our hands. He makes no distinctions among people. . . .

A visit to Washington gives one some idea of how wonderfully well-equipped men are to calculate future events. Forty years ago, when choosing a capital for the Union became a matter of public concern, the first step, reasonably enough, was to decide upon the most favorable location. The place chosen was a vast plain along the banks of the Potomac. This wide, deep river bordering one end would bring European goods to the new city; fertile fields on the other side would keep markets well provisioned and nourish a large population. People assumed that in twenty years Washington would be the hub of the Union's internal and external commerce. It was bound, in due course, to have a million inhabitants. Anticipating this influx, the government began to raise public edifices and lay out enormously wide streets. Trees that might have hindered the construction of houses were felled by the acre. All this was nothing but the story of the milk-jug writ large:

> Il était quand je l'eus de grosseur raisonnable.
> J'aurai . . .[3]

The farmer's wife and Congress reasoned in much the same way. The population didn't come; vessels did not sail up the Potomac. Today, Washington presents the image of an arid plain scorched by the sun, on which, scattered here and there, are two or three

3. "[The pig], when I bought it was reasonably fat. / When the time comes to sell it . . ." The verses are from La Fontaine's fable *La Laitière et le pot au lait* [The Milkmaid and the Jug of Milk], in which a farmer's wife, balancing a jug of milk on her head as she walks to market, daydreams about all that the sale will buy her: more chickens, a pig, a cow, and a calf. She jumps for joy at the prospect, and spills the milk.

sumptuous edifices and five or six villages that constitute the city. Unless one is Alexander or Peter the Great, one should not get involved in creating the capital of an empire.

I've backed myself into such a corner that I don't have time to discuss the memoir you sent me. But I hope to be with you a week or ten days after this letter arrives, and I shall expatiate upon the subject more satisfactorily than on paper. What I can do right now, my dear father, is thank you; your work sheds light on subtleties that help me understand the administration of this land. One's mind, as you know, is enlightened only by comparing one thing to another. Your memoir has already served as the basis for many very useful questions. You say in one of your letters to me, dear father, that you are counting on me to do something beneficial in this world; I desire it no less than you—I daresay, even more for your sake than for my mine. Embrace Mama for me, and my brothers and sisters. May God preserve you all! The thought that henceforth I shall not take a step that doesn't bring us closer to one another gladdens my heart.

Tocqueville to his brother Édouard, New York, February 9, 1832

I decided, my dear friend, to send this brief message by way of Liverpool informing you that our departure has been delayed ten days. We shall leave New York on the 20th rather than the 10th. The decline in commercial traffic between America and France has muddled the schedule of packets. I am writing to you rather than to my father so that you may, as you see fit, impart the news to the entire family or keep it to yourself. There are drawbacks, either way, you will be the judge of that. If it is thought that I left on the 10th, my failure to arrive might cause anxiety; on the other hand, knowing that I've left on the 20th might plant in people's minds some of the silly notions current among landlubbers about the equinox. As for the latter fear, I have already seen enough of the sea and sailors not to be greatly troubled by it. This transitional time of year, between winter and spring, is unquestionably a bad season to be at sea, but the dangers are neither more nor less great than a month before the equinox or on the day itself. That is an indisputable fact, but people don't know it. I therefore give you carte blanche to do what you feel is most sensible. My own advice, however, would be to transmit the letter only if you see that nerves are badly frayed.

The Liverpool packet is weighing anchor and I don't have time to add anything except that I am cruelly disappointed by the delay that's left me stranded in New York when, possessed as I am by the idea of rejoining you in France, I can take no interest in the men and things around me.

Farewell, I embrace you with all my heart. I include Alexandrine and Denise.

On February 20, 1832, the travelers boarded *Le Havre*, the same packet that had brought them to the United States. They reached Paris in late March.

Even with prodding from Beaumont, Tocqueville was slow to undertake work on their study of American prisons. Domestic rearrangements necessitated by the cholera epidemic took his mind away from it, but most distracting were political imbroglios. True to their reputation for extravagance, a group of ultra-royalists, among them Tocqueville's cousin Louis de Kergorlay, arrived at Marseille on April 28, 1832, aboard a Sardinian steamer chartered by Charles X's widowed daughter-in-law, the duchesse de Berry. These "legitimists" were hoping to spark an insurrection, overthrow Louis-Philippe, and make the duchess a regent for her young son, whom they considered the "legitimate" heir to the French throne. It was supposed to be another "return from Elba," but their Napoleonic fantasy exploded in their faces. Several of the plotters, including Kergorlay, were caught and imprisoned at Marseille. Tocqueville traveled south to visit him. While there, he learned that Beaumont had been dismissed from government service for refusing to serve as public prosecutor in a case clearly rigged by the régime to advance Louis-Philippe's material interests. Tocqueville thereupon resigned his own post and began in earnest to collaborate with Beaumont in writing their report on prisons. Written at full tilt (principally by Beaumont), their work, *Du Système pénitentiare aux États-Unis, et de son application en France* [On the Penal System in the United States and Elements of It Applicable to France], with folio volumes of documents appended, was submitted to the ministry of the interior in October 1832.

APPENDIX

Tocqueville on Civil Law in Pennsylvania

To Ernest de Chabrol, Aboard the *Fourth of July* on the Ohio River, November 26, 1831

Today I shall fulfill my long-standing promise to tell you about civil justice in America. But I must warn you that my treatment of this subject will be very superficial, first because it is too vast for a letter, and second because my notions are still incomplete—I haven't had time to systemize them.

I shall limit myself today to the *Order of Jurisdictions*, which is what seems to interest you most. And in speaking about it, I shall necessarily touch upon several other important points.

I shall limit myself to Pennsylvania law, which, being the simplest in the Union, is what I know best. Pay close attention, for we are about to enter a world absolutely new to you. Abandon any idea of making analogies between these people and us.

In the United States there are two entirely distinct civil justices: federal justice and the justice of each state. Each state constitutes an independent sovereignty—that's the basic principle. The states have ceded some portions of their law to the *Union*—that's the exception.

Thus, certain trials involving people's rights, trials that pit one state against another, those of citizens from one state bringing suit against citizens from another, of Americans and foreigners suing one another, are judged by special tribunals called *United States Courts*.

I need not deal with their organization today. Suffice it to say that jurisdiction is rather well defined, so I am told that jurisdictional disputes are rare. I shall now address the matter of civil justice as each state has established it within its domain to settle the interests of its own citizens, and I shall take Pennsylvania as my example.

The permanent judicial body in Pennsylvania consists of two courts: the first, called *Inferior Court* or *Court of Common Pleas,* has twelve judges; the second, called *Superior Court,* has five members.

Their names may lead you to conclude that the two courts stand in much the same relationship as our Tribunal of First Instance and our Royal Court, with the one receiving appeals from the other. However, such appeals occur only in special cases, on which it would be useless to dwell as they are all exceptional.

In general, it can be stated that what we mean by *appeal* has no place in the civil procedure of Pennsylvania. You will best understand how things work here by following a suit as it makes its way through the inferior court, without comments from me. Pennsylvania is divided into twelve judicial districts, which encompass a number of subdivisions, called *counties.* These counties have many features in common with our subprefectures. Attached to each of the twelve judicial districts is one of the judges of the inferior court.

Every three months, this judge must appear at the county seat and, with the aid of a jury, hear suits ready for litigation.

I'll pause here, my dear Chabrol, long enough to tell you that you owe me a debt of gratitude, for one cannot conceive of labor more thankless than the writing of this account, bad though it may be. The subject is immense; to abbreviate I must constantly pare away flesh, cut right and left without respect for logic. In this concise version you will get an absolutely incomplete idea of the material, but no matter— reward the intention, not the result.

As I said, the tribunal consists of two parts: judge and jury. Different guaranties were needed against the judicial shortcomings of these two different bodies.

The guaranties furnished by American law against the blunders of the jury are very curious indeed, and I doubt that you have any conception of it. This subject alone would deserve a letter. Do you know that a judge theoretically has the right to *immediately* quash a jury's verdict not only on the basis of *law* but on the basis of the jury's finding of *fact*?

That is the principle. Note, however, that in practice the judge invokes *fact* to set aside a verdict only when jurors have grossly erred or obviously favored their passions. Points of law are another matter. There the judge ruthlessly annuls a verdict if his legal opinion takes exception to it. Never mind appearances and received opinion: I assure you that when it comes to meting out justice in the system derived from English common law, the power of the jury is a mockery. The jury speaks, but it is the judge ventriloquizing.

This being the case, why not clearly separate the judge's task and the jury's? A good question. I believe that I could provide excellent reasons to justify the common law method. But I am swept along in the current of my subject and will not digress.

So much for the first guaranty offered to unsuccessful plaintiffs. Should the judge choose not to annul a verdict instantly, if he lets it stand, what then? The loser has recourse to a kind of appeal called *writ of error*. He addresses not a higher tribunal but the one that meets every three months, on which his judge sits. He rehearses his suit, offers new grounds, produces new witnesses. He argues that either the jurors made a mistake or that the judge instructed them incorrectly in the law.

After deliberation, the tribunal, on which the judge himself sits, either dismisses the appellant's case outright, or annuls the verdict but renders no judgment, sending the whole matter back to the same judge who has twice pronounced an opinion. One can appeal this new judgment, again and again, to the end of days *theoretically*.

But in practice, when the assembled court has twice quashed a judgment, the judge who handed it down relents, and the jury follows his lead.

Now you are more or less familiar with the English system as practiced in Pennsylvania. You see that I was right in saying that the system does not provide for an appeal, in the true sense of the word. Cases are referred from a judge to himself, so to speak. The second tribunal proceeds more like our Court of Cassation than our appeals courts, with this difference—it judges fact as well as law, and holds a case hostage to one judge.

But you will want to know in that case what is meant by Superior Court. The latter, with exceptions, is unrelated to Lower Court. It functions in a higher, but totally independent, sphere. Matters of a certain gravity rightfully fall under its jurisdiction. It is a more enlightened tribunal, placed above opinion but not *hierarchically* superior to the Court of Common Pleas. It functions like the latter in its own sphere of action, and follows absolutely the same rules.

You now have an incomplete but general idea of the judiciary system of Pennsylvania. What distinguishes this state from others in the Union is the fact that, unlike them, it has removed special courts from the English model. Thus, there is no *Court of Doctors Commons*, the court responsible for ruling on questions related to marriages and wills.

Unknown as well is the *Court of Chancery*, which constitutes such an important part of the English judicial system. Pennsylvanians have assigned the business of these tribunals to the *Court of Common Pleas*, resulting in simpler but less complete jurisprudence—less complete because these special courts can do certain things not allowed the *Court of Common Pleas*.

An example would be the execution of contracts. According to English custom, which still has the force of law here, the Court of Common Pleas can only exact damages from the party that has not honored a contract. In the *Court of Chancery* that party could be compelled to execute its commitment to the letter.

That's all I can tell you today about civil law. I repeat, it's a pity to abridge such material. I have many notes and an abundance of observations. It seems to me that I could write a whole volume on this subject (for better or worse), especially in regard to the jury, its constitution, its elements, and its usefulness.

I hope that one day we shall converse about these subjects to our heart's content. I must leave you now. I haven't told you anything about Justices of the Peace, because I covered that subject in a letter to Elie, who must have shown it to you. What I said is accurate, but my remarks about many other matters are off-the-cuff—it would be dangerous to take them too literally.

In my next letter I shall try to speak about the criminal law; it will be simpler and easier.

Adieu, my good friend. I embrace you whole-heartedly; convey friendly greetings to our colleagues.

INDEX

In subheadings, AT is Alexis de Tocqueville and GB is Gustave de Beaumont

religion: American attitude toward, 30, 65, 85, 88–93, 224; AT's beliefs, 181–82; in Canada, 171, 172, 173–74, 176, 224; church-state separation, 149, 226–27; and education, 207–8; in France, 89, 149, 226n; of Indians, 139; intolerance, 149, 159; penal system and, 64–65; religious mania, 40; Sabbath, 31, 85, 88; tolerance, 88–89, 93, 134; in the West, 148–49, 156. *See also* Catholicism; Protestantism; Quakers; Shakers; Unitarianism

Rémusat, Charles de, 2

Revolutionary War (American), 230, 231

Richard, Fr., 133–34

roads, 115, 125, 139–40, 237, 248

Rosambo, Louis de (father of Louise de Tocqueville), xi

royalist movement, 85, 109, 215–16, 232, 232n, 240–41, 269–70

Sabbath, 31, 31n, 85, 88

Saginaw, Mich., journey to, 134–37, 139–45

Saint-André, baron de (French consul), 28

Saint Lawrence River, 172–73, 174–75

Salverte, Eusèbe de, 190, 190n

Sandy Bridge inn (Tenn.), 244–46

Sault Ste. Marie, Mich., 151–54, 160

Say, Jean-Baptiste, 12–13n, 12

Schérer, Édouard, 5, 5n, 102, 108–9, 215, 221

Schermerhorn family, 73, 73n

Sears, David, 187, 187n

Sedgewick, Miss, 184

Séguier, Armand Pierre, baron, 63, 63n

Sérurier, M. (Fr. ambassador), 263–64

Shakers, 123–25

Sing Sing prison, 49, 51–52, 55–58, 63–64, 78, 116n

slavery, 229, 245, 249, 250, 261

snakes, 135, 138, 145

society: aristocracy's decline, 94; AT and GB's status, 200–201; Boston, 186–88, 191–92, 198–99; family trees, 32; New York, 28–29, 73–74, 82–83, 103–5; Philadelphia, 210–11; social distinctions, 49. *See also* class

the South, 107, 249, 261. *See also* Indians: forced from lands; Mississippi River voyage; *and names of specific cities and states*

the Spanish, 253, 254

Sparks, Jared, 192

Spencer, John Canfield, 132–33, 132n

stagecoaches, 125

steamboats: Hartford to N.Y., 198; Hudson River trip, 111–13, 122–23; on Lake Erie, 146; Mississippi River trip, 252–53; Ohio River trip, 230, 235, 238, 238n, 246–47, 263; R.I. to N.Y., 19, 21; safety, 235, 238n, 263; Saint Lawrence River trip, 100, 172; *The Superior*, 146, 147–51, 202

Stöffels, Charles (letter), 218–20, 218n

Stöffels, Eugène (letters), 84–86, 84n, 216–17

The Superior (steamship), 146, 147–51, 202

Taschereau, M., 173

Tennessee, 244–49, 251

theater, 106, 210

Thomson, Miss, 150

Throop, Enos, 117–18

toasts, 48, 74, 198

Tocqueville, Alexandrine de (sister-in-law of AT): about, 26n; AT concerned about, 26, 77; father's death, 261–62; health, 101, 183, 212; letters to, 41–42, 81–84, 197, 212–15, 257–59; pregnancy, 183, 183n, 212, 263

Tocqueville, Alexis de: absent-mindedness, 83; anxieties and self-doubt, xviii, 219–20; appearance, 2; birth, xii; book planned, 221–22, 262, 266; busy life, 197, 201; childhood, xii–xiii; education, xiv–xv, xvii–xviii; English spoken, 10, 23 (*see also* English language); excitement craved, 217; family history, viii–xiv; family loved, 70, 75, 81–82; friendship with GB, xvi–xvii; goal of understanding America, 53; grief over Lesueur's death, 180–83, 192–93, 200; on happiness, 38, 183, 218–19; health, 15, 15n, 259; on his American sojourn, 262–63, 266; on his own character, 39; homesickness, 53, 70, 102–3, 110; news from home

desired, 16–17; oath of loyalty, vii–viii, 98n; prison report written, 269–70; as prosecutor, xvi; questioning attitude, xiv–xv, xviii; religious beliefs, 181–82; and the royalists, 215–16; on seeking to understand American government, 194–95, 196; stage fright, xvi; swimming, 158; voyage's advantages questioned, 193

Tocqueville, Denise de (niece of AT), 77, 81, 214–15

Tocqueville, Édouard de (brother of AT): about, xii, 26n; gloves requested of, 44–45, 50; letters to, 43–45, 180–84, 230–31, 261–63, 268–70; marriage and family, 26n, 77, 81–82, 183, 212n, 217, 263; travels in Europe, xv–xvi, 183; verses sent, 214

Tocqueville, Émilie de (sister-in-law of AT): about, 20n; AT behind on correspondence, 197; AT's affection for, 234–35; health, 101, 178; house designs for, 20; letters to, 70–73, 128–33, 177–79, 232–35

Tocqueville, Hervé-Bonaventure de (father of AT): about, viii, xi–xiv, xvi; letters to, 15–17, 51–55, 108–10, 159–62, 195–98, 265–68; thanked by AT, 268

Tocqueville, Hippolyte de (brother of AT): about, xii, 20n; letters to, 197, 239–41; and the royalists, 232, 232n

Tocqueville, Louise de Rosambo de (mother of AT): about, x–